W9-CPE-806

Casey Stengel

CASEY STENGEL

A Splendid Baseball Life

Richard Bak

Taylor Publishing Company

Dallas

Published by Taylor Publishing Company
1550 West Mockingbird Lane
Dallas, Texas 75235

Designed by David Timmons

Library of Congress Cataloging-in-Publication Data
Bak, Richard, 1954–
Casey Stengel : a spendid baseball life / Richard Bak.
p. cm.
Includes bibliographical references (p. 000) and index.
ISBN 0-87833-929-9
1. Stengel, Casey. 2. Baseball managers—United States—Biography. 3. New York Yankees (Baseball team)—History.
I. Title.
GV865.S8B35 1997
796.357'092—dc20
[B] 96-41909
CIP

Printed in the United States of America
10 9 8 7 6 5 4 3 2 1

For Mary, Hilary, and Rosemary

Mets

Contents

One	*A Boy with Baseball Knuckles*	1
Two	*K.C. at the Bat*	17
Three	*Wake Up, Muscles*	39
Four	*Casey, Where Are Your Pants?*	57
Five	*Still in the League, Barely*	71
Six	*That Clown in Pinstripes*	93
Seven	*Most People My Age Are Dead*	131
Eight	*An Amazin' Exit*	155
	APPENDICES	
	You Could Look It Up	181
	Washington's Original "Great Communicator"	183
	Bibliography	192
	Index	195

Life is just a game of base ball
If you get in it
you want to win it
But some times the mgr dont give you a chance
But leave you setting there on the bench.
Just give me a left handers fast ball
and I will sock it a mile
And if the empire calls it a foul
laugh and dont say your blind as a owl
Life is just a game of base ball
so win or lose with a smile.

— Ring Lardner, *Lose with a Smile*

ONE

A Boy with Baseball Knuckles

To Casey Stengel, a man whose personal experience in baseball spanned some sixty seasons, the game's great history was like a giant pail of protoplasm, into which he could dip his gnarled hands and pull out an anecdote or reference point as needed. Ask him a simple question and odds were good that he would launch into a long, circumlocutory discussion that would bring to life such disparate characters as John McGraw, Nap Lajoie, and Grover Cleveland Alexander, with Wee Willie Keeler thrown in for good measure. One young reporter was dazed and more than a little confused after a pregame session with Casey. Asked who the Yankees' manager was starting that day, the reporter replied, "I'm not sure, but I think it's Christy Mathewson."

"I want to thank my parents for letting me play baseball, and I'm thankful I had baseball knuckles and couldn't become a dentist."

Conversely, one of Stengel's greatest strengths was that, though he referred frequently to the past, he never chose to live in it. He saw the penny newspapers, handlebar mustaches, and John Philip Sousa marches of his youth give way to television, Afros, and acid rock and hardly gave it a thought. Change was inevitable, so why resist it? If nothing else, that philosophy kept an old person young. When someone approached Casey shortly before his death in 1975 and asked him what he would most like to be, the wry and

Facing Page: **Two-year-old Charley Stengel in 1892.**

Kansas City, Missouri, in 1890, the year Charles Dillon Stengel was born.

wrinkled paterfamilias of the national pastime sanguinely replied, "An astronaut."

Biographies are bound by literary convention to turn at some point to the distant past, which in Stengel's case means a cursory look at 1890, the year of his birth. Benjamin Harrison was in the White House, John D. Rockefeller controlled 95 percent of the country's petroleum supply, and such figures as humorist Mark Twain, industrialist Andrew Carnegie, showman P.T. Barnum, and reporter Nellie Bly (who had traveled around the world by ship and train in a record seventy-two days, six hours, and eleven minutes) were familiar names to all but the newest citizens. In early July, Idaho and Wyoming were admitted into the Union. This made six new states in little more than a year's time, forcing exasperated seamstresses to guess where to sew the forty-third and forty-fourth stars onto the flag. (There was no set pattern.) In late December the last Indian battle was fought at Wounded Knee, South Dakota, but by then the director of the census had already announced that the fabled American frontier was now officially closed.

It was a time of gaslights, horse-drawn streetcars, and six-day work weeks. A pound of pork roast cost eight cents; a pound of butter, a quarter. Electricity and indoor plumbing were still luxuries. Housework was so labor intensive even middle-class families needed servant girls to help with the cooking, washing, and sewing. Such inventions as Singer's electric sewing machine, Kodak's camera, Edison's kinetoscope, Otis's electric elevator, and Hollerith's tabulating machine were finding their way to market, the last being used to tabulate the nation's decennial census. The headcount revealed the population to be a tad under 63 million, a staggering forty percent increase in just one decade. Also in 1890 Ellis Island opened to help process the thousands of immigrants arriving daily in New York Harbor.

To be sure, accommodating the flood of newcomers was just one of many problems facing the country as it headed into a decade that would become known as the Gay Nineties. In 1890 Jacob Riis published *How the Other Half Lives*, his now classic study of New York slum life. Though Riis's disturbing photographs offered proof that America's sidewalks were not really paved with gold, few citizens considered the nation's problems too great to be handled. Storybooks and popular magazines continued to describe a society where a boy could grow up to be just about anything he set his mind to be. Maybe not the president of the United States or the head of Standard Oil (who would want to be like the cold and humorless Harrison or the roundly despised Rockefeller, anyway?), but certainly a dentist or an engineer. As Casey himself might have said, the possibilities were amazing.

All things considered, then, America was a splendid place to be on the evening of July 30, 1890, when twenty-nine-year-old Jennie Stengel of Kansas City, Missouri, expanded the nation's roster by one with the delivery of a husky baby boy named Charles Dillon Stengel.

Jennie Jordan Stengel was a loving mother and a fine cook. "We liked everything my mother cooked," her famous son recalled many years later. Of particular note were her mashed potatoes and gravy: "We'd push mashed potato on the plate, drown it in gravy, and put a big hunk of steak on top. . . . Nowadays people say, don't eat gravy, it's bad for you, but I've been taking gravy all my life."

The newborn's father, Louis Stengel, had grown up in Rock Island, Illinois, a farming community on the other side of the Mississippi River from Davenport, Iowa. His own father, Karl Schtengal, was a German immigrant who had died of tuberculosis in 1865 when Louis was only four. The boy was raised by his mother Katherine and, after she remarried, by his stepfather, Charles Wolff. A few years later Wolff left farming to open a gunsmith shop on the Mississippi, near the ferry that serviced Rock Island and Davenport.

Exactly how and when Louis first met Jennie Jordan has been forgotten, but it's known that the young lady's family initially frowned on the relationship. Like Louis, Jennie was a first-generation American, the Jordans having emigrated from Ireland sometime around 1850. Her family was considerably more prosperous and established than the Stengels, however. Jennie's father, John, was a successful businessman; her maternal grandfather, John F. Dillon, was a prominent railroad attorney who later became a federal judge. Over time the Jordans' objections to Louis softened, and in early 1886 he and Jennie were married. Shortly thereafter, the newlyweds moved 300 miles southwest to Kansas City, where Louis had acquired a job (possibly through the Jordans' connections) as an agent with the Joseph Stiebel Insurance Company.

Thanks to the coming of the railroad, Kansas City was experiencing a boom when the Stengels arrived. The onetime frontier trading post, officially known as the City of Kansas until a new charter was adopted in 1889, had become a major Midwestern trade center with train yards, meat-packing plants, warehouses, factories, stores, and banks sprouting like the numerous dandelions alongside its many railroad tracks. Despite its growth, Kansas City has always retained an open, don't-fence-me-in feel, boasting several large public parks and more miles of boulevard than Paris. The city was even more spacious a century ago, the many empty lots, fields, and dirt roads making it an ideal place for a youngster coming of age.

Charley was the last of three children born to Louis and Jennie Stengel. The first, Louise, born at the end of 1886, was followed one year later by a son, Grant. Physically, the future Casey resembled his father. He was stocky and strong, with a long, narrow face, light blue eyes, and large ears. "I think the thing I remember about him most was that he almost never cried," Louise told a reporter many years

A game in progress at the Parade at the turn of the century. The large, open park was just one of several sandlots that Stengel learned to play ball on with his talented older brother, Grant.

later, after her youngest brother had become known far and wide as Casey Stengel. "He was a very active baby, talked early, and was a good eater."

Stengel's lively and gregarious nature owed more to his mother. Both parents were patient with their children, giving them plenty of freedom to play and welcoming their friends. "The best thing I had was that the family allowed everybody to come to our home," Charley once said. "My mother always liked everyone in the neighborhood, and they could all come and use our yard."

The yard changed frequently over the years, as the Stengels rented a succession of houses. As a salesman living on commissions, Louis Stengel was not terribly successful, though the low cost of living mitigated the effects of his meager pay. There always was plenty of food on the table, particularly Charley's favorite meal, steak and gravy over mashed potatoes. To supplement his regular trips to the market, Louis did what many folks in those days did: he raised chickens in the backyard and grazed a cow on an adjacent lot. The milk, butter, and eggs were either put in the family larder or sold to neighbors.

Charley's best friend when he was growing up was his older but smaller brother, Grant. Together the pair managed to get into mischief on a regular basis. One of their earliest and most perilous adventures involved a trip to Grandpa Wolff's place in Rock Island when Charley was four. Grant was pulling Charley in a wagon when Charley somehow fell into a ditch filled with water. Disaster was narrowly avoided, said the Rock Island paper, which reported that "little Charles Stengel was saved from drowning" by an alert passerby.

Charley's other grandfather, Grandpa Jordan, played a key role in one of the classic stories of his youth. One hundred years ago mothers often dressed their young sons in dresses and let their hair grow until they had reached the age of four or five. Charley, with his long, curly hair, was especially striking. The female members of the family loved to fuss over him.

Charley, on the other hand, liked to imitate his mother's father, following him around the house and even pretending to chew tobacco and spit like him. Charley couldn't help but notice that Grandpa Jordan's hair was considerably shorter than his. One day while the family was visiting in Davenport, Charley said, "I'd like to get my hair cut short like you."

And so he did. His grandfather gave him fifteen cents and sent him to the town barber, who obligingly sheared off several years' worth of glorious blond growth.

"When I came back," Charley remembered, "and my mother and my aunt and my grandmother saw me, they took and grabbed me and slapped me for getting those curls cut off. They said, 'Who told you you could get your hair cut?' And I said, 'My grandfather.' They sure did jump on him." In tears, Jennie Stengel rushed to the barbershop, where she swept the clipped ringlets off the floor. There was nothing she could do with them, however, except save several locks in an envelope—a souvenir she kept for many years.

Charley could be rambunctious and ornery. For the most part, his childhood was typically Midwestern: He went ice skating, sledding, swimming, roller skating, and fishing, and played games of baseball, tag, and hide and seek. He shot marbles, teased girls, wrestled boys, rode his bicycle, and explored the mysteries of the countryside. He raised pigeons and taught the family's dog, Sport, to perform tricks.

One favorite activity that got him into occasional trouble was snowballing. He and Grant and their friends would hide behind cover, wait for a wagon to pass by slowly, then cut loose on the unsuspecting teamster. Charley perfected his aim—he was a left-handed thrower—by trying to knock the pipe out of the driver's mouth or the hat off his head. It was great fun, especially when the infuriated victim jumped down and gave chase.

"We usually got away," he said, "but once in a while they'd catch one or two of us and beat us up."

Being a southpaw was considered not only odd, but slightly wicked in those days, and it caused Charley some grief in school. He entered Woodland Grade School in 1896 when he was six years old. The first time he picked up a pencil in his left hand, his teacher grabbed him by the ear and put him in the closet. Forced to learn how to write with his right hand, his penmanship suffered for the rest of his days. As unnatural as switching hands was, later in life he would claim that it actually paid off for him as a ballplayer.

"I was naturally lefthanded and in baseball that helps you out to have a well-developed right hand as well," he explained. "That's the hand I used to catch the ball and if you look it up you would see I caught a lot of 'em."

Charley did most of his early shagging on the sandlots around Kansas City, often playing with and against

Ivy Olson, who played every position but pitcher and catcher during his 14-year big-league career, was known as the playground bully when he and Stengel attended grade school together in Kansas City. "They let him be the boss because he *was* the boss," recalled Stengel, who later played several seasons with Olson in Brooklyn.

Stengel entered Central High School in January 1906. He would leave four years later to play professional ball, just a few credits shy of earning his high school diploma.

boys several years older than he was. For many years he played weekends for the Parisian Cloak Company on a team sponsored by haberdasher Siggy Harzfeld. Charley was considered a good ballplayer, but still not Grant's equal. In fact, in years to come when the name "Stengel" first started appearing in box scores, many who remembered the boys' diamond exploits naturally assumed that it was Grant Stengel who was making good on his potential.

Charley once summarized his brother's assets. "He was skinny—he claimed that was because I got most of the food at home—and he wasn't a slugger, but he could hit, and he could place the ball, and he very seldom struck out. He could run like a deer and he was very sharp and bright on the bases. He was a good fielder and an accurate thrower. He had what was wanted in those days before the lively ball."

Grant's ambitions were squashed because, as a teenager, he had his heel sliced off when he tumbled off a surrey while returning from a game. The injury barely affected Grant's view of life. Amiable and not terribly ambitious, he would wind up drifting through a series of jobs before finally becoming a taxi driver in Kansas City. "He no doubt would have advanced to the big leagues if he hadn't had that accident," claimed Charley. "He was a better ballplayer than I was."

Charley, looking to contribute to the family welfare, had a number of part-time jobs as a youngster. His very first employment was turning the organist's pump at St. Mark's Episcopal Church, where the family worshiped. (Papa Stengel was a Lutheran and Mama Stengel a Catholic, so the Episcopalians represented a comfortable compromise.) Charley got a quarter a day. Later he worked at a local drug manufacturer, filling bottles with medicine, then corking, glueing, and labeling them. He received a dollar for every five cases of bottles he filled. For a time he also worked for a floral shop, delivering bouquets on his bicycle. One summer he earned three dollars a week as a water boy on a construction site, a job that he felt helped build strength in his arms.

He also helped his father operate a water sprinkler truck owned by the insurance company for which Louis Stengel worked. Eventually, the elder Stengel bought the operation, naming it the Kansas City Improved Street Sprinkling Company. The horse-drawn truck would wind its way through the city, wetting down the dirt streets. Charley got a kick when Grant would expertly aim the water at a passerby he recognized.

Grant dropped out of school to work full-time on his father's truck, but the road-sprinkling business slowly died with the advent of paved roads. "If I hadn't put that boy on the water wagon," his father lamented, "he'd have gone through high school and college."

As the country's premier humorist of the day reminded his readers, "Training is everything." After all, pointed out Mark Twain—a fellow Missourian who shared Charley's sense of the absurd—"Cauliflower is nothing but cabbage with a college education."

Charley, like Grant, figured to remain cabbage. He entered Central High School in early 1906 when he was fifteen and a half years old, not sure of much except that he didn't especially like school, at least not the book-learning part. He had a quick mind, but no patience for reading and writing assignments.

Athletics was another story. He had developed a body built for roughhousing: strong arms and legs and a thick chest. Unfortunately for him, his ears kept pace. Boys in the neighborhood called them "sails." It had taken some time, and a few fights, before kids quit teasing him with calls of "going sailing, Charley?" By the time Charley entered high school he had acquired a new nickname, "Dutch"—a popular and inevitable consequence of his German ancestry.

Charley "Dutch" Stengel was a big man on campus at Central High. In 1908 the school fielded a football team for its only season. Charley, a junior, was its fullback and captain. The game, played in straight-ahead fashion without helmets, suited his tough and unsubtle nature. To Stengel's dismay, the school disbanded the eleven after one of its players was seriously injured by a kick to the head.

Charley also played three years of basketball, with one contemporary describing him as "mostly all arms and legs and always moving." Basketball, like football,

Steady and unspectacular "Dutch" Stengel (third from right) played right forward for Central's basketball team, which won the city championship in 1909. "He could always be depended upon to furnish the same consistent work," reported *The Centralian* yearbook. "Moreover, though considered the roughest man on the team, he committed, on an average, fewer fouls per game than any of his mates."

was still a static affair, with low scores and an emphasis on brawn. Charley's most productive season consisted of 22 baskets in 17 games, but he was enough of an offensive threat to be the catalyst of the team that captured the city championship in 1909. One of his teammates was a tall, thin, deep-voiced fellow, William Powell, who occasionally dressed in women's clothes for school plays. "He wasn't no sissy, though, you can be sure of that," said Charley. "One time when we were playing basketball we both went up for a ball. He came down with the ball and I came down with a cracked tooth from his sharp elbows." Powell went on to Hollywood where he starred with Myrna Loy in the *Thin Man* movies of the 1930s.

Fern Carper was attending St. Joseph High School the winter Charley led Central to the roundball title.

"Oh, he was a monkey on the basketball court," said Carper. "He kept looking at the stands every time he put a basket in. He was built nicely, with wavy blond hair. After the game he came over and said, 'Hi, I'm Charley Stengel.' I remember that because we all knew him as Dutch Stengel, but I guess he thought that was too rough for our sweet young ears."

Central High's roundball hero, accompanied by his sister Louise, took Carper and her friend out for ice cream cones. "We were all thrilled that the star wanted to take us out. We were just sophomores and he was a senior," said Carper. She later married another Dutch, Eddie "Dutch" Zwilling, an outfielder for three different big-league teams in Chicago. The Zwillings and Stengel became lifelong friends.

Stengel captained the last football team at Central High. The school discontinued the sport in the fall of 1909 after one of its players was seriously injured by a kick to the head.

Although Charley was never the leading man that Powell was to become, he did enjoy a certain reputation with the opposite sex. He was shy, to a point, but he was never the foot-scuffing, "aw shucks" type. He often had his sister introduce him to girls he was too timid to approach. Once acquainted, he was secure enough in his own masculinity to endure the whistles and catcalls from his friends as he twirled his date around the dance floor. Charley cut a mean rug, exhibiting grace and stamina. According to a high-school chum, he once won five dollars in a marathon that required him to show up at the dance hall fifty straight nights. Dancing would remain his favorite leisure-time activity throughout his entire life.

More than anything, though, Charley excelled at baseball. He made the varsity team as a freshman, playing second and third base as a left-handed fielder, then became its number-one pitcher for the next three seasons. In 1909, his senior year, he pitched Central to the state high-school championship with a thrilling, 7-6, 15-inning victory over Joplin. Meanwhile, he commanded three dollars a game from Siggy Harzfeld, for whom he continued to play on weekends.

His reputation extended outside Kansas City. In the summers of 1908 and 1909, he barnstormed with a semipro team, the Kansas City Red Sox, traveling as far west as Utah and Wyoming and as far east as St. Louis. He made one dollar a day, plus food and lodging, and discovered that he loved the life of a professional ballplayer—the bawdy humor and horseplay, the camaraderie and competition, the adulation and sense of freedom. A classroom seemed terribly cramped and suffocating to a nineteen-year-old who'd had a taste of the world and was anxious to sample more.

One of his buddies, a short, colorful character by the name of Runt Marr, described how the gang would hang out at the Grand Billiard Parlor in downtown Kansas City. They'd shoot pool, smoke cigarettes, and argue the merits of big-league stars like Ty Cobb, Johnny Evers, and—Charley's favorite—Pittsburgh shortstop Honus Wagner, a fellow dutchman.

"We had these little picture cards, see, the ones that came in the cigarette packages," Runt recalled, "and we'd study their faces and their batting stances and the way they wore their caps and the way they buttoned their uniforms and we'd copy them. We all knew baseball was a tough life, but we knew Dutch Stengel could make it. He was tough as a boot."

Charley never finished high school. He attended Central in the fall of 1909, looking to graduate the following January, but discovered that he was a few credits short. At the same time he was being wooed by the Kansas City Blues. The Blues played in the American Association, a Triple-A league that was just one step removed from the majors.

The choice between finishing his degree and playing pro baseball was a no-brainer for Charley, but the would-be Blue was underage and needed his father's signature.

"Here, Pop, sign this, will you?" he asked one day as his father read the newspaper.

Startled, Louis Stengel responded, "What about school?"

"Aw, I'm finished with school. The Blues will pay me $135 a month."

This was a substantial amount of money to Louis Stengel, who had been raising a family of five for years on as little as ten or twenty dollars a week. "So I put down my paper and signed," he said. "You never could change that boy's mind anyway."

On the wintry morning of March 15, 1910, Charley boarded the Union Pacific

William Powell, destined to gain fame in Hollywood in the 1930s, had his first acting experiences at Central High. Powell, seen here standing fourth from left in the school's Christmas production of "The Rivals," also played varsity basketball with Stengel. An indifferent student, Stengel would cheerfully greet budding dramatists at school with the cry, "Ye gods, men! And how are you today?"

Stengel, seated second from left in the middle row, was the eighteen-year-old pitching star of the team that won the high school baseball championship in the spring of 1909.

Railroad for Excelsior Springs, Missouri, where the Blues were holding spring training. His mother and brother saw him off.

"Now just listen to what they tell you before you go to arguing," advised Grant before the train chugged off into the snow.

"I wanna play in the big league, don't I?" replied Charley. "Why would you argue with anybody if you ain't made the team yet?"

This was a very real concern. Charley's pay was contingent on him making the final cut, no sure thing with an abundance of talented players competing for the limited number of jobs. At the turn of the century, baseball was truly the national pastime. Literally and figuratively, it was the only game in town. Only recently, during the 1890s, had Americans either invented or imported such sports as basketball, ice hockey, badminton, water polo, and volleyball. Football was largely a college game, and prizefighting was a back-alley spectacle only slightly less odious than cockfighting. Consequently, the best athletes gravitated toward baseball.

The Blues staged their first exhibition game against Smoky Joe Wood and the Boston Red Sox. Wood, a Kansas City native who was just a couple of summers removed from pitching for the Blues, was a big local favorite. The Kansas City park on Brooklyn Avenue was packed. The entire Stengel family and more than a score of friends turned out to watch Charley go head-to-head with the Boston speedballer.

Instead they watched him tote a water pail. "Hey kid," yelled manager Danny Shay, "get the water bucket and bring it out to the regulars." His eyes down, Charley did as he was told while his friends hooted.

Shay, a former journeyman shortstop for several big-league teams, put Charley on the mound the next day against the Baby Blues, a semipro team financially supported by the Kansas City Blues. He was rocked for several hits. His second start a few days later in Omaha, Nebraska, was a failure, too. Charley apologetically told Shay that he was really an outfielder.

Shay was soon unimpressed by the failed pitcher's ball-hawking skills. "You're built like a horse, with that big rear end of yours," he told him. "No wonder you can't catch a fly ball."

Charley hadn't played much in the outfield before, but his options were limited. He couldn't pitch, and because he was a lefty, he couldn't be an infielder or a catcher. So under Shay's instruction he ran himself ragged chasing fungoes hit far over his head and balls that bounced crazily off the outfield fences. One day he'd finally had enough of Shay's incessant cries to "Play the angles! Play the angles!"

"If you want somebody to play the angles," he suggested, "why don't you hire a pool player?"

"You ought to be a pool player," responded Shay. "You've got a head as hard as a billiard ball." Players listening to this exchange gleefully dubbed Charley "Billiard Ball Stengel."

A couple of veterans, Bill "Spike" Shannon and Pat Flaherty, took pity on the awkward but conscientious youngster. Both had bounced around the big leagues before settling in Kansas City. Shannon hit balls by the hour until Charley gradually learned how to judge flies and to play caroms off the fences. Flaherty administered a more painful lesson, drilling Charley in the stomach with a quick pitch one day during batting practice. "I just wanted to give you a tip," explained Flaherty. "Never take your eye off the baseball."

Or, he might have added, the train schedule. Charley soon found himself optioned to Kankakee, Illinois, about fifty miles south of Chicago. Kankakee belonged to the financially ailing Class C Northern Association. He moved into a boardinghouse for four dollars a week (including meals) and made friends with a pair of young pitchers, Bill McTigue and Willard Sheetz, who were cousins from Tennessee. All the players collected their mail and paychecks at a funeral parlor operated by one of the team owners, a mortician named Hickey.

Before leaving for Kankakee, Charley had been instructed by Shannon and Flaherty to work on his sliding skills. He did so, albeit in a fashion that rubbed some of his teammates the wrong way. While shagging flies in practice, he would intermittently heave his mitt a few

Stengel as a member of the semipro Kansas City Red Sox. In the summer of 1908 the Red Sox barnstormed as far west as Utah, the players earning a dollar a day and meal money. It was the youngster's first taste of life as a traveling, professional ballplayer, and he fell in love with it.

Stengel was already a teenager when the first modern World Series was held between Pittsburgh and Boston in 1903. As he grew older his hero remained Honus Wagner, a perennial batting champion and fellow Dutchman who was at his usual position, shortstop, when Stengel broke into the big leagues late in the 1912 season.

Charles "Kid" Nichols, who lived across the street from the Stengels, was the owner of a record 362 National League victories when Charley came by to ask his advice upon signing with the Kansas City Blues. "Don't be arguing all the time," the retired pitcher told his young neighbor. "Listen to your manager. Or if you have an old player teaching you, listen to him. Never say, 'I won't do that.' Always listen. If you're not going to do what he says, don't tell him so. Let it go in one ear, and let it roll around in there for a month, and then if it isn't any good let it go out the other ear. But if it *is* good, memorize it and keep it. You do that and you'll learn something, and you'll keep out of a lot of trouble."

yards away, then race toward it, concluding his sprint with a slide.

The Kankakee State Hospital, an asylum for the mentally ill, sat on the other side of the outfield fence. One day the regular second baseman, a big-nosed fellow named Gilligan, commented to a teammate, "Stengel is one guy who won't be playing here next year." Asked where he'd be going, Gilligan pointed to the asylum and said, "Over there."

"Lefthanders have more enthusiasm for life. They sleep on the wrong side of the bed and their head gets more stagnant on that side."

The butt of the joke didn't much appreciate it. In a game shortly thereafter, he and Gilligan both converged on a short fly ball. Charley accidentally spiked the second baseman's foot, putting him out of commission for a few games. The feud carried over to Hickey's funeral parlor, where the players ran into each other a couple of days later. Gilligan accused Stengel of trying to get him dropped (clubs couldn't afford to carry injured players on the payroll). Charley called his accuser "duck nose," and the battle was on. As fists flew, Charley smashed into an empty coffin on display, and it crashed to the floor. Hickey finally broke up the melee, tossing Charley off the premises with the warning never to return.

Charley might have thought that playing in the shadow of an insane asylum while having a funeral home as a mailing address was as bad as things could get, but there remained one last blow. In mid July the league folded, throwing him out of work. He was still owed a half-month's salary. Figuring (correctly) that he would never see his check, he took his wool Kankakee uniform with him when he left.

He wasn't unemployed long. In short order he was wearing the flannels of the Shelbyville, Kentucky, team in the Class D Blue Grass League, where he had been reassigned by the Kansas City Blues. On the Shelbyville roster was Isador Sanders, a local product who always remembered his more talented teammate for his never-give-up attitude and nonstop banter. Stengel, Sanders noted, was "blessed with unique lungs."

Shelbyville, like Kankakee, proved a losing proposition in the standings and at the box office. In late August the last-place team was purchased by businessmen in Maysville, Kentucky. Once again Stengel was on the move, this time to a small town on the Ohio River.

The peripatetic outfielder enjoyed his stay in Maysville. After hitting the first homer of the season for the new owners, he was given a box of candy and a safety razor, and the local paper ran a succinct and flattering headline: "Stengel." A few days later another home run earned him a three-dollar hat. The gifts and compliments from Maysville's boosters eased the sting of a combined .236 batting average spread across 128 games with Kankakee, Shelbyville, and Maysville. The Blues, however, liked his power, intensity, and baserunning ability. When he returned home, they put him in uniform for the last six games of their schedule. He batted three times, banged out one hit, and had the satisfaction of concluding his first professional season as a .333 hitter for his hometown nine.

That and a nickel could buy him a mug of beer in the off-season. "You'd better have something to do if baseball doesn't work out," his father warned him. Charley,

For a couple of years Stengel juggled baseball and offseason studies at Western Dental College. Although he posed for this graduation photo—where he sits at the extreme left of the third row—he dropped out before gaining his diploma. Dentistry was a steady profession, but the big leagues were calling.

not certain of his diamond prospects, took it to heart. He paid fifty dollars to enroll at the respected Western Dental School in Kansas City.

As he did when playing ball, Charley brought hard work and humor to the task at hand. He was diligent in his studies and slightly outrageous in his pranks. He could be counted on to jam a cigar into the mouth of a corpse in anatomy class or to conceal himself under a sheet and rise suddenly, ghoul-like, from a slab. Once while walking around with the severed thumb from a corpse in his coat pocket, he came across an old friend, Harold Lederman. "We're talkin'," Stengel said, "and then I had to go and I put my hand in my pocket, felt that loose thumb, put it in my hand, and shook hands goodbye with Harold. Only I left the thumb in Harold's hand."

In later years Stengel would always recount with relish stories of his misadventures as a dental student. His first patient, he said, was "a guy who must've been nine feet tall and who was the strongest man around." While a supervising instructor looked on, Charley wrapped his arm around the patient's head and struggled to yank a tooth from his jaw. Soon a simple extraction turned into a cross between a taffy pull and a wrestling match. The more he pulled, the taller the patient seemed to grow, until finally the only thing he seemed capable of extracting was the patient from the chair.

Stengel blamed his woes on being a left-handed practitioner in a field dominated by right-handers, or on having banged-up, oversized "baseball knuckles"—

too large, presumably, to maneuver deftly in and around a patient's mouth. In reality these handicaps would have made little or no difference. The truth was that, despite his image as the class clown, he was a capable student. Had he not chosen a baseball career, he almost certainly would have become a dentist—Doc Stengel, one supposes.

In the spring of 1911 the Blues assigned the budding dentist to Aurora, Illinois, a member of the Wisconsin-Illinois League. Before leaving, he was able to wrangle a raise to $175 a month. He earned the increase by leading the Class C circuit in batting (.352), hits (148), and stolen bases (50). That he was able to hold onto his raise owed a lot to the advice of Al Tebeau, the club's owner. During a train trip, Tebeau—whose list of properties also included a brothel, saloon, and gambling hall—watched his star player lose heavily in a poker game with his teammates.

"You look to me like you can go to the big leagues," Tebeau told him the next day. "But if you want to be a big leaguer, you'd better quit playing cards. If you don't, you'll be broke every payday. I know, that's my bread and butter, this gambling business. And you sure can't play cards." Charley, who usually was very careful about money, took the advice to heart—one reason he would die a fairly rich man.

He didn't abandon his crowd-pleasing slapstick antics, however, not in Aurora and not in Montgomery, Alabama, where he spent the following summer toiling for the Brooklyn Dodgers' Class A team. The Dodgers had drafted him off the Aurora roster for $500, then paid him $150 a month—a twenty-five dollar pay cut—to see what he could do in the Southern Association.

What he did was shift his vaudeville act from one minor league to another. In Aurora he had sneaked up to an umpire who had just called him out on strikes and, as the umpire bent over dusting off the plate, whacked him full in the fanny with a bat. That episode cost him a twenty-five dollar fine and a two-day suspension. In Montgomery he crawled into a manhole in the outfield, then emerged in time to flag down a fly ball. Charley was talented, eager to learn, but just as eager to play the fool.

He undeniably had the attention of scouts. One, asked for his appraisal of Stengel's big-league potential, replied, "Well, he handles the bat well, and he can run and field and throw."

Stengel was "a dandy ballplayer," the scout concluded. "But it's all from the neck down."

☞ TWO

K.C. AT THE BAT

If Charley "Dutch" Stengel's inclination toward baseball burlesque didn't exactly enhance his chances for making the big leagues, neither did it prevent him from moving quickly to the majors once his talent was recognized. For several days during the 1911 season, a scout, Larry Sutton, had watched him play for Aurora and had liked what he'd seen. "Good hands, good power, runs exceptionally well, nice glove, left-handed line drive hitter," Sutton, a bird dog for the Brooklyn Dodgers, wrote in his notes. "Good throwing arm. May be too damn aggressive, bad temper."

The prospect's temper got worse when, having been sold by Aurora, where he'd made $1,050 for the season, he was expected to accept a salary of $900 to play for Montgomery. The $150 difference in pay was enough to make him threaten to quit the game for dental school. Sutton, an old pro who had been responsible for delivering the likes of Zack Wheat, Jake Daubert, and Otto Miller to Brooklyn, where they all developed into stars, talked Charley into reporting to Alabama for the 1912 season. Sure, there was a short-term financial loss, he told him. But if he proved he had the goods, in a couple of years he could expect to be called up to Brooklyn, where he would then make a big leaguer's salary.

"I knew he was right," the reluctant outfielder said. "I was still a long way from finishing dental school, and I knew I couldn't get a job in Kansas City for $150 a month."

The scenario Sutton described to Stengel developed more quickly than either

Facing page: **"K.C." Stengel in 1913, his first full season in Brooklyn.**

Norman "Kid" Elberfeld was a crusty veteran who had a big influence on Stengel's career. "Listen," said the old shortstop and former big-league manager when the two were at Montgomery, "if you want to get to the big leagues, watch me." Elberfeld, who had started his professional career in the Gay Nineties, ended it as Stengel's teammate on Brooklyn in 1914.

had imagined. During his 136 games with Montgomery, Stengel batted .290 and led the Southern Association in outfield assists. He also demonstrated considerable baseball savvy, thanks in part to the daily instruction he received from an old-timer named Norman "Kid" Elberfeld, a rough-and-tumble shortstop who had entered the professional ranks not long after Stengel had been born.

Elberfeld, who had signed with Montgomery after being dropped by Washington, saw something of himself in Stengel, who turned twenty-two that summer. They were practically inseparable, talking baseball while seated inside restaurants and hotel lobbies, executing plays on the diamond. Stengel found Elberfeld's stories of insider baseball and the personalities that made up the big leagues fascinating. A favorite tale was how Elberfeld, when playing shortstop for the New York Highlanders, had broken in Ty Cobb in his first major-league game back in 1905. The Georgia Peach tried to steal second base with a headfirst slide—then considered a bush-league tactic—and the feisty Elberfeld had administered "the teach," slapping the tag on the rookie and then rubbing his face into the dirt. Stengel was spellbound. The veteran helped instill in him an appreciation of the game's colorful past and an understanding of its evolving strategy, stretching back in some cases to before the Spanish-American War.

Elberfeld also had an impact on his protege's sense of style. When Stengel got the call to join the Dodgers at the end of Montgomery's season, Elberfeld insisted Charley dump his old clothes and cardboard suitcase and spend twenty-two dollars for a new suit and seventeen dollars and fifty cents for a leather bag. Charley considered these kinds of purchases frivolous, but Elberfeld prevailed. "You gotta dress like a big leaguer before they believe you are one," he stressed. Stengel would heed Elberfeld's advice to always go first class for the rest of his life.

The newest Dodger reported to Brooklyn's decrepit Washington Park on the afternoon of September 16, 1912, still bleary eyed from his farewell party and the ensuing thousand-mile train trip from Alabama. He parked his suitcase and watched from the stands as his new team, destined to finish seventh, lost to Pittsburgh. "I can play as good as these guys," he thought. After a full night's rest in a Manhattan hotel, he came to the ballpark early the next day, eager to test himself against one of baseball's perennial powerhouses.

On the mound for the Pirates that bright and warm Tuesday afternoon was right-hander Claude Hendrix, a teammate of Stengel's when both had played for the semipro Kansas City Red Sox in 1908. The newcomer was stationed in center, alongside left fielder Zack Wheat, another familiar face from his hometown. "When I get to the big leagues," Stengel had told his pool hall cronies back in Missouri, "I'm going right up to Cobb and Wagner and all them fellas and just say I'm anxious to show you what I can do."

In the bottom of the first inning, he smacked a Hendrix pitch to center field for a single. Exhilirated, he then tried to introduce himself to the Pirates' first baseman, Dots Miller. "Hi, my name's Stengel and I just come up."

Miller wasn't interested. He opened his mouth just long enough to direct a squirt of tobacco juice at the busher's new shoes. "Some of them fellas in the big league weren't really friendly then," Stengel remembered.

In the second inning Stengel singled past third to drive in the Dodgers' go-ahead run, 2-1. The score was tied at three runs apiece when he batted a third time. This time he singled to center, knocking in what proved to be the winning run. Then, for good measure, he stole second base. He repeated his performance in his fourth trip to the plate, lining a base hit to right field off reliever Jack Ferry and then swiping second.

In his fifth and final at-bat, Stengel faced a hard-throwing lefty, Sherry Smith. With the Dodgers up 7-3 in the bottom of the eighth, the rookie Stengel felt cocky enough to experiment. He shocked his manager, Bill Dahlen, and the four thousand in attendance by crossing over to the other side of the plate and batting right-handed. Smith, possibly flustered, walked Stengel, who promptly stole his third base of the afternoon.

It was quite a debut. His performance—four hits in four at-bats, a walk, three stolen bases, and two runs batted in, including the game-winner—had not only ended Pittsburgh's twelve-game winning streak, it caused some in the press to compare the phenom to more established greats. "I broke in with four hits and the writers promptly decided they had seen the new Ty Cobb," he recalled. "It took me only a few days to correct that impression."

His teammates were not in awe. His first few days he was frozen out of batting practice, the regulars' traditional method of reminding a rookie of his place. Stengel solved the dilemma in his own inimitable way. He had cards printed up and presented one to the veterans' ringleader, first baseman Jake Daubert: "Hi. My name is Charles Dillon "Dutch" Stengel and I would like to take batting practice." This cracked everybody up. Soon the busher was batting, drinking, and gambling with the regulars.

There remained the problem of what to call the new guy. During his first year or so in the majors, Stengel was interchangeably known in the press and in the clubhouse as Charley, Dutch, and even Jake (after a nineteenth-century ballplayer named Jake Stenzel). Some players referred to him as Kansas City or, more frequently, by the initials stenciled below his name on his luggage, K.C. During this period Ernest Thayer's 1889 poem, "Casey at the Bat," was gaining widespread popularity, thanks to actor DeWitt Hopper's overheated per-

Stengel's first major-league at-bats were against Claude Hendrix, with whom he had played on the Kansas City Red Sox. Hendrix, from Olathe, Kansas, compiled a 143-117 record with a 2.65 ERA in the National and Federal leagues before he was banned from organized ball in 1920 for allegedly fixing a game.

formances of it in vaudeville houses across the land. In short order, K.C. Stengel became Casey Stengel. It was an easy, inevitable, and permanent transition for players and fans to make, especially after Vitagraph released a one-reeler, *Casey at the Bat*, in 1913, followed by a full-length drama by the same name (starring Hopper) three years later. The nickname would stick for the rest of Casey's life, though his family would continue always to refer to him as Charley.

Burleigh Grimes, a veteran of 19 National League seasons, recalled Casey at the bat. "He stood at the plate with a closed stance and that big butt of his in your face," said the old spitballer. "He was what I called a long swinger. His bat came from way behind his ear to way out front. He always stood with his right foot closer than his left to the plate, sort of looking over his right shoulder at the pitcher. He would move his feet around in the box a lot. If he moved that front right foot up he was trying to get you to pitch inside so he could pull the ball. If he moved back, he was looking for an outside pitch he could slap to left field. A real smart fellow, that Stengel."

Smart enough to know when to exercise caution on the base paths. Contrary to stories that he liked to tell on himself (a favorite was "I steal a couple of bases, which is embarrassing for me because there's already runners on them"), Casey was an aggressive but heads-up base runner. During his minor-league days, one of the qualities scouts had remarked upon was his manner of sliding, which employed a "fadeaway" style similar to Ty Cobb's. As a base stealer, Casey would turn out to be a pale imitation of the Georgia Peach, swiping 131 big-league bases but getting tossed out a nearly equal number of times.

After breaking in with three stolen bases against Pittsburgh, Stengel next faced the Chicago Cubs. While stepping into the box his first time up, he had a conversation with the Cubs' ace backstop, Jimmy Archer.

"I see you broke in pretty good," Archer said.

"Yeah, pretty good," agreed Casey.

"Well," said Archer, "when you get on there, let's see you run."

"Not today, Mr. Archer," replied Casey. "I know you." In three games against the Cubs, Stengel didn't test Archer's arm once.

Stengel liked everything about Brooklyn except the ballpark. Washington Park was a cramped, wooden facility several years older than Casey. In fact, one part was older than the country itself. A stone structure that had once served as George Washington's headquarters stood on the site and had been converted into a ladies' room. Construction of a new concrete-and-steel stadium was already under way when Casey reported to the club. The following spring the Dodgers would be playing in a modern 24,000-seat park, Ebbets Field, named after club president and co-owner Charlie Ebbets.

The Cubs' diminutive second baseman, Johnny Evers, got an early sample of Stengel's aggressive baserunning. "You fresh busher!" he yelled after the rookie slid hard into second base on a force play. "You come into me like that again, and I'll stick this ball down your throat. If you ever cut me, you'll never play another game in the big leagues." The rookie's response: "That's the way I slid in the bushes, and that's the way I'll slide up here."

April 9, 1913: The Phillies beat the Dodgers 1-0 in the first game at Ebbets Field. Stengel played center field and batted lead-off, becoming the first Dodger to come to the plate at Brooklyn's new ballpark. A few days later he had the distinction of hitting the first home run there.

Casey hit well in his 17-game rookie tour: 18 hits in 57 at-bats for a .316 average. He also drove in 13 runs and stole five bases. He would wind up batting a respectable .284 over 14 major-league seasons. He was a somewhat impatient hitter, often jumping at the first pitch he saw, though usually content to spank the ball to all fields. He gripped the bat like a power hitter, holding his hands close to the end of the handle. He had a big swing, making him susceptible to change-ups, curves, and other slow stuff. He also had trouble with fastballs high and inside, especially from left-handers. During his career he would strike out about once every ten plate appearances (including walks and sacrifices), higher than the norm in those days. However, his power numbers were consistent with his sturdy 5-foot-9, 175-pound frame: a .410 slugging average and 60 home runs in a career spent mainly in the dead-ball era.

He returned home after his rookie season something of a local hero, but amidst the backslapping and glad-handing, he remained merrily self-deprecating about his batting skills. He got his first look at Walter Johnson that autumn when baseball's "Big Train" pitched the first five innings of an annual charity game for his hometown of Coffeyville, Kansas. Thirteen batters, including Stengel, went down on strikes as Johnson effortlessly fogged them in. Casey took the first two pitches for strikes before deciding the cause was hopeless. As Johnson once again went into his windup, he threw his bat down and headed for the bench.

"Come back here, you blind fathead," the ump yelled after him. "He threw that last ball to first base."

"They brought me up to the Brooklyn Dodgers, which at that time was in Brooklyn."

"That's all right," Casey shouted from the bench. "I didn't see the other two either."

That fall Stengel didn't return as usual for off-season studies at dental school. Although he had posed for the graduation photo taken the previous spring, his month in Brooklyn convinced him that his destiny was yanking fastballs, not molars. If he was wrong about his future, he could always go back. But of course, he never did.

In the spring of 1913 he reported to camp to begin his first full big-league season. He got the accompanying major-league salary Larry Sutton had told him about, but only after holding out all winter. Charlie Ebbets, looking for ways to reduce his overhead because of the cost of building his new stadium, finally relented and gave Casey the $350 a month—$2,100 for the season—that he wanted.

Stengel continued to demonstrate a flair for the dramatic. On April 5, 1913, Ebbets Field was formally opened with an exhibition between the Dodgers and New York Yankees. An overflow crowd of twenty-five thousand was on hand. In the bottom of the first inning, Stengel, batting leadoff, became the first Dodger ever to bat at Ebbets Field. He grounded out. However, in the fifth inning he drove the ball to left-center field. It shot off the rock-hard dirt (the outfield grass had yet to be installed) and headed for the fence, aided by the center fielder's inadvertent boot when he tried to cut it off. By the time the ball was recovered and relayed home, Stengel had circled the bases. He was credited with the first ever home run at Ebbets Field. To silence anyone unkind enough to point out that the historic feat had come in an exhibition and had been aided by a generous scorer, three weeks later, against the New York Giants, he slammed a two-run shot over the fence for the first regular-season home run hit at the Brooklyn ballyard.

Thanks in part to Casey's blistering hitting—his average soared past .350 in May—the surprising Dodgers climbed as high as second, but then came the long, slow fade. Ankle and shoulder injuries caused Stengel to miss 30 games. He still managed to hit .272, tie for the team lead in home runs with seven, and throw out 16

The 1913 Dodgers, managed to a sixth-place finish by Bill Dahlen. Stengel is standing second from the left in the back row, next to the mascot.

This studio portrait of Stengel was taken when he was in his early twenties. By now he was increasingly known as "Casey."

One of Casey's early heroes was Detroit's fiery Ty Cobb, whom he tried in vain to pattern himself after on the basepaths. "I never saw anyone like Cobb," he said. "No one even close to him. When he wiggled those wild eyes at a pitcher, you knew you were looking at the one bird nobody could beat."

base runners. The Dodgers finished sixth. It wasn't a big improvement from the previous year's seventh-place finish, but there was reason for optimism. The nucleus of young talent included Jake Daubert (who had won the batting championship and a new Chalmers automobile as the league's most valuable player), Zack Wheat, second baseman George Cutshaw, and catcher Otto Miller. Like Stengel, who had been hailed early in the season as a "center fielder extraordinaire," they were solid performers at bat and in the field.

It wasn't long before Casey emerged as one of the team's leaders. To Casey, tedium was to be avoided at all costs. It was the reason he had dropped out of school, never went to church, and often found his mind wandering during the monotony of practice or in the late innings of a 12-1 ball game. He did what he could to enliven matters at all times. Whether it was entering (and winning) a greased-pig contest, leading a knot of revelers in a night on the town, playing to the fans in the stands, or cutting up in front of some cute girls on the Coney Island beach, he clearly enjoyed being the center of attention. "There wasn't a day around Casey that I didn't laugh," said Zack Wheat. Years later when sportswriter Joe Williams described Brooklyn as "the last frontier of baseball fiction, the lone surviving outpost of big-league romance," it was implicitly understood that the rascally Stengel had played a major role in shaping that image.

So did the Dodgers' new manager, Wilbert Robinson, who replaced Bill Dahlen after the 1913 season. The chubby, paternal, and eternally patient ex-catcher, dubbed "Uncle Robbie" by the press, had learned his baseball playing for the storied Baltimore Orioles teams of the 1890s. One of his teammates, John McGraw, had gone on to become famous as the manager of the New York Giants. McGraw admired Robinson's keen baseball mind and ability to handle players and hired him as a coach. However, their friendship came to an end when McGraw accused Robinson of blowing a sign in the Giants' loss to Philadelphia in the 1913 World

Series. Charlie Ebbets jumped at the chance to sign Uncle Robbie as the Dodgers' new skipper.

"It's hard to remember today what an unusual personality Uncle Robbie was," said Bill Hallahan, who pitched several seasons for him. "I remember coming out of Ebbets Field after a game one day and there he was, talking to a group of cab drivers, explaining to them what had happened in the game and giving the reasons for his strategy. Can you imagine a manager doing that today?"

Or trying to catch a grapefruit dropped from an airplane? That was Robinson's most famous stunt, one that Stengel may or may not have had a hand in.

"It was rougher then....When I broke in, you just knew they were throwing at you. The first month I was in the league, I spent three weeks on my back at the plate."

During spring training in Daytona Beach, Florida, prior to the 1915 season, talk turned to the possibility of catching a ball dropped from an airplane. Ruth Law was in the area, and Charlie Ebbets had arranged with the famous aviatrix to go up in her flying machine and drop the ceremonial first pitch opening the exhibition season. Ebbets chickened out—flying was still a dangerous novelty then—but Uncle Robbie figured it was a stunt worth pursuing. After all, the old catcher reasoned, Gabby Street had once caught a ball thrown off the top of the Washington Monument, and he was every bit the backstop Street was.

Robinson bragged he could catch a ball delivered from a low-flying airplane. So it was that one rainy Saturday a plane bearing Law and Brooklyn trainer Frank Kelley appeared in the sky, about five hundred feet above the Dodgers' training site. Down below was Robinson, standing, as arranged, on the pitcher's mound, his neck arched and his glove at the ready. Kelley leaned over the fuselage and let something go.

Stengel is thrown out trying to steal third in a game against the Phillies early in his career. Putting the tag on him is Hans Lobart.

The Brooklyn Tip-Tops and their opponents from Buffalo gather in front of the scoreboard for ceremonies marking the opening day of the 1915 Federal League season at Washington Park, former home of the Dodgers. The renegade league, which started play in 1913, lasted only three years but was responsible for getting hundreds of major-league players pay raises they never would have gotten without the increased competition for their services. Casey saw his salary jump from $2,500 in 1913 to $6,000 in 1915, a direct consequence of owner Charles Ebbets's desire to hold on to his best players.

Zack Wheat was a quiet and undemonstrative product of Hamilton, Missouri, who batted .317 over nineteen big-league seasons. "He was the most graceful left-handed batter I ever saw," Stengel said of his Hall-of-Fame outfield mate and life-long friend. "With the dead ball, many of his line drives were caught, but they were just shot out of a cannon almost every time up."

Uncle Robbie, then approaching his fifty-second birthday and some forty pounds overweight, circled uncertainly around the slippery mound as the missile gathered speed and then—splat!—exploded against his chest. The force of the impact drove him to the ground.

Several players rushed to his aid. "Jesus, I'm killed!" Robinson exclaimed, his hands frantically wiping at the gore covering his face and upper torso. "I'm dead! My chest's split open! I'm covered with blood!"

It took several long moments before everybody realized that their manager had not been cleaved in two by a baseball, but floored by a grapefruit. Kelley, known as a clubhouse comedian, had substituted it for the ball. Pulp, juice, and fruit fragments were everywhere. At this point the laughter became uncontrollable. Players rolled around teary eyed while Robinson turned the air blue with curses. Uncle Robbie immediately suspected Stengel was behind the gag.

Wilbert Robinson, the beloved "Uncle Robbie" of Brooklyn, took over the team in 1914 after a falling-out with John McGraw and managed it for nearly two decades. Robinson was as responsible as anyone for the team's screwball image, once starting a "Bonehead Club" for players who made stupid mistakes and then becoming its first member by giving the wrong lineup card to the umpire. Robinson guided the Dodgers into two World Series, in 1916 and 1920, but came out on the short end each time. Nonetheless, he was inducted into the Baseball Hall of Fame in 1945.

Actually, Casey was one of the few players not to take Law up on her offer of a free flight during her stay in Daytona Beach. He had come to camp in awful physical shape, the result of a bout with typhoid. At the time neither the press nor the players suggested he was a conspirator, though Robinson remained unconvinced. But after thousands of retellings over the years, the details of the story became blurred beyond repair, to the point that Stengel even started boasting that *he* had dropped the grapefruit. Not only that, he'd say in late-night bull sessions as Yankees manager, he'd dropped the fruit bomb on Uncle Robbie *while sitting on a chair on the plane's wing!*

It would have been a fairly simple matter to check the facts with Law and others there that day. Indeed, some writers knew or suspected that Casey had had nothing to do with the famous grapefruit incident—a confession he later made in his autobiography. But if he didn't, then he *should* have, the popular thinking went, and for that reason it remained an integral part of the Stengel legend.

In his prime, Casey was a better-than-average player, a fact often lost in the laughter. "Because of his clowning," wrote one reporter early in Casey's career, "Stengel is lightly esteemed as a player by many folks who should know better. The truth is that it's doubtful whether there is a man on the Brooklyn ball team who has more baseball instinct than this same comical cuss."

"I was fairly good at times" was Casey's own assessment of his ability. "But a lot of people seem to remember some of the stunts I pulled better than they do the ball games I helped win."

He had his finest all-around big-league season in 1914, Uncle Robbie's first year at the helm. Robinson moved him from center to right field, which was the sun field in Brooklyn, but Stengel learned how to deftly track fly balls in the glare (aided by a new innovation, sunglasses). He also became adept at playing the weird bounces off the beveled fence, often practicing for hours before a game. Casey batted .316 in 126

Ruth Law advertised herself as "The Champion Explorer of the Sky," but today the pioneer aviatrix's place in history largely revolves around the grapefruit she, or a passenger, dropped on Uncle Robbie one day during spring training.

games as Uncle Robbie's Dodgers moved from seventh to fifth place. The final averages released by the National League office showed that only four players, including a trio of teammates, hit higher:

	AB	Hits	Avg.
Jake Daubert, Brooklyn	474	156	.329
Beals Becker, Philadelphia	514	167	.325
Zack Wheat, Brooklyn	533	170	.319
Jack Dalton, Brooklyn	442	141	.319
Casey Stengel, Brooklyn	412	130	.316

The following season was a downer for Stengel, though the Dodgers won 85 games and crept up a couple more notches to third place. His .237 average, a drop of 79 points from the previous summer, would be the lowest of his career. He also was being platooned more regularly. Nonetheless, Robinson, who was to have a great influence on Casey the manager, was "wonderful to work for," said Casey the player. "He would make you think he thought you were better than you were."

Uncle Robbie, noticing Stengel's difficulty in handling left-handers, sat him down against tough southpaws, but always did so apologetically. "If he put Jimmy Johnston in there and Johnston didn't get a hit," Casey recalled, "Robbie would call me over the next day and say, 'Gee, I couldn't sleep last night. I made such a terrible mistake not putting you into that ball game.' And if it happened another time, he'd say, 'I made that mistake again.'

"Now he hadn't made any mistake and he knew it. He just liked to keep you feeling good."

Another of Robinson's assets was his care and feeding of veterans, which Casey observed closely. "Robbie loved old players—men that were experienced," Stengel said. "He loved to get an old pitcher who had a bad arm, because he knew the man was brighter than when he was young and could throw harder. He took Rube Marquard and Larry Cheney and several others that were supposed to be over the hill and made exceptional pitchers out of them, because he showed them how to take advantage of their experience."

Former Giants catcher John "Chief" Meyers was one of several veterans Robinson brought on board and coaxed productive seasons out of. "I always maintained that Stengel won one more pennant than the record books show," Meyers told Larry Ritter a half century later. "That was in 1916, with Brooklyn. Of course, Robbie was the manager. But Robbie was just a good old soul and everything. It was Casey who kept us on our toes. He was the life of the party and kept us old-timers pepped up all season. And we knew so much baseball that we just outsmarted the rest of the league and walked off—or, you might say, limped off—with the pennant."

That summer the Dodgers won 94 games, tops in the majors. Several reclamation projects had a hand in the pennant, including shortstop Ivy Olson, third baseman Mike Mowrey, and pitchers Larry Cheney, Rube Marquard, and Jack Coombs, who combined for 44 victories after their previous teams had given up on them. The ace of the staff was Jeff Pfeffer, who won 25 games.

One day in 1910, Casey had been told to "Watch the angles, kid," when a ball bounced away from him. To which the brash minor leaguer had replied, "If I wanted to learn to play the angles, I wouldn't be here, but down at Johnny Kling's pool hall." Stengel changed his tune in the big leagues. By 1915 he had become an expert at handling the balls that caromed off the beveled right-field fence at Ebbets Field.

Stengel contributed a .279 average and eight home runs, one fewer than team leader Zack Wheat. His most important round-tripper came on September 30 in the second game of a Saturday doubleheader against the Phillies. Philadelphia had won the opener to squeeze a half game past the Dodgers and into first place. The second game was tied 1-1 when Stengel led off the bottom of the fifth. Grover Cleveland Alexander, on his way to a 33-win season (including an astonishing 16 shutouts and a major-league low 1.55 ERA) was on the mound. "Every ball that he threw would break, even his fastball," said Casey.

After delivering the first pitch low to Casey, Alexander came back with a belt-high fastball. This one apparently didn't break. Stengel turned on it, sending the ball flying over the right-field wall. The blast turned out to be the margin of victory as the Dodgers moved back into first place to stay. To the end of Casey's days, his dramatic home run off Ol' Pete remained one of his favorite baseball yarns.

The World Series began October 7. The Boston Red Sox, who had manhandled the Phillies

Casey always savored the home run he hit off Grover Cleveland Alexander on September 30, 1916. It helped beat Philadelphia and pushed the Dodgers past the defending National League champions into first place.

in the previous World Series, were once again the American League's representative. Boston, which depended on superior pitching and airtight defense, was hoping to win its fourth world championship in seven years. The team was so deep it could afford to lose two key members of the 1915 squad because of salary disputes: Smoky Joe Wood sat out the season while star center fielder Tris Speaker was traded to Cleveland. A twenty-one-year-old pitcher named George Herman "Babe" Ruth more than took up the slack, however. Ruth led the staff with a 23-12 record, topped the junior circuit with a 1.75 ERA and nine shutouts, and tied the club lead in home runs.

The Series opened in Boston with right-hander Ernie Shore opposing Marquard. Stengel, batting in his customary third spot, rolled weakly to second base in his first postseason at-bat. But in the fourth he opened the inning with a single past second, then came around to score the tying run on Wheat's triple. The Red Sox built a 6-1 lead going into the ninth, then narrowly survived a four-run rally (including another single by Stengel) for the win.

Fred Merkle, who was never allowed to forget a baserunning blunder that cost the Giants the pennant in 1908, was one of several veteran acquisitions that secured a flag for Brooklyn in 1916. Later, as manager, Stengel would emulate Wilbert Robinson's strategy of picking up experienced hands late in the pennant chase.

Ruth started game two. Under Uncle Robbie's platoon system, this meant replacing Stengel with the right-handed hitter Jimmy Johnston. Casey watched from the bench as Ruth and Sherry Smith hooked up in one of the classic pitching duels of all time, with the Sox finally prevailing 2-1 in 14 innings.

With the Dodgers down two games to none, the venue shifted to Ebbets Field. Casey was back in the lineup and in the middle of the action as Brooklyn eked out a 4-3 victory. Afterward Stengel was his usual loud and demonstrative self, shouting in the dugout, "We've got Boston on the run!" But the Sox banged out easy 6-2 and 4-1 victories the following two afternoons to win the Series. Casey, who'd managed to get into every game except the second, wound up leading all hitters with a .364 average—four hits in 11 at-bats. His losing share for less than a week's work was $2,835, roughly half of his regular-season salary.

It never seemed to be enough, however. By now Stengel was the leader of a hell-raising clique known as the Grumblers. They moaned about the food on train trips and about the cockroaches in their hotel rooms. Most of all, they bitched about their low salaries. Casey was dubbed King of the Grumblers.

Charlie Ebbets was growing weary of Stengel's shenanigans and chronic complaining. Once during the 1916 season, the owner called Casey into the office to hear Casey's side of a fight he'd had with a teammate at Coney Island. "What kind of hoodlums do we have on this club, anyhow?" Ebbets wanted to know.

Casey flashed four fingers. He'd had only four beers, he said, launching into a convoluted explanation.

"Yeah, he only had four beers," Uncle Robbie snorted, "but they were big as pails." For the rest of the season, players and fans around the league flashed four fingers at Casey and yelled, "I only had four!"

New York's nightlife appealed to Casey. He danced, drank, gambled, and bedded his share of baseball Annies. (Some sportswriters maintained that it was a case

of venereal disease, not typhoid, that accounted for his abysmal 1915 season.) But dissipation costs money, and Casey liked to live beyond his means. One irritated saloonkeeper taped nearly two dozen checks Casey had written him to the front window of his Flatbush Avenue establishment; each bore a bank stamp reading Insufficient Funds.

Stengel was never satisfied with what he made. In fact, he held out every season he was at Brooklyn. Before the start of the 1914 season, he used the threat of the new Federal League, which had placed a team in the borough, as leverage to get a two-year deal for $6,000 a season—a tactic Ebbets didn't appreciate. Casey's contract expired at about the same time the Brooklyn Tip-Tops and the rest of the Federal League did; coming off a .237 season, he had little choice but to sign a lesser contract for $5,400.

In 1917 Casey batted .257 as the defending National League champions plummeted to seventh. Although he had led thc club in games, hits, runs, doubles, triples, home runs, and RBI, that winter he was asked to take another pay cut, this time to $4,100, for the 1918 season.

Casey returned the contract with a note to Ebbets: "Dear Charlie, I received the contract but know it wasn't mine when I saw the figures. You must have sent me [batboy] Red Monahan's by mistake."

The Dodgers' owner wasn't amused. The next contract he mailed slashed

First baseman Jake Daubert won batting titles in 1913 and 1914, but he was a bust in the World Series against Boston. In the third game, played October 10, 1916, he was tagged out by catcher Pinch Thomas after trying to leg out an inside-the-park home run. Stengel, the on-deck batter, can be seen observing the action at extreme right; moments later he would come close to getting tossed out of the game for loudly protesting the umpire's call. Daubert's dash foreshadowed Casey's more famous—and more successful—race around the bases in the opening game of the World Series exactly seven years later.

Pitching aces Babe Ruth (left) and Ernie Shore accounted for three of the Red Sox's four wins as Boston took the 1916 World Series four games to one. Stengel, who was benched against Ruth, hit .364 in the Series, tops among all Dodgers.

Stengel's salary by another $400. Casey asked if he could sign the original offer. That was fine with Ebbets, who then traded his malcontent to Pittsburgh.

"I knowed I shouldn't have been such a smart aleck," Casey told a friend back in Kansas City.

The trade of January 9, 1918, sent Stengel, George Cutshaw, and $20,000 to the Pirates in return for shortstop Chuck Ward, pitcher Al Mannix, and Burleigh Grimes. The diamond in the rough was Grimes, a 3-16 pitcher for Pittsburgh who would rack up four 20-game seasons in Brooklyn and lead it back into the World Series in 1920.

Stengel had been an extremely popular figure during his six seasons in Brooklyn and was sorely missed by the press and the fans. For his part Casey hated Pittsburgh, with its belching smokestacks and soot-stained sidewalks. Some of his new teammates even insisted on calling him Charley. That summer the transplanted King of the Grumblers showed that he hadn't lost his crown in the move. After he was booed by fans at Forbes Field for not sliding in a close play at the plate, he retorted, "With the salary I get here, I'm so hollow and starving that I'm liable to explode like a light bulb if I hit the ground too hard."

He'd always had a quick temper, but as a Pirate he seemed more confrontational than ever. Thumbed out of a game at the Polo Grounds, he ripped off his jersey, threw it over his shoulder, and stalked across the outfield lawn to the center-field clubhouse. When the league president wired him that he had been fined twenty-five dollars, Casey showed up for the next game with the yellow telegram pinned to his sleeve. He wore it during the entire game, prompting a second fine of two hundred dollars.

By now even a world war was looking good. Leon Cadore, a close friend of Stengel's when both played in Brooklyn, had joined the army as America mobilized millions of men to join in the European fighting. After listening to Cadore, Casey figured the service was a better option than the National League. With the government issuing a "work or fight" order and curtailing the baseball season, he figured on going in sooner or later anyway. Why not do it now and save two hundred dollars? The league office wouldn't dare try to collect the fine from someone serving his country.

On June 13, 1918, he showed up at Ebbets Field and announced that he had joined the navy. The doctor administering the physical had "pronounced me a perfect man," said Casey. Grant Stengel wasn't impressed. As Casey's older brother pointed out, he had given up his baseball salary of four thousand dollars a year to

Never afraid of innovation, Casey was one of the first major-leaguers to wear a new-fangled invention called "sunglasses" to cut down on the late-afternoon glare in the outfield.

"Bullet Joe" Rogan (standing at far right) and the rest of the Kansas City Monarchs assemble for a team picture in 1920, their first season in Rube Foster's newly created Negro National League. Although Casey could hardly be considered a pioneer in race relations, he was responsible for rescuing the fastball pitcher and several others from obscurity. In 1919 the Pirates had traded Stengel to Philadelphia; rather than report, he had gone on a barnstorming tour of the Southwest. One day Stengel's team played against a former army team stationed at Fort Huachuca, Arizona, that included Rogan. When Casey returned to Kansas City that winter, he tipped off J.L. Wilkinson, a local businessman then helping to organize the Monarchs, to what he had seen. Rogan and several of his black teammates wound up becoming the core of the league's most prosperous team. Twenty-five years later one of Stengel's most severe critics, Jackie Robinson, would break into professional ball with the Monarchs.

Casey and two of his fellow Philadelphians, Gavvy Cravath (center) and Fred Luderus (right), in 1920. That summer saw the second of three straight last-place finishes for the hapless Phillies.

Philadelphia's Baker Bowl was a ballpark with the dimensions of a cigar box. Stengel played right field there for parts of two seasons, 1920-21: "I had the wall behind me, the second baseman in front of me, the foul line on my left, and Cy Williams on my right. The only time I had to catch the ball was when it was hit right at me."

avoid paying a two hundred dollar fine. "Now you can live on navy pay of fifteen dollars a month," said Grant.

Casey got no closer to France than the Brooklyn Naval Yard during his six-month tour of duty. He was originally assigned to painting ships, but after his superiors realized who the genial fellow in bell-bottoms was, they took away his brush and bucket and handed him a bat and ball. He was put in charge of the yard's baseball team. He arranged games with teams thrown together from the crews on incoming ships. The naval yard compiled an admirable record. It helped that its opponents still had sea legs.

"I used to board them ships as soon as they got in," said Stengel, "and make a date for a game the next day. I found if they'd been on land too long, we couldn't beat them."

One day when Casey and his shipyard nine were practicing at Prospect Park, he handed his wallet to a youngster for safekeeping. Casey was out in the field when he saw the boy on a bicylce pedaling like mad away from the park. To a swabbie making fifteen dollars a month and no guarantee of a major-league salary after the war ended—and who knew when that would be?—it was a discouraging sight, to say the least. "I can still see that kid riding away with my fifty bucks," Casey would say many times over in the coming years. "The moral of the story is, never trust a boy on a bicycle."

Casey was discharged over the winter. The Pirates wanted him back, but at a modest price. He haggled with owner Barney Dreyfuss over his contract before finally caving in and signing. Baseball was all he knew.

He saved what was perhaps his most famous stunt for his old friends in

Stengel was not alone in considering seven-time batting champion Rogers Hornsby one of the most gifted hitters ever. Even more impressive to Casey was the moody Texan's guts. One afternoon at Baker Bowl he watched from the outfield as Phillies pitcher Lee Meadows fired three straight fastballs behind Hornsby's head, then broke a curve over the plate. Instead of falling away as expected, Hornsby stepped into the pitch and walloped a hard, flat line drive to left field. "That was the roughest I ever saw a man pitched to in the big leagues," Casey said admiringly. In the 1930s, when Casey was managing in Boston, he'd bring up Hornsby's name whenever one of his players complained about having to play in windswept Braves Field. "Yes, it is a shame," he'd say with heavy sarcasm. "Mr. Hornsby played here only one season [1928] and he hit only .387."

Flatbush. One May afternoon in 1919 when the Pirates were at Ebbets Field, Casey was standing in the bull pen area between innings, kibitzing with his old friend Leon Cadore. Suddenly a sparrow flew past them and plowed headfirst into the grandstand wall. Casey scooped up the dazed bird and stuck it under his cap—filed away, as it were, for future reference.

In the top of the seventh, he came up to bat. Casey was all set to dig into the batter's box when inspiration hit. Pretending that he had a cinder in his eye, he called time and backed out of the box. And then with a grand flourish, he bowed to the grandstand, doffed his cap, and out flew the bird, wings flapping furiously as it climbed into the sky. Needless to say, the Brooklyn crowd loved this impromptu performance, as did both benches. Even the home plate umpire, Cy Rigler, laughed.

Reporters sought comment from Casey's old manager. "Well, there's no use getting excited about it," Uncle Robbie said. "He's got birds in his garrett, that's all."

Some stuffed shirts, particularly Barney Dreyfuss, didn't care for the comic relief. "The higher-ups complained I wasn't showing a serious attitude by hiding a sparrow in my hat," offered Stengel, "but I said any day I got three hits, I figure I am showing a more serious attitude than a lot of players with no sparrows in their hats."

This kind of logic was lost on Dreyfuss, who that August peddled Stengel to Philadelphia for outfielder George "Possum" Whitted. Casey sent a telegram to Phillies owner William Baker, a former New York City police commissioner who had bought the team in 1913: "There's not enough money here. Stop. Will need more to go over there. Stengel."

Baker fired off a reply: "There's not much money here, either." To which Stengel responded: "If there isn't enough money in Philadelphia I'll be in Kansas City, Missouri." With that he left Pittsburgh on a train bound for Kansas City.

Casey spent the balance of 1919 barnstorming through Kansas, Oklahoma, Texas, New Mexico, Arizona, and California with a semipro team he'd organized. In the fall Phillies left fielder Emil "Irish" Meusel joined the team. Meusel helped persuade Casey to sign with Philadelphia. A big-league salary with a last-place team was still preferable to kicking up dust in towns named Chilocco and Ropesville.

For the next year and a half, Stengel and Meusel wound up flanking Cy Williams in the outfield at Baker Bowl, the Phillies' cigar box of a ballpark. A forty-foot-high wall and screen ran from the center-field clubhouse to the foul line in right where Casey was stationed. "It might be exaggerating to say the outfield wall cast a shadow across the infield," Red Smith once wrote, "but if the right fielder had eaten onions at lunch the second baseman knew it." It was only a cozy 280 feet from home plate to the foul pole, making Casey feel damn near claustrophobic as he fielded the barrage of balls hit his way from left-handed batters.

To Casey, everything about the Phillies was a hoot. He and Williams had to contend with a large hump in the grass in right-center where an underground train tunnel ran from the yards of the adjoining Philadelphia and Reading Railroads. And instead of using lawnmowers to keep the grass low, the team employed sheep, who were released from their home under the stands to graze in the outfield between games. In this kind of environment, Stengel was noticeably less than serious, occasionally catching easy fly balls behind his back and once treating the small Baker Bowl crowd to his now famous bird-in-the-hat routine.

The Eighteenth Amendment, national prohibition, shut down old-time

Philadelphia breweries like Schmidt's, Poth's, and Bergdoll's and threatened to make the summer of 1920 the first dry one of Stengel's professional career. But he, Meusel, and several other fun-loving teammates had no trouble finding speakeasies in the heavily industrialized section of North Philadelphia that surrounded Baker Bowl. In a sense they were the Philadelphia chapter of the Grumblers, moaning about their penurious owner, the dilapidated ballpark, and whatever else crossed their minds. By their second season together in 1921, Stengel and Meusel had acquired a reputation as slackers, as well, but that was unfair. Casey had chronically sore legs and a bad back while Meusel was trying to nurse a tender throwing arm. So it was only natural that they let the conscientious Cy Williams take every fly ball he could get. Stengel's and Meusel's cries for help became a standing joke between them for years afterward: "Hey, Cy! You take it!"

Then, on June 30, 1921, as Casey was being administered to by the trainer, he was handed a message. He, second baseman Johnny Rawlings, and pitcher Red Causey had been traded to the Giants for Goldie Rapp, Lee King, and Lance Richbourg.

New York? Casey jumped off the trainer's table with a shout.

"I thought you had a bad back, damn it," growled his manager, Bill Donovan.

"I don't anymore," said Stengel, overjoyed to be heading back to where all top performers belonged: center stage in the Big Apple.

THREE

Wake Up, Muscles

Casey Stengel wasted no time in reporting to the Giants. Unlike Johnny Rawlings, who decided to wait over a day, Casey grabbed the 6:14 train from Philadelphia to New York, then took the midnight train from New York to Boston, where the Giants were finishing up a series. As Stengel later explained, "I wasn't taking any chances on the deal being called off."

He could hardly be blamed for disbelieving his luck. He had suddenly been shipped from a deadwood team to the winningest, classiest organization in baseball. Between 1903 and 1925, a span of twenty-three seasons, the Giants would win ten National League pennants and finish second nine other times—a standard of excellence no other team could approach. Just as remarkable was the fact that the winning would span the dead-ball and lively ball eras, two distinct periods in baseball history.

The one constant was John J. McGraw, whom many considered then (and now) the greatest manager ever. McGraw hated the nickname Mugsy, but an alternative, Little Napoleon, was kinder and a bit more descriptive. Like the French emperor, he was short, pugnacious, and despotic, and he viewed the world in hard, practical terms. As a boy, McGraw had lost his mother and four siblings to a diphtheria epidemic; his emotionally devastated father beat him so severely that McGraw finally ran away to be raised by a neighbor. To further compound his sense of fatalism, as a young man, he lost his first wife to a ruptured appendix. As the fireplug of the old Baltimore Orioles of the 1890s (where he was credited with inventing the hit-and-run play with Wee Willie Keeler), McGraw had scrapped and clawed to

***Facing page:* Casey as one of John McGraw's Giants.**

Baseball's most famous manager looks out from a tobacco ad. "I learned more from McGraw than anybody," said Stengel.

gain the smallest tactical or psychological advantage over his opponent. This warrior mentality brought him great success after his playing days when he jumped from the upstart American League to the Giants at the end of the 1902 season. He was a brilliant strategist, among the first managers to recognize the importance of relief pitching and platooning. He was also a caustic and profane autocrat who did his utmost to control every facet of his players' lives, on and off the field.

One of the signs of McGraw's genius was his adaptability. His teams had excelled at a time when trick pitches, cavernous outfields, and lopsided baseballs had put a premium on bunts, stolen bases, and airtight pitching and defense. But a new era was suddenly upon him thanks to the shorter fences of the modern concrete-and-steel parks being built, the outlawing of the spitter, and the introduction of several new balls into play each game. Rather than resist change, McGraw went along with the flow. He continued to stress fundamentals—defense, pitching, smart baserunning—but he now peppered his lineup with strategically placed power hitters. It was the reason he had dealt for Stengel, and Casey knew that. When Casey took his first look around the Polo Grounds, he said to himself, "Wake up, muscles. We're in New York now."

He was joining a team of fine young stars including outfielder Ross Youngs, second baseman Frank Frisch, shortstop Dave "Beauty" Bancroft, and first baseman George Kelly—all future Hall of Famers. The acquisition of Rawlings allowed McGraw to put Frisch on third, a move that solidified the infield.

The acquisition of Stengel didn't do the same for McGraw's unsettled outfield. Casey was used sparingly. He got into just 18 games, batting a mere 22 times (mostly as a pinch hitter), while McGraw fiddled with his outfield combination. Less than a month after obtaining Casey, McGraw sent $30,000 and three players to the Phillies for Irish Meusel. Casey's buddy was ecstatic about leaving Philadelphia, where he had been suspended for indifferent play. He wound up batting .343 between the two clubs, good for fifth in the league. With Meusel in left, old pro George Burns in center, and Youngs in right, the Giants overtook Pittsburgh in the last weeks of the season for the pennant. Stengel pitched in where he could, jockeying opponents, riding umpires, coaching first base, and trying to keep things loose in the clubhouse. He also observed carefully as McGraw drove his team to the top.

"I chased the balls that Babe Ruth hit."

The Giants took on the Yankees, their cotenants at the Polo Grounds, in the first all–New York World Series. Most of the fans turned out to see what the game's greatest sensation, Babe Ruth, could do against the Giants' less-than-illustrious pitching staff. Ruth had hammered 59 into the seats during the season (16 more than Stengel had hit in his entire major-league career thus far) and scored 177 runs while driving in another 171.

The Yankees won the first two games by identical 3-0 scores, then went into the tank. Remarkably, McGraw used only thirteen players in the entire Series, including four pitchers. Casey was one of ten subs who watched from the bench as the Giants'

As these two shots from his Giants days illustrate, Casey could be serious or he could be a clown. In either mode he was a valuable member of a team that won pennants in each of the three seasons he played at the Polo Grounds.

The 1921 edition of the Yankees' Murderers Row included (from left) Wally Pipp, Babe Ruth, Roger Peckinpaugh, Bob Meusel, and Frank "Home Run" Baker. Despite the presence of such power in the lineup, it took the Yankees three tries before they were able to beat the Giants in a World Series.

regulars rebounded to win the best-of-nine tournament five games to three. Once again, Casey the bench warmer did what he could to contribute, getting tossed out of the fifth contest for protesting too vigorously an umpire's call from the dugout. Nobody complained about the lack of playing time, for the payoff was a winning share of $5,265 per man. As Casey remarked: "I made more money sitting with the Giants than I ever made standing with anybody else."

McGraw's set lineup in the 1921 Series was at odds with his platoon mentality, from which Casey would reap great benefits over the next two seasons.

"My platoon thinking started with the way McGraw handled me in my last years on the Giants," Casey later explained. "He had me in and out of the lineup, and he used me all around the outfield. He put me in when and where he thought I could do the most good. And after I got into managing I platooned whenever I had the chance, long before I came to the Yankees. . . ."

Stengel feasted on right-handers, batting .368 in 1922, a figure exceeded only by Rogers Hornsby of St. Louis. He added seven home runs and 48 RBI in 84 games. "I never hit that high before," said Casey, "and I said to myself, that's amazing. But I woke up on the last day of the season and found that Hornsby was leading the league

Casey at the bat in 1922. That year he hit .368 in part-time action with the Giants.

On May 7, 1923, Casey got into a brawl with Phil "Lefty" Weinert when the big Philadelphia pitcher dusted him off with a fastball at his head. Casey, who had been hit by Weinert his first time up, threw his bat and charged the mound. It took several policemen to break up the ruckus, which resulted in a ten-day suspension. Casey wasn't able to crack the lineup again until July, but wound up hitting .339 for the season as the Giants won a third straight pennant.

33 points higher." (To be fair to Chicago first baseman Charlie Grimes, one should note that Casey fell short of having the necessary number of plate appearances to qualify for the batting championship. Officially, Grimes finished runner-up to Hornsby with a .354 mark in 138 games.)

In October the Giants met the Yankees in the World Series. For the second straight year, the Giants prevailed, this time whipping the Yanks in four straight (or five straight if you count the 3-3 tie in game two). Ruth hit an abysmal .118 and frequently lost his cool as Giants players rode him unmercifully. When he wasn't screaming derogatory comments about Ruth's ancestry or personal hygiene, Casey chipped in with base hits in each of the two games he started. He hit .400, based on two hits in five at-bats. Afterward he picked up another handsome winning player's share, this time $4,470.

Despite two straight world championships, success never changed the boss's routine, said Casey. "McGraw worked us hard. He'd sit on a chair in front of the boxes behind home plate and watch the entire workout. He wouldn't allow us to stand around the cage between turns at batting practice, the way I'd done on some clubs. You were supposed to bunt the last ball, then run and circle the bases, then go out and practice fielding until your next turn at bat. If he caught you loafing, he'd make a circular motion with his finger, and that meant you had to run and circle the ballpark."

Casey had a good rapport with the demanding McGraw. By 1923 he was coaching the Giants' B squad in spring training and frequently visiting the manager's fashionable brick home in Westchester County. The pair often discussed strategy and tactics until the sun came up. Mrs. McGraw would often wake up in the morning to find student and master frying bacon and eggs while still gabbing baseball.

A lot of what Casey later practiced as a manager was learned in these marathon bull sessions and reinforced in game situations. "He wanted you to be a fighter at the plate and not just give in to the pitcher, whatever happened," said Casey. "Stand in there, don't back off an inch, and get a piece of the ball. Something may happen.

"He also was very alert on when to start the runners, when to start double steals, and he was very good at not having you caught off a base. He hated to see you just walk off a base sluggishly. He said the first two steps off a base, if the batter hits the ball, might make you be safe at third or safe at home plate."

If it was great to be young and a Giant, as Ross Youngs had once enthusiastically proclaimed, Casey discovered that it wasn't too bad being middle-aged and a Giant either. If there was one thing that was missing from his life, however, it was a woman.

A pair of Casey Stengel trading cards from the early twenties.

Babe Ruth and broadcaster Graham McNamee at the 1923 World Series. Years later, asked if Ruth used a heavy bat, Casey replied, "He could have used his sleeve or a rolled-up copy of the *Police Gazette.* Wouldn't have made a bit of difference."

Casey had had his share of one-night stands. Conquests were especially easy in New York, where young, attractive women hung around hotel lobbies hoping to latch on to ballplayers. Whether a fellow was married or single, it was hard to turn away the prospect of a romp in the sheets with a girl eager to tell her friends that she had bedded a fellow who spent his afternoons playing for the famous and glamorous New York Giants.

McGraw, aware of the possibilities of blackmail, disease, and general physical dissipation, tried to make such sexual rendezvous more difficult by using detectives, curfews, and surprise bed checks. Casey recalled how he used to cover for his roommate, a young pitcher named Hugh McQuillan. "McGraw had a system about that time when his chief detective would go around the hotel at midnight, knocking on your door. When he said, 'Stengel?' I would sing out 'Here!' in my baritone voice. Then he would say 'McQuillan?' and I would yell 'Here!' in my tenor voice. There was never a dull moment."

Casey was impressed by McGraw's creativity in keeping tabs on his players' nocturnal habits, such as his practice of checking breakfast stubs—a trick Casey would borrow when he became a manager. "You know that the guy who has orange juice, cereal, bacon and eggs, toast and coffee, or an order like that hasn't been up fooling around all night," Stengel explained. "It's those who order double tomato juice and black coffee who go out to mail letters at three o'clock in the morning."

After a dozen big-league seasons, Casey had grown wiser in his pursuit of the opposite sex. "Going to bed with a woman never hurt a ballplayer," he would later preach to his troops. "It's staying up all night looking for them that does you in. You gotta learn that if you don't get it by midnight, chances are you ain't gonna get it, and if you do, it ain't worth it." Not wanting to offend McGraw, a man he admired tremendously, undoubtedly had a lot to do with Casey's change of heart. Although he had some flings with showgirls and other big-city party girls, the one-night stands were losing their appeal. Stengel was now in his early thirties and looking for a deeper, more lasting relationship. One day at the Polo Grounds, he was introduced to the woman who would become his partner for life.

Casey was a regular visitor to the apartment of Irish Meusel and his wife, Van. In the summer of 1923, the Meusels were entertaining a friend from the West Coast, a slim and attractive brunet named Edna Lawson.

Edna, born August 31, 1895, in Menominee, Michigan, was an educated, refined, and somewhat worldly woman. After her father had made and then lost a good deal of money in the logging business, he uprooted the family for Glendale, California, in 1914. There he entered the real estate and construction businesses, quickly becoming a financial success in a part of the country that was ripe for development. Meanwhile, Edna finished her last year of school at Glendale High, then tried her hand in the fledgling movie business.

Second baseman Frank Frisch was a slashing hitter and heir apparent to John McGraw until his unexpected trade to St. Louis for Rogers Hornsby in 1927. There he helped the Cardinals to four pennants and two championships. He and Casey were close friends. Later, when Frisch was piloting the Pirates, he enjoyed poking fun at Casey's woes while managing the Braves. After Casey was run down by a taxi in 1943, Frisch sent a telegram to his hospital room. "Your attempt at suicide fully understood," cabled Frisch. "Deepest sympathy you didn't succeed."

Casey slides across the plate just ahead of the throw to complete his famous inside-the-park home run against the Yankees in the opening game of the 1923 World Series.

The couple of studios in Glendale provided occasional work for locals as extras. Edna was attractive, and she didn't have to say much (this, after all, was the silent-film era), but she found the work less than glamorous. "I was a good dancer so they put me in western dance-hall scenes," she recalled. "Once I knocked over the whole set. Nobody made much money in those days. The most I ever got was $85 a week. But I acted with Lillian Gish and Hoot Gibson and other stars. I guess I photographed well, but it wasn't for me." Always good with numbers, she took up bookkeeping and started a new career as an accountant.

"Edna was a very solid personality," remembered John Lawson, the youngest of Edna's three siblings and a future mayor of Glendale. "She was the stabilizer of the family, very mature as young girl and very secure in her own self."

Edna enjoyed travel. Every summer she took a two-week vacation to a different part of the country. On one such trip to Menominee, she met Van Meusel, with whom she kept in touch. Van invited her to visit New York to take in the fine restaurants, night spots, and Broadway shows. She'd have to hurry, though, Van wrote Edna, as she didn't know how much longer her husband would be playing for the Giants. Duly warned, Edna canceled a planned trip to Oregon and instead took a train east.

Van Meusel took Edna to the Polo Grounds and told her to keep an eye on the Giants' center fielder, a bachelor who could make her laugh. Edna wasn't quite sure who Van was talking about. Although Edna had enjoyed such activities as basketball, tennis, and swimming in school, "I didn't know enough about baseball to know where center field was," she confessed. "But I saw somebody out there between two other fellows, so I figured that must be center field."

After the game Casey walked Edna back to the Meusels' apartment and secured

Emil "Irish" Meusel, pictured here with his brother Bob and his sister-in-law, played with Stengel in Philadelphia, New York, and Toledo. They remained good friends with him until Meusel's death in 1963.

Some Dashing Prose from a Casey Admirer

Damon Runyon, the veteran sportswriter of the *New York American*, did as much as anybody in the media to establish the Stengel legend. His front-page account of Casey's inside-the-park home run that beat the Yankees in the opener of the 1923 World Series has become nearly as famous as the dash itself, the reason it's reprinted here:

STENGEL'S HOMER WINS FOR GIANTS, 5-4

60,000 Frantic Fans Screech as Casey Beats Ball to Plate.
Warped Legs, Twisted, Bent in Years of Campaigning,
Last Until He Reaches Goal

Damon Runyon: "This is the way old 'Casey' Stengel ran...."

By Damon Runyon

This is the way old "Casey" Stengel ran yesterday afternoon, running his home run.

This is the way old "Casey" Stengel ran running his home run home in a Giant victory by a score of 5 to 4 in the first game of the world's series of 1923.

This is the way old "Casey" Stengel ran, running his home run home, when two were out in the ninth inning and the score was tied and the ball was still bounding inside the Yankee yard.

This is the way—

His mouth wide open.

His warped old legs bending beneath him at every stride.

His arms flying back and forth like those of a man swimming with a crawl stroke.

His flanks heaving, his breath whistling, his head far back.

URGES HIMSELF ON

Yankee infielders, passed by old "Casey" Stengel as he was running his home run home, say "Casey" was muttering to himself, adjuring himself to greater speed as a jockey mutters to his horse in a race, that he was saying: "Go on, Casey! Go on!"

People generally laugh when they see

Another view of Casey's dash.

old "Casey" Stengel run, but they were not laughing when he was running his home run home yesterday afternoon. People—60,000 of them, men and women—were standing in the Yankee stands and bleachers up there in the Bronx roaring sympathetically, whether they were for or against the Giants.

"Come on, Casey!"

The warped old legs, twisted and bent by many a year of baseball campaigns, just barely held out under "Casey" Stengel until he reached the plate, running his home run home.

Then they collapsed.

"CASEY" SLIDES

They gave out just as old "Casey" Stengel slid over the plate in his awkward fashion with Wally Schang futilely reaching for him with the ball. "Billy" Evans, the American League umpire, poised over him in a set pose, arms spread wide to indicate that old "Casey" was safe.

Half a dozen Giants rushed forward to help "Casey" to his feet, to hammer him on the back, to bawl congratulations in his ears as he limped unsteadily, still panting furiously, to the bench where John J. McGraw, the chief of the Giants, relaxed his stern features to smile for the man who had won the game.

"Casey" Stengel's warped old legs, one of them broken not so long ago, wouldn't carry him out for the last half of the inning, when the Yankees made a dying effort to undo the damage done by "Casey." His place in center field was taken by "Bill" Cunningham, whose legs are still

> **"I've had a pretty checkered career. They call me superannuated now. I'm thirty-three. I'm no wonderful runner and I wouldn't expect to set the Mississippi River afire with my brains. I guess I'm a bookkeeper that had a lucky day."**

a date for the following evening. For seven straight nights they went out—dinner and dancing, followed by a movie and some hand holding—then made plans to meet again a few days later when the Giants were in Chicago. There, Casey looked into her brown eyes and asked her to marry him. Edna, who'd never had a truly serious suitor, was startled. She said she'd have to think it over. Then she caught the train back to California while Casey and the Giants resumed their pursuit of the 1923 pennant.

Bill Terry was a rookie first baseman during Stengel's last season with the Giants. "He wasn't much of a ballplayer by then," remembered Terry. "He couldn't hit lefthanded pitching, his fielding was slow, and his legs and arm were gone. But he was a funny fellow, kept everybody alive on the bench, and contributed as much to a ball club off the field as some guys do on the field." In 75 games Casey contributed a .339 average and 43 runs batted in. Moreover, his .505 slugging average was highest among all Giants with at least 200 at-bats. With Frisch leading the league in hits, Ross Youngs in runs, and Meusel in RBI, the Giants outlasted Pittsburgh and Cincinnati for their third straight flag.

Once again their opponent was the hated Yankees. "Hated" was not too strong a word for McGraw, for he truly detested the American League in general, his crosstown rivals in particular, and Babe Ruth most of all. McGraw's acidity and petulance were apparent from the start when he refused to have his team dress in Yankee Stadium, the magnificent new park the Yankees had built across the Harlem River from the Polo Grounds. Instead, the Giants put on their uniforms in their hotel rooms, then rode out in cabs to play in "the house that Ruth built."

The third annual Battle of Broadway commenced on October 10, 1923. The opposing pitchers were John "Mule" Watson for the Giants and Waite "Schoolboy" Hoyt for the Yankees. A noisy crowd of 55,307 people—at the time, the largest crowd ever to watch a big-league game—filled the seats. For Stengel, who was playing center field and batting sixth in McGraw's lineup, the stage was set for the most memorable moment of a career that was already becoming crowded with them.

Watson, a journeyman pitcher McGraw picked up from the Braves during the season, was chased after giving up three runs in two innings. Hoyt, a future Hall of Famer, didn't fare much better, giving way to Bullet Joe Bush in the top of the third as the Giants rallied to take a 4-3 lead. Bush shut down the Giants for the next six innings. Meanwhile, the Yankees managed to knot the affair at 4-4 with a single run in the seventh off reliever Rosy Ryan.

There matters stood as the Giants came to bat in the top of the ninth. Ross Youngs lined to center and Irish Meusel grounded to third for the first two outs of the inning. Up stepped Casey. Bush worked the count to three balls, two strikes, then wound up and put everything he had behind a fastball.

Even for someone who had been around as long as Casey, baseball rarely got more dramatic than this: bases empty, two outs, and a full-count pitch in the ninth inning of a tied World Series game with the whole world watching. Bush's pitch was a bit high and outside, but Casey solidly put wood to ball. He crashed it to left-center field, the most cavernous region of the new park. The line drive appeared innocent enough at first; one press-box observer, Fred Lieb, said, "It looked to me like a single." But the left fielder, Irish Meusel's younger brother Bob, wary of Casey's reputation for slicing the ball, had pulled over close to the foul line. The center fielder, Whitey Witt, had figured Stengel might try to pull the pitch, so he was shaded toward right. As a result, the ball skipped through the vast expanse of grass between Meusel and Witt and headed like a scared rabbit toward the wall 450 feet from the plate.

Casey, his adrenalin flowing and the roar of the crowd rushing like a freight train past his ears, pumped his arms and stretched his legs for all he was worth. The pad he'd installed in his shoe to protect a bruised heel began to slip, causing him to alter his stride. He kept his balance and continued churning around the bases, his mouth wide open and his head back as he sucked in air and egged himself on. "You could hear him yelling, 'Go, Casey, go, go, go, Casey, go,'" said the Yankees' Joe Dugan, who watched Casey peel around third base. "It was the damnedest thing."

By now Stengel felt that his lungs and legs were both near collapse, but home plate was directly ahead. Somewhere in the whirling kaleidoscope of sound and movement, he was aware that a throw was coming. Witt had retrieved the ball and tossed it to Meusel, who possessed the best outfield arm in baseball. Meusel pegged a strike to shortstop Ernie Johnson, who in turn relayed it to catcher Wally Schang. Johnson's throw was a little bit up the first baseline. The ball bounced harmlessly away as Casey, completely gassed, slid across the plate, popped up onto one knee, and made some kind of comical hand gesture that the *New York Times*' reporter interpreted as "well, there you are."

Casey was pummeled by exultant teammates, then caught his breath on the bench as Bill Cunningham took his spot in center field and Rosy Ryan retired the Yankees in the bottom of the ninth to close out an unforgettable 5-4 victory.

Had Casey's fifteen-second sprint happened in Cleveland or St. Louis, it would have been just as funny and equally exciting, but it probably would have stopped short of reaching folkloric proportions. However, this was New York, the center of hype and hyperbole, and thus it was accorded bouquets appropriate for any world-class performance in Manhattan.

That the Series was being broadcast on that new-fangled invention, radio, also helped. While Casey circumnavigated the bases, Grantland Rice and Graham McNamee transmitted the excitement of the moment from their carbon microphone to hundreds of thousands of radio listeners. The new electronic medium added immediacy to Casey's improbable dash and, thanks to the theater of the mind, created an aura of mythic quality. Casey, as media-savvy as any player who ever lived, always appreciated what the press did to perpetuate his legend. "It caused that writer Damon Runyon to compose some beautiful words about how it was done," he said.

Damon Runyon, soon to become famous for his "guys-and-dolls" takes of New York City low life, wrote his column for the *New York American*, which syndicated it around the country. His now classic account began: "This is the way old 'Casey'

Stengel ran yesterday afternoon, running his home run home." It went on to describe in overblown but stirring prose the race between man and ball that Casey won on his wobbly, ancient legs.

Although Runyon's is the best remembered of all the news accounts, it was just one of dozens of florid and overheated stories hammered out in the Yankee Stadium press box under deadline pressure and reprinted in newspapers across the country. In keeping with the spirit of the man of the moment, sportswriters had a lot of fun with Casey's home run. Here was Heywood Broun: "The dust flew as Casey tossed one loose foot after another, identified each one and picked it up again. Perhaps he didn't go so fast but he ran determinedly. It would have been a thrilling sight to see him meet an apple cart or a drugstore window." Grantland Rice was unafraid to dust off the old Casey-at-the-bat analogy while Hype Igoe characterized the thirty-three-year-old Stengel as "gimpy, crooked-fingered, spavined, halt, squint-eyed and mebbe a grandfather."

This first World Series home run hit at a park that would see many more in the years to come had given John McGraw a leg up on an unprecedented third straight world championship. It also made Stengel a nationally recognized name. It didn't, however, win the Series. The following afternoon at the Polo Grounds, Babe Ruth reminded everybody who the *real* sultan of swat was, bopping two into the right-field seats for the deciding runs in a 4-2 Yankees victory.

As it turned out, the Babe hadn't completely knocked Casey off center stage. Both teams assembled at Yankee Stadium for game three. This time another record crowd of 62,430 people watched Sam Jones and Art Nehf exchange goose eggs for six innings. In the top of the seventh, Casey dug his cleats into the batter's box as the Yankees' bench gave him raspberries. With the count two balls and one strike, Jones threw a screwball that didn't break. Casey whipped his heavy bat around and drove the mistake through the tobacco haze and into the left-field bleachers.

Once again it was show time. As Casey made his way around the bases, he flashed two fingers to the Giants' dugout, signifying his second home run of the Series. He thumbed his nose at the Yankees' bench and then blew them a kiss. It was the first time in 117 World Series games stretching back to 1903 that a home run had broken up a scoreless tie. Casey's dramamtic blast held up, Nehf shutting down the Yankees the rest of the way for a 1-0 victory.

Afterward, Yankees owner Jacob Ruppert harrumphed that Stengel's behavior had made a mockery of the sport. He thought the commissioner of baseball should fine or suspend him. "No, I don't think I will," responded Judge Landis. "A fellow who wins two games with home runs may feel a little playful, especially if he's a Stengel."

The two games Stengel won for McGraw turned out to be the Giants' last victories of the Series. The Yankees stormed back to capture the next three games and the championship, their first in what would become a long line of World Series titles. Although McGraw would lead the Giants to a fourth straight postseason berth the following year, he would never win another championship. By the time McGraw left the team in the middle of the 1932 season, Babe Ruth's Yankees had eclipsed the Giants as baseball's symbol of excellence.

Casey's performance—he had batted .417, tops among Series regulars—earned him a postseason check of $4,113. Six weeks later the toast of Broadway was just plain toast. On the evening of November 12, 1923, he was traded with Bill Cunningham and Dave Bancroft to the lowly Boston Braves for pitcher Joe Oeschger and outfielder Billy Southworth. Stengel received the news back home in Kansas City, where he had taken to recreating his famous slide for friends on the sawdust-covered floor of the neighborhood speakeasy. He was stunned, but he didn't lose his sense of humor.

"What do you have to do?" he said. "I suppose if I'd have hit three home runs they'd have sent me to the Three-Eye League."

FOUR

Casey, Where Are Your Pants?

The seventh-place Boston Braves, fortified by Casey's presence in the lineup, dropped to last place in 1924. At thirty-four, old for an everyday outfielder, he played in 131 games (the most since his Brooklyn days), rang up a .280 batting average (third best on the club), and even managed to coax a team high of 57 runs and 13 stolen bases out of his now famous bowed legs. Casey knew his best days were behind him. His legs and his knees ached, and his back continued to give him problems. "I felt that year like I was carrying a ten-pound sack of potatoes on my back" is how he later described his last full season as a big-league player.

It was far from being a lost summer, however. "Boston is a fine town with a wonderful river," he had written Edna Lawson shortly after being traded from the Giants to the Braves. In the same letter Casey wondered if the California girl he was courting might not take her vacation in the East again in 1924. She didn't. But she did meet him halfway, traveling to St. Louis, where on August 18, 1924, she and Casey were married in a small Catholic ceremony. The only other attendees were Edna's brother Larry, a career army officer stationed nearby, and his wife.

Edna, who was just a couple of weeks shy of turning twenty-nine, was to remain married to her man for the next half century. Their tongue-and-groove relationship was predicated on mutual respect and consideration and a good deal of genuine affection. No matter how the outside world perceived Casey—as a clown, a crank, a ruffian—Edna would always find him charming, sensitive, attentive, and

Facing page: **Stengel as a Boston Brave in 1924, just a few months removed from World Series glory.**

Casey (back row, second from right) was invited to join a group of White Sox and Giants on a 1924 tour that took them to Canada, England, and France.

courtly. "That was a great love affair from the first day to the last," Edna's brother John said. "I don't think I have ever seen or heard of two people being closer."

The newlyweds moved into the St. George Hotel in Brooklyn, Casey's bachelor quarters when he had been with the Dodgers, for the rest of the season. Afterward, they went on a two-month barnstorming trip to Canada, England, and France, courtesy of organizers John McGraw and Chicago White Sox owner Charles Comiskey. The trip was a financial bust, but Casey did get to meet King George V and his heir, the Duke of York, while Edna sipped tea with Queen Mary (though she later confessed she would have preferred to be anyplace else). Upon their return in early December, they stayed a week at the McGraws' home, then headed for California, where the Lawson clan met Casey for the first time.

The elder Lawson liked his new son-in-law well enough to build a new two-story house for the couple at 1663 Grandview Avenue. The street, lined with palm trees, wound its way to the foothills of the Sierra Mountains a couple of miles away. Under Edna's fine eye, the house became one of the prettiest in Glendale, with a swimming pool, tennis court, large gardens, orange and lemon trees, and an interior decorative scheme that slanted heavily toward Oriental. The scenery and fruit-scented air acted like a balm on Casey's baseball-frazzled nerves. He and Edna moved in during the winter of 1924–25 and called the place home for the rest of their lives.

In February Casey reported to camp with the Braves, an aging second-line outfielder on a team going nowhere. He barely played, getting into just a dozen games, most of them as a pinch hitter. At the same time he was riding the pine, Braves owner Emil Fuchs acquired the Worcester club of the Eastern League. In mid-May, Fuchs appointed Casey the president and playing manager of this minor-league team, which was in last place with a 9-15 record. Fuchs recognized that Stengel had some managerial ability and could still hack it as an everyday player (at least in the low minors). Also, with his antics and World Series home runs still fresh in the public mind, his name had a certain marquee value.

The move to Worcester, Massachusetts, quickly and unceremoniously ended Casey's major-league career—as a player, anyway. Even at that point in his career, he was confident he would one day return as a big-league manager. He had been working toward the goal practically his entire professional life, picking the brains of masters like McGraw and Uncle Robbie and carefully observing and cataloging whatever went on around him. Worcester represented the first step in the journey that could ultimately get a person one of the coveted sixteen managerial positions available in the American and National Leagues.

In his first stint as a manager, Casey took the moribund Worcester franchise and whipped it into shape, with the team making a run for the pennant before fading to third. Casey "was one of those guys who mastered the details from the start," said Ken Smith, then a sportswriter for the *Hartford Courant* (and later director of the Baseball Hall of Fame). "You know, one of those managers who watch the other team's batting practice." Stengel penciled his own name onto the lineup card nearly every day, finishing with a .320 average and 10 home runs in 100 games. He also got his first suspension after he threw a ball into the stands to protest an umpire's call.

Travis Jackson shakes hands with King George V in London during the 1924 tour as Stengel, to the English monarch's immediate right, looks on.

Edna Larson married Casey in 1924 and remained his partner for the next fifty-one years.

"It used to be that you had to catch the ball two-handed because the glove was so small. Why, when I got married I couldn't afford dress gloves, so I wore my baseball mitt to my wedding and nobody even noticed. That took care of my right hand, and I was smart enough to keep my left hand in my pocket."

Casey figured to follow the Worcester team's move to Providence, Rhode Island, for the 1926 season. But in the fall of 1925, an opportunity became available in Toledo, whose American Association team, the Mud Hens, was partly owned by John McGraw. The Mud Hens had two openings, for a manager and an outfielder, the result of an administrative slipup that cost the Giants the services of Lewis "Hack" Wilson. The squat, powerful center fielder had been farmed out to Toledo during the 1925 season but was expected to be recalled to New York in September. However, the Chicago Cubs—acting on a tip from soon-to-be-dismissed Toledo manager Jimmy Burke—drafted Wilson off the Mud Hens' list of unprotected players before the Giants could formally exercise their option. McGraw was livid over losing his prospect on a technicality. Once he calmed down, he decided to send one of "his" men, Stengel, to Toledo to replace both Wilson and Burke.

There was a glitch, however. Contractually, Casey still belonged to the Braves. Even if Emil Fuchs let him go, the Braves would expect to receive some cash or players from McGraw in return. To avoid this, Casey hit on the perfect solution. He was still the player-manager-president of the Worcester club. So, as president, he released himself as a player and fired himself as manager. Then Casey the president resigned, making himself free to sign a contract for $8,500 a year to manage the Mud Hens. Fuchs protested the stunt, and Judge Landis was ready to force Stengel back to Boston or out of baseball when the Braves' owner finally relented and let Casey go his merry way. He'd never really cared for the fellow anyway.

Stengel wound up spending six seasons in Toledo, a term of managerial service to be exceeded only by his dozen years with the Yankees. It was quite an experience. Toledo's image as a wide open, two-fisted kind of town had gotten a national boost six and a half years earlier when tens of thousands of ruffians and oddball characters had poured in to watch Jack Dempsey hammer the hell out of the giant heavyweight Jess Willard in their famous Fourth of July championship fight. A year later

In 1927 Stengel (middle row, fourth from right) led the Toledo Mud Hens to the American Association pennant and the Little World Series title over Buffalo. Helping the cause were several former big leaguers, including ex-Tiger Bobby Veach (top row, third from left) and ex-Giant pitchers Jesse Barnes (front row, second from left) and Rosy Ryan (middle row, far right). Another was shortstop Everett Scott (front row, far right), who at the time owned the major-league record for consecutive games played.

Downtown Toledo, circa 1930, with its many blind pigs, gambling dens, and whorehouses. "Toledo was a tough town," said Jocko Conlan, a Mud Hens outfielder under Stengel who later became an American League umpire.

Roy Parmelee, a member of the Giants' starting rotation during the middle 1930s, broke into professional baseball with Casey at Toledo. "He was very tough on the veterans," recalled Parmelee. "He could really get on them. But us rookies—he was like a father to us."

Prohibition merely added a touch of adventure to Toledo's traditional vices of gambling, drinking, and prostitution. Some commentators reckoned that Toledo had more whorehouses per capita than anywhere in the country. Nobody bothered to count the speakeasies.

Harry Illman, an attorney and the author of *Unholy Toledo*, sold newspapers and hawked Mud Hens programs during the Roaring Twenties. Illman remembered his town as rivaling Al Capone's in terms of the easy availability of vice and the official corruption that allowed it to flourish. In fact, reporters often referred to the wide open Ohio city as "Chicago on Lake Erie." Ballplayers desiring a postgame drink could choose from such popular establishments as Chateau LaFrance, Casino (where the vice cops gathered), and the Villa. Those looking for a craps game could

By the time Casey returned to Brooklyn as a coach in 1932, Ring Lardner had become cynical about the game he had once loved and which had inspired some of his best writing. However, in Stengel the author of *You Know Me, Al* recognized a broad streak of vaudeville that had always appealed to him. Lardner, just a year away from dying, wrote Casey into several short stories that appeared that summer in *The Saturday Evening Post.* He also offered Casey a bit of advice: never "give" a reporter a story; just keep on talking and the reporter will eventually find it.

Max Carey, the National League's premier center fielder and ten-time stolen-base champion, followed Wilbert Robinson as Dodgers manager in 1932, but lasted only two seasons.

choose between two major houses: Jimmy Hayes' Jovial Club or the Dugout, operated by Tom Worland, presumably a baseball fan. The most notorious brothels were Mother H's, Pappy's, and Gypsy Joe's, where girls named Silver Tongue Elsie and Little Egypt acquired quite a following. Chicken Charlie's was a more convenient stop, offering food, drink, and women, all under one roof. Pool rooms, cigar stores, and blind pigs featured poker, rummy, and faro games, off-track horse betting, and slot machines. In some, a Western Union ticker was present for the benefit of those who liked to wager on major-league games.

Some of this kind of action ordinarily would have appealed to Casey, but he was older, married, and in charge of the team. Not that he and Edna, who typically spent the season with her husband, were averse to having fun. They drank top-grade bootleg hooch with important friends, danced at such emporiums as Tabernilla, Coliseum, and Madison Square Gardens (most of which served liquor), and placed bets at local racetracks.

On game day Edna sat near the dugout at Swayne Field, enjoying the praise heaped on her husband when the Hens won and cringing at the verbal abuse he took when the Hens lost. In 1926, Casey's first season in Toledo, the team won 87 and lost 77, moving from seventh to fourth in the standings.

"I see a lot of you reading about the stock market, and I know you're thinking about it. Now, I'm gonna do you a favor, since you're so interested in Wall Street. I'm gonna give you a tip on the market. Buy Pennsylvania Railroad—because if you don't start playing better ball there's gonna be so many of you riding trains outta here that railroad stocks are a cinch to go up."

Outside of actor Jamie Farr (who regularly wore a Mud Hens jersey in episodes of the 1970s television hit, *M*A*S*H*), Casey remains the best-known person ever associated with Toledo. Nearly seven decades after he left town, a few old-timers can still remember the pennant he delivered in 1927. As they invariably will tell you, it was Casey Stengel's (and the Mud Hens') first championship.

That summer he adroitly guided his mix of young players and crusty veterans to the top. Although he appeared in just 18 of the team's 168 games himself, he showed he could still deliver in the clutch. One afternoon at Swayne Field, he belted a pinch-hit home run—his first (and only) as a Mud Hen and his last as a professional—to pull out a last-licks, extra-inning victory in an important midsummer contest.

The Mud Hens' roster included many familiar names from Casey's recent past: Irish Meusel, Rosy Ryan, Jack Pfeffer, Bullet Joe Bush. There also were Bobby Veach, a three-time RBI champ who had played several years in the Detroit outfield alongside Ty Cobb and Wahoo Sam Crawford, and shortstop Everett Scott, a veteran of five World Series with the Red Sox and the Yankees who at the time owned the major-league record for consecutive games played.

Although in those days all minor-league teams of higher classification fielded at least one or two former big leaguers, from the start Casey demonstrated an affinity for veterans whose savvy and experience compensated for diminishing physical skills. He knew that baseball smarts won as many games as brute strength or youthful vigor. "Just because your legs is dead," he liked to say, "doesn't mean your head is." The Mud Hens won the pennant on the last day of the season, touching off a two-day civic celebration, and then went on to beat Buffalo of the International League, five games to one, in the Little World Series. Casey, once the toast of Broadway, was now the toast of Toledo.

Owing perhaps to the town's overall combativeness, as well as to his own desire to prove himself, Casey seemed more pugnacious than usual during his time in Toledo. He was suspended late in the 1927 pennant race for allegedly inciting Mud Hen fans to attack the umpire after the Hens dropped a Labor Day twin bill to their bitter rival, Columbus. "Several hundred spectators rushed from the stands and attacked the umpire, who was forced to retreat in the dugout, where police reserves came to his rescue," reported the *New York Times*.

Stengel was involved in at least three major altercations in 1929 alone. On May 23 he was charged with assault and battery for punching a fan in the jaw. On July 4 he was suspended after fighting a Minneapolis player during a game in St. Paul. Three days later he attacked the Columbus third baseman, precipitating a riot. Police intervened, quieting the crowd while hustling Casey away from the park in a taxi.

Another infamous Mud Hen moment occurred the following year when umpire Joe Rue ruled that a triple by Toledo outfielder Jocko Conlan (himself later an umpire) was actually a ground-rule double. The decision ultimately cost the Mud Hens the game and Rue nearly his life. After the final out, a wave of angry Toledo fans swept out of the stands, hoping to administer some frontier justice. The umpire somehow escaped, though Conlan got caught up in the melee. "I got hit pretty good three or four times and they weren't even after me," Conlan recalled. "Toledo was a tough town." Once again Stengel was accused of inciting the crowd. At the request of Tom Hickey, the president of the American Association, Judge Landis held a hearing on the matter. But he refused to throw Casey out of organized ball, as the angry Hickey had suggested. Landis knew that Toledo's picaresque baseball fans usually needed little encouragement to express a sentiment.

Casey himself was the object of the fans' cries after one humorous episode. Stengel liked to punctuate his clubhouse lectures by smacking a wooden spit box with a bat. On one such occasion he banged a bit too enthusiastically, spraying tobacco juice all over a player's brand-new suit. Casey exited the clubhouse, leaving his horrified and possibly murderous victim behind, and trotted out onto the grass at Swayne Field, the Mud Hens' home.

Jocko Conlan was with him. A number of comments followed the two as they passed by the grandstands. "Oh, my!" several women said. Casey waved to them and continued on his way. Gradually he became aware of the growing murmur of the crowd. "What are they hollering about?" he asked Conlan. Finally he looked down. "Why, I haven't got my pants on," he said in astonishment. In his rush to leave the scene of the crime, Casey had walked out half-dressed.

"Why didn't you tell me I didn't have my pants on?" Casey said, cracking a bat across Conlan's legs before hustling back into the clubhouse. For some time after-

Facing page: **John McGraw plays bottlecaps with Connie Mack at the 1933 All-Star Game, one of the dying manager's last public appearances. On February 24, 1934, Stengel was introduced to the press as the Dodgers' new manager. That evening McGraw fell into a coma at his New Rochelle home and passed away the following morning, possibly unaware that his one-time student had joined the exclusive ranks of big-league managers.**

wards Mud Hen fans greeted Casey with cries of "Casey, where are your pants?"

Minor-league rosters change dramatically from season to season; players are sold, drafted, recalled, and traded at a sometimes dizzying pace. The revolving-door nature of the business gave Casey headaches. It also provided valuable experience in maneuvering players in and out of the lineup and in dealing with the ever changing cast of personalities in the clubhouse. It would pay off down the road during his glory years with the Yankees.

After capturing the championship in 1927, Toledo finished sixth in 1928, eighth in 1929, third in 1930, and eighth again in 1931. Casey batted for his final times as a professional that summer. He was forty-one years old, but he was still able to bang out three hits in eight at-bats, two of which were doubles. The only time he picked up a bat after that was to hit fungoes.

The Great Depression killed off several minor leagues and caused the Mud Hens to pass into receivership. Although the Toledo franchise survived, Casey found himself out of work after the 1931 season. All told, he had lost eight more games (498) than he'd won in Toledo. His teams had won as many as 100 games in one season (1927) and had lost that many twice (1929 and 1931). The Hens' up-and-down performances mirrored his personal fortunes during this period. The crash took most of what he and Edna had invested including stock in the Mud Hens. Although they were still living better than the majority of Americans, it would take several years for them to recoup their losses.

There were an estimated 9 million people out of work by the end of 1931, but Casey was one of them for only a short while. In December sixty-eight-year-old Wilbert Robinson was fired as the Dodgers' manager after 18 up-and-down seasons. Replacing Uncle Robbie was former Pirates outfielder Max Carey, who Stengel knew from his days in Pittsburgh. At baseball's annual winter meeting, Stengel approached Carey about coming back to Brooklyn in some capacity. On January 4, 1932, it was announced that an old Ebbets Field favorite, invariably described as "colorful" in press reports, had been hired as a coach.

Max Carey exercised a businesslike approach to the game, which in Brooklyn—accustomed to zanier behavior—meant dull. Stengel, determined not to slip on this next rung on the ladder to becoming a big-league manager, stayed as low-key and serious as his normally effusive nature would permit. He worked hard with the players, hitting fungoes by the hour, and shared whatever wisdom he had acquired from more than two decades of playing professional baseball.

Still, the writers were hoping for more. Ring Lardner gave Casey some advice. "Just keep talking," the famous writer told him. "When a newspaperman comes around, don't try to feed him a particular story. Chances are it'd be nothing he could use. Just keep talking and he'll get his story."

Lardner was best known for being the sardonic author of *You Know Me, Al* and other pieces of fiction featuring a semiliterate ballplayer named Jack Keefe. Lardner had grown disillusioned with the game after the 1919 Black Sox scandal, but he had always enjoyed watching and talking to the hustling and picturesque Stengel. During the 1932 season, he wrote a half-dozen stories for the *Saturday Evening Post* featuring correspondence between a fictional Dodgers outfielder, Danny Warner, and his girlfriend back in Illinois, Jessie Graham. Lardner injected Casey into his stories, Danny describing him to Jessie as "a kind of asst mgr and coach of the club." More than a coach, Casey serves as a surrogate father to the youngster with the inflated ego. As Danny writes: " . . . he kind of took me in toe the 1st day we beggin to work out and now mgr Carey has got him rooming with me so it looks like there taking a special interest in how I get a long as Stengel sets and talks to me by the hr about the fine points of the game that comes up durn practice."

Danny also fancies himself a lyricist. Lardner had Casey providing guidance in that area, too. In one installment of the story, Stengel takes Danny to a music publisher, then offers inspiration for what is called "The Dad Song." One of the lines just happens to contain the name of Casey's wife. As Danny explains to Jessie, Casey "made me put Ednas name in." The song turns out to be as big a joke as Danny's abbreviated major-league career. In the end, he is sent down to Jersey City, and the girl he has worked so hard to impress rushes east to marry him. Casey got a kick out of reading the installments as they appeared between April and September of 1932, during which time the *real* Dodgers were busy finishing third.

The new, improved Dodgers proved to be as illusionary as Lardner's fiction. The following year the Danny Warner stories were collected into a book called *Lose with a Smile*, something Dodgers management refused to do as Brooklyn collapsed to sixth place. To make matters worse, the hated Giants won the season series between the two clubs as well as the National League pennant. There was a good deal of grumbling in the front office that winter. A change was coming in Flatbush, thanks to a wisecrack that for once did not originate in the mouth of Casey Stengel.

B
BROOKLY

FIVE

Still in the League, Barely

Bill Terry, best remembered today for being the National League's last .400 hitter, was known to his contemporaries as a cocksure, swaggering man with a sharp tongue and an almost unhealthy love of the almighty dollar. His disposition was the main reason writers took their good, sweet time before finally voting him into the Hall of Fame in 1954, thirteen years after he had retired with a smokin' .341 average.

Terry cared not a whit what people thought of him, not even his boss of many years, John McGraw. In fact, at one point the strong-willed first baseman and his manager didn't speak to each other for two full seasons—a snub that didn't prevent McGraw from naming Terry his successor two months into the 1932 campaign. Under Terry, the Giants rebounded from a seventh-place finish in 1932 to win it all in 1933. As the playing manager of the defending world champion Giants, Terry fielded questions from a battery of reporters one January day in 1934.

"I'll have the same team that won the pennant," Terry said.

"You mean the team we picked for sixth place last year?" a writer asked.

"The same team," Terry said with a laugh. "Anybody want to bet a hat we don't win again?"

Finding no takers, Terry added, "Pittsburgh, St. Louis, and Chicago will be the teams to beat."

"Do you fear Brooklyn?" he was asked.

"Brooklyn?" he replied. "Gee, I haven't heard a peep out of there. Is Brooklyn still in the league?"

***Facing page:* The Dodgers' rookie manager in 1934.**

Hack Wilson.

Terry's rare attempt at humor would not only come back to haunt him, it would also open the door for Casey Stengel to become a big-league manager. Although Max Carey was above responding to Terry's verbal slight—which was turned into a minor sensation by Roscoe McGowan and other writers looking for a preseason angle—Dodgers management, particularly business manager Bob Quinn, was incensed. When Carey refused to be drawn into the silly but growing controversy, he was fired. The front office, and the press, immediately began considering candidates.

"The report that Mr. Casey Stengel may replace Mr. Max Carey as manager of the Brooklyn Dodgers is too good to be true," Joe Williams wrote in the *New York World-Telegram* on February 13, 1934. "Mr. Stengel is so pre-eminently the man for this delicate and delicious assignment it just isn't in the cards for him to be named. Just as there is no limit to the obtuseness of a baseball magnate, I have my doubts that there is any beginning to his astuteness, and thus I am not optimistic that plain logic will prevail."

For once logic *did* prevail in Flatbush. Eleven days later, on Saturday, February 24, Casey faced the press at the Hotel New Yorker to announce that he had signed a two-year contract for $12,000 a season to manage the Dodgers.

"The first thing I want to say," he commented, "is that the Dodgers are still in the National League. Tell that to Bill Terry. And I don't care what you fellows call my club—the Daffiness Boys, the Screwy Scrubs, or anything, as long as they hustle."

"Casey Stengel has a grave duty to perform," Ring Lardner's talented son John wrote in the *New York Post* at the start of spring training. "He must give Brooklyn a ball club that is both efficient and screwy. Brooklyn fans enjoy victory, but they enjoy it most with a large dose of what scientists call Flatbush folly, or red hook raving, or dementia greenpointensia, or plain, ordinary phrenitis."

Terry, for one, felt he had nothing to fear from the bungling Bums. He watched one spring game where, on two separate occasions, a pair of Casey's Dodgers wound up heading for the same base at the same time. "How long have these guys been down here?" Terry remarked. "They're in midseason form already!"

The Dodgers and Giants faced each other for the first time in early May, with Terry's troops sweeping the series. "However," Dan Parker of the *New York Daily Mirror* warned prophetically, "it's a long lane that has no ashcan and Casey Stengel doesn't forget easily. Maybe Bill will live to rue his remarks before the season is over. It's bad business stirring up the fighting blood of a team that in the past has specialized in knocking off the Giants in the home stretch when they were pennant contenders and victories were as precious as radium." When Casey obligingly posed with Terry for the usual grip-and-grin photographs of opposing managers, Brooklyn fans screamed at Stengel to stay away and tossed firecrackers at him. Brooklynites remained hostile toward Terry throughout the season and for many years to come.

As Terry drove his team to what looked to be another pennant, Casey did what he could to keep the Dodgers from dropping into the cellar. Despite the Dodgers' sorry record (they would wind up 71-81, finishing ahead of only Cincinnati and Philadelphia), the rookie skipper was occasionally hailed as a managerial success. In early July Chester L. Smith of the *Pittsburgh Press* predicted that Casey "will someday be recognized as one of the great managers. Underneath his clowning is a keen perception of what it takes to win and an ability to lead that are found in few men."

There was some evidence for Smith's assertion. In an early-season game in St. Louis, for instance, Casey ordered a double steal with the game tied in the eighth and slugger Hack Wilson at the plate. This daring and surprising play worked and the Dodgers won. After the last out was made, Casey "danced a sedate fandango on the dugout steps" before disappearing into the clubhouse.

Casey was popular with the press and the fans, but he was not universally loved by his players. At times he could be caustic, sarcastic, and impatient, particularly with those who exhibited few baseball smarts. "Everybody was a dummy to him," maintained Art Herring, a veteran pitcher who joined the club after five seasons in Detroit.

Bill Terry grew to rue the day he made his flippant remark about the Dodgers. "The Giants thought we gave 'em a beating Saturday and yesterday," Stengel said after his Dodgers spoiled the Giants' season. "Well, they were right. But I'm sorry for them when I think of the beating they still have to take. Wait till their wives realize they're not going to get those new fur coats. I've been through it, and I know."

For several days in 1934 Herring roomed with Hack Wilson, the former Cubs outfielder who had once played briefly with Stengel in New York. Four years earlier Wilson had smashed 56 home runs and set a still standing big-league record with 190 RBI for Chicago. But Wilson, whose idea of a balanced lifestyle was to tote a highball in each hand, was a notorious rounder. As a result, he was now playing out the string under Stengel.

When Brooklyn visited Wilson's old stomping grounds for a series with the Cubs, it was suggested that Herring, a conscientious, clean-living sort, room with him. Immediately after checking into their Chicago hotel, Herring laid down the law.

"Now, I go to bed about nine o'clock, Hack," he said. "Here's the password." Herring handed Wilson a piece of paper with the password spelled out. "If you're too drunk to say 'Aunt Fanny from Hillsboro, Texas,'" he warned, "you won't get in."

Many years later Herring sat inside his mobile home near Gas City, Indiana, and recalled what happened next. "I didn't see him again until five o'clock the next morning. He knocked at the door and I said, 'What's the password?' Well, he didn't get in.

"We had to report for a game at eleven o'clock that morning, and you know what? He

Nick Tremark Remembers Casey

Nick Tremark's brief career as a Brooklyn Dodger, from 1934 to 1936, exactly paralleled Stengel's three-season stint as manager of the team. The short, stocky outfielder was a native of Yonkers, New York, and a fine minor-league hitter. He never did much in the big leagues, but he was always grateful for the chances he did get from his first and only major-league skipper. Tremark, today a retired schoolteacher living in Hurlingen, Texas, recalled some of the elements of the Stengel legend, including his playfulness, remarkable memory, and affection for young players who hustled and were eager to learn.

Nick Tremark at spring training with the Dodgers.

There wasn't anybody better than Casey. In fact, my demise, you might say, was when they let Casey go and hired Burleigh Grimes. He always put me in when he had that chance. When I first came up, I'd be talking to him on the field and somebody in the stands would say, "Hey Casey, who's that with you?" And he'd say, "That's my boy." He gave me every opportunity that he could.

One day he put me in to pinch-hit against Dizzy Dean. We were behind 8-7 in the ninth inning, and Johnny Babich, the pitcher, was due up. Casey said, "Traymark"—he always called me Traymark instead of Tremark—"bat for Babich."

He scared the shit out of me. This was for the money. You know, sometimes you go up and pinch-hit and it doesn't matter to the opponent whether you get a hit or not. The game is lost or they're way ahead or something. But this was early September, and the Cardinals were fighting it out with the Giants for the pennant.

I came up with men on second and third and two outs. I got a base hit, over short, drove in two runs. That made it 9-8. The Cardinals still had to come up, and Casey put in Van Mungo. He was a fastball pitcher, the best on the squad. Van was never a reliever, but Casey put him in for that one inning. The Cardinals didn't score and so we won, 9-8. That was my big moment.

I was a lefty. That was my downfall. You know, I was only five-foot-five, and I couldn't play the infield because I was a lefty. I could've played first, but there you've got to be big. I couldn't pitch or catch, of course, so I had to play the outfield. I'm not blowing my horn, but after my rookie year Brooklyn farmed me out to Redding in the New York-Pennsylvania League, that's Class A, and I hit .333, played every game. Redding moved to Allentown, and I was farmed out there in 1936. Played every game and hit .379. Batted in a hundred and some-odd runs and was runner-up for most valuable player of the league and so on and so forth. I came up and finished the season with Casey.

I was pretty stocky, weighed about 170 pounds. I was pretty strong. I just didn't hit that long ball. Like Hack Wilson? Well, Hack was a monster. Hack spent his last season with Brooklyn. That was in 1934, the year I graduated from Manhattan College in New York. I signed with Brooklyn, and they kept me for the rest of the season. When Hack was released during the season, I took his spot on the active roster.

I don't know why Casey took such a liking to me. Well, I was cocky. I never saw a short guy who wasn't cocky anyways. I know I was always kind of a favorite with the fans in Brooklyn. They'd razz me, but in a good way. They'd call me King Kong, all of that. It was just in fun. I think maybe it was because a couple of times Casey put me in the lineup and I delivered. I don't know. We just clicked.

I was starting in center field this one time in Brooklyn. I think it was Bill Klem who was umpiring. It was time to start and Klem yells, "Play ball!"

All of a sudden Casey comes running out of the dugout, calling time.

Klem says, "What's the matter, Casey?"

Casey says, "I've only got eight men out there."

Klem looks around. He sees that we're all in position. "Naw, Casey," he says. "There's nine men out there."

"Oh, no," Casey tells him. "I haven't got a center fielder."

And Klem looks out to center field and sees I'm standing there. "Well, there's Tremark out in center field," Klem says.

So Casey stands on his tiptoes and cups his hands over his eyes like they're binoculars, and he says, "By God, you're right! I'm gonna have to tell those groundskeepers to keep that grass cut low from now on."

Casey was talking Stengelese even then. You could listen to Casey talk for ten minutes, then back off and say to yourself, "Now what the hell did he say?" I think this was his natural way of talking. You'd eventually understand what he was trying to say, but my God, you'd have to decipher it.

He was the best storyteller. Coming back on a Pullman from St. Louis was a pretty long trip, so we'd all sit around Casey and he'd tell stories. He'd tell one about Hack Wilson. Casey was trying to get Hack to stop drinking because that's about all he liked to do.

He showed Hack a glass of booze once. "See this, Hack?" he told him. "This is what you're drinking. Now pay attention. I want to show you something." Then Casey took a live worm and dropped it into the glass. Well, naturally, in a short while the alcohol killed it. "See?" he says. "The worm's dead. Now, Hack, did you learn anything from this?"

Hack said, "Yeah. If you drink liquor, you won't get worms."

During the winter of 1936, the Dodgers fired Casey and hired Burleigh Grimes. I knew I was gone then. You know, everybody that comes in new likes to bring their own people in. Brooklyn invited me to spring training, and I had a hell of a good camp. We were getting ready to leave spring training when they sold me to Louisville. I was really, really disappointed because I thought that I had done well, and my record showed that I deserved a chance. I know that one of the Brooklyn sportswriters wrote that I would've made a good leadoff man for anyone—except for Burleigh.

So, before reporting to Louisville, I went up to Burleigh. "Listen," I said, "I've done everything you've wanted. I had a pretty good season at Allentown and I thought I had a good spring. Tell me, just what is wrong?"

And he said, "Nick, you're big league in everything but size."

I quit baseball in 1940 and moved to Texas in 1956. A couple of years later the Yankees had a testimonial dinner for Casey at some New York hotel. My uncle lived in New York at the time, and I asked him to get Casey's autograph on the banquet program.

My uncle went up to him and said, "Casey, would you mind autographing this for my nephew, Nick Tremark? Do you remember him?"

Casey said, "Oh yeah. Smallest outfielder I ever had. And a pretty good hitter." He signed it: "To Nick Tremark, with future success. Casey Stengel. P.S.—You could always hit Dizzy Dean."

Now, this was twenty-five years after the hit I'd gotten off Dean. With all the ballplayers he'd managed and played against, and all the good ones that should stick in his mind, and all the games he had been involved in, for some reason he remembered me. He had a remarkable memory.

The last time I saw Casey was about 1963 or '64, one of his last seasons with the Mets. I was visiting my daughter in Houston when the Mets came to town. I said to myself, "I'm going to find out what hotel they're staying at and I'm gonna look him up."

So I called him up on the phone and Casey said, "Hello, Nick. How are ya? Come on down to the hotel lobby in fifteen minutes and we'll chat."

I went down and he said, "Hi, Nick. You seen Dizzy lately?" That was Casey. He never forgot.

hit two home runs that day. I roomed with him for three days in Chicago and then I asked waivers on him. But he was some guy."

Like Herring, Stengel was alternately intrigued and exasperated by Wilson. During another road trip that summer, Wilson made the rounds of Philadelphia's speakeasies and reported to Baker Bowl nursing a head-splitting hangover. The Brooklyn pitching staff being what it was, Wilson spent a good deal of the afternoon chasing down long fly balls under a boiling sun. He finally got a reprieve when Stengel came out to the mound to yank his starter, Walter "Boom-Boom" Beck.

Beck, an ex-Phillie, had acquired his nickname for the sound of the many base hits that opposing batters had rattled off Baker Bowl's fabled tin outfield wall. Boom-Boom was unhappy with his performance and even less happy with Casey's hook. Instead of handing the ball over, he angrily fired it toward right field, where Wilson was bent over, his tongue hanging out and his back to the diamond. The ball struck the wall, startling Wilson out of his stupor. He pounced on it and, as Casey and the

The beneficiaries of Brooklyn's season-ending victories over the Giants were the St. Louis Cardinals, who found themselves in the World Series against Detroit. Here the fabulous Dean brothers—Dizzy on the left, Paul on the right—greet Lynwood "Schoolboy" Rowe before the Series opener. Dan Parker of the *Daily News* suggested a monument to Stengel be erected in St. Louis's Plaza. "He's a Kansas City boy, anyway, and it wouldn't be out of place," wrote Parker. "The slogan at the bottom of such a granite shaft might well be: 'Pardon my Brooklyn axes.'"

entire ballpark watched in wonderment, pegged a perfect strike to second base.

Now *that*, said Herring, was Brooklyn.

The Giants moved into first place in early June and stayed there for three and a half months, though Frankie Frisch's "Gas House Gang" Cardinals kept nipping at their ankles. On Labor Day the Giants enjoyed a six-game lead, but then came a September swoon. On September 28, Dizzy Dean blanked Cincinnati to put St. Louis in a flat-out tie with the Giants for the pennant. Both teams were 93-58 with two games left to play. To the joy of dramatists everywhere, the Giants would have to close out the season at home against the Dodgers.

The borough was in an uproar, and writers delighted in fanning the emotional fire. "The World Series will be an anti-climax to those two brawls at the Polo Grounds," wrote Paul Gallico in the *New York Daily News*. "The most rabid, vituperative, hysterical rooter in the world, the Brooklyn fan, will troop across the bridge by the thousands, bringing cowbells, sirens, razzberries, whistles. A pennant and thousands of dollars will hang on every pitch, every hit, every error, every putout. The Giants are faltering, and the Brooklyns are frantic to get even. The big iron trough beneath Coogan's Bluff will be an absolute bughouse."

Stanley "Frenchy" Bordagaray dared flout convention by growing a mustache. "Go shave it off," commanded Stengel, "before someone throws a ball at it and kills you."

The impending drama moved John Kieran of the *New York Times* to verse. His clever "Ballad of Bitter Words" ended:

> Bill, get out the bandages; set up the cot;
> Trouble looms up in this bitter intrigue.
> Stengel is handing out powder and shot:
> Brooklyn, dear fellow, is still in the league.

Beyond settling the issue of territoriality, the games represented a form of personal vindication for Casey. "Probably no pair of games ever played in major league baseball could mean so much to a manager who has not enjoyed a salubrious season," observed the *Brooklyn Eagle*'s Ed Hughes. "In these two games, Stengel can provide an almost satisfactory substitute for a winning team. Next to the Dodgers winning the pennant, what is dearest to a Flatbusher's heart? Beating the Giants out of a pennant, of course. If Stengel can do this, all will be forgiven. . . . The World Series for Brooklyn and Casey Stengel will be staged tomorrow and Sunday at the Polo Grounds."

The Dodgers had dropped 14 of 20 previous meetings with the Giants in 1934, but they came out as loose and confident as the Giants were tight and dispirited. On Saturday, September 29, the Dodgers rode Van Lingle Mungo's fastball to a 5-1 victory. Meanwhile, Dizzy's younger brother, Paul, pitched the Cardinals past the Reds,

"I had this player in Brooklyn and you could ask him for a match and find out what bar he was in the night before. After we traded him to another club I always went up to him before the game and asked for a match. If he pulled out a match from some bar, I knew he had been out late and I could pitch him fastballs."

6-1. This dropped the Giants to one game behind the Cardinals with one game left to go. New York would have to beat Brooklyn, then hope that last-place Cincinnati could somehow beat St. Louis, to force a play-off for the pennant.

There was no play-off. On Sunday the Dodgers overcame an early four-run deficit to beat the fading Giants, 8-5, making moot Dizzy Dean's thirtieth victory of the season against the Reds. The Cardinals had won the pennant by two games, though Brooklyn fans relished saying that New York had *lost* the pennant by two games—against their beloved Bums.

The mood inside the Polo Grounds ranged from jubilation to dejection. As Casey, clad in a bath towel, led his team in giving three cheers for the rabid Brooklyn fans, in a more subdued corner of the center-field clubhouses, Terry bitterly contemplated blowing the pennant. "If Stengel's team had played as hard as it did the last two days," he mumbled, "it would not be in sixth place."

A less emotional analysis was that Casey had squeezed whatever he could out of a talent-thin lineup. He surely would have preferred an outfield like the Pirates' or an infield like the Tigers' or a pitching staff like the Yankees'. Having any of those would have made his job as manager infinitely easier. But he had to be content with playing the cards he'd been dealt.

Walter "Boom Boom" Beck was going places, but not fast enough to suit Casey. Seeing the volatile pitcher kick a water cooler after another in a long line of dismal performances, Casey warned him, "Stop that. If you break a toe I won't be able to get anything for you."

Len Koenecke was a once-promising outfielder whose dissipations included heavy drinking and rumors of homosexuality. After being given his release by Stengel in St. Louis late in the 1935 season, he drank heavily and got into an argument with the pilot and copilot of a private plane on a flight back to Buffalo. In the ensuing scuffle he was bludgeoned to death with a fire extinguisher—a development that left Casey in a state of near-shock when he heard the news. Stengel, perhaps blaming himself for Koenecke's death, always refused to talk at length about the tragedy.

This included a joker by the name of Stanley "Frenchy" Bordagaray, an outfielder obtained from the White Sox after the 1934 season. Bordagaray first called attention to himself during a spring training game, getting tagged out on an impulsive attempt to steal home with two outs in the ninth. "You ain't seen nothing yet," he reportedly told Casey.

He was right. Bordagaray played just two seasons in Brooklyn, time enough to write several new chapters in the club's already loony history. There was the day he was picked off second base, though Casey was convinced that Bordagaray had had his foot planted firmly on the bag.

"No, he's right, Case. I'm out," Frenchy admitted when Stengel came out to protest the call.

"How could you be out?" Casey demanded. "You were standing on the base!"

"I was tapping my foot," explained Bordagaray, "and I guess he got me between taps."

On another occasion Bordagaray lined a ball off Stengel's noggin during batting practice. That afternoon the Dodgers broke a long losing streak. Afterwards Bordagaray suggested to Casey that, for good luck's sake, he hit him on the head with a ball every day.

The daily press, hungry to fill pages, seized upon such occasional incidents, embellished them, and made them out to be signs of the club's incurable daffiness. Casey was wise to the ways of newspapering, courting what he liked to call "my writers" in bull sessions that often involved a fair amount of alcohol. He was happy to deflect attention from the standings, which during his three seasons in Brooklyn revealed nothing but second-division finishes: sixth in 1934, fifth in 1935, and seventh in 1936. The one thing Stengel didn't lose was his sense of humor. Settling into a barber's chair for a shave after a tough doubleheader loss, he instructed the man wielding the razor: "Don't cut my throat. I might want to do that myself later."

"I remember a crazy incident that could only happen in Brooklyn," said backup catcher Ray Berres. "We were out in front by several runs one afternoon at Ebbets Field, but it was raining. Casey was hoping to have it called; maybe he figured that was the only way we were going to win."

The umpires would have nothing to do with Stengel's pleas to call the game. Frustrated, he decided to be a bit more demonstrative about the soggy playing conditions. "Casey took his shoes and stockings off and went out to coach third base in his bare feet," chuckled Berres. "He was walking around the coach's box, squishing his toes in the mud. The umpire ran him out of the park, but he still didn't call the game."

The team's woeful performances could hardly be laid at Casey's feet, bare or otherwise. Penurious owners, a weak farm system, and a poor gate were to blame. He did what he could. He particularly enjoyed teaching young players, taking them under his wing, just as McGraw and Uncle Robbie and Kid Elberfeld had once done with him. "What else are you gonna do when you get a second-division ball club?" he said. "You've got a couple of young players on it, you work on them. Who else are you gonna work on? You keep after them. You ask them why they didn't make that

throw. You ask them why they played that man there. Then for somebody else they turn out to be good ballplayers, but what of it? You helped to make them good ballplayers, didn't you?"

Part of a young player's appeal to Casey was that, unlike a veteran, he usually gave the manager his undivided attention. "Naturally I was impressed with him," said Berres, who was a rookie under Casey in 1934. "I'd heard and read about him while he was managing in Toledo. Like any other lad coming up, I was just happy to get to the big leagues and I did what I was told. If Casey was right or wrong, he was the manager—which always made him right."

It didn't always make him employed, however. After Bob Quinn left the Dodgers' front office to join the Boston Braves, Casey's days in Flatbush were numbered. In the fall of 1936 he was fired with a full year left on his contract. Burleigh Grimes, the grizzled spitballer for whom he had once been traded, replaced him.

With the Dodgers paying Casey $15,000 not to manage in 1937, he and Edna tried to enjoy the time off, taking in swank nightclubs, theaters, and fine restaurants in upper-middle-class style. It wasn't nonstop revelry, however. That year both of Casey's parents died. In addition to taking care of their affairs, he had to assist his sister, a spinster who had never left home.

Burleigh Grimes (right) replaced Stengel as manager of the Dodgers in 1937, a move that was unpopular with fans and the press. "The newspapermen didn't like the idea of seeing him go," said Grimes. "He was always a favorite with those guys, and with good reason. In fact, they didn't even invite me to their dinner that winter. They were sore at me because I'd taken Casey's job."

Casey was out of work but, thanks to a journeyman outfielder named Randy Moore, was still in the money. Moore, a Texan whose family was involved in the oil business, had joined the Dodgers in 1936 after several seasons with the Braves. Upon his advice, Casey and Edna invested $10,000 in oil properties, an investment that paid off handsomely. As always, it was a joint business decision, but Edna was the undisputed brains of the outfit, which was exactly the way Casey liked it. She looked over the business interests—theirs as well as her family's—freeing Casey to concentrate on baseball.

Another investment the two made was plunging $43,000 into the Boston Braves, a perennial loser that Bob Quinn was hoping to turn around. Longtime Braves manager Bill McKechnie had left for Cincinnati, conveniently creating an opening for that newest of stockholders, Casey Stengel.

Boston proved to be a barrel of yuks, both in the standings and inside the clubhouse. During Casey's six seasons at the helm, 1938 through 1943, the Braves never finished higher than fifth. For four straight years they finished seventh. "But life was

"Whenever I decided to release a guy, I always had his room searched first for a gun. You couldn't take any chances with some of those birds."

made tolerable by the pranksters we had," first baseman Elbie Fletcher told Donald Honig, "guys like Al Lopez, Tony Cuccinello, Danny MacFayden."

Fletcher went on to describe a typical stunt. One day Cuccinello and Lopez nailed MacFayden's favorite pair of shoes to the floor, then used a razor to cut along the soles.

"After the game MacFayden showered and dressed and then slipped his feet into the shoes and got up and took a few steps and stopped. He looked down and found himself wearing the tops of his shoes. The laughter went all around the clubhouse till Stengel finally came over to see what it was all about. There was MacFayden still standing there dumbstruck, wearing the tops of his shoes and looking back over his shoulder at the soles nailed to the floor. Stengel just shook his head."

As was his custom when saddled with a losing ball club, Casey regularly joined in the high jinks. During a 1939 doubleheader at the Polo Grounds, for example, he tried to get the umpires to stop the second game—another losing effort—at dusk. When they refused, he somehow found a railroad lantern and returned to the diamond, saying, "Don't want no trains to run over me in this here darkness." It rained during the following day's game against the Giants. When the umpires again refused his request to cancel the affair, he emerged from the dugout sporting an umbrella, raincoat, and galoshes.

John A. "Bob" Quinn was responsible for hiring Casey to his first two big-league managerial jobs—with Brooklyn in 1934 and with the Braves in 1938. That both teams were perennial also-rans presumably didn't faze Quinn, a veteran baseball executive who had previously served in the front offices of woeful American league clubs in Boston and St. Louis.

One of Casey's favorites on the Braves was Ernie Lombardi, a catcher with enormous hands and a schnozz to match. The heavy-legged Lombardi moved only slightly faster than glaciers melted, which made his two batting titles a truly remarkable achievement. His line drives, however, threatened to rip infielders' ears off. On one occasion Casey, noticing the third baseman playing back on the outfield grass, signaled for a bunt. Lombardi did as he was told. He dropped the ball perfectly on the grass, chugged for all he was worth down the first baseline, and incredibly, beat the throw. As the crowd went nuts, Lombardi looked around for Casey. He finally spotted him—on his back in the coaching box, having pretended to keel over in a dead faint.

With little else going on with the sad-sack Braves, writers started paying a little more attention to a style of communication dubbed "Stengelese." Since he was a child, Casey had always talked fast, words tripping over each other as his speech attempted to keep up with his lightning-quick wit and his powers of observation and recall. Stengel could be devastatingly clear when he wanted to get a point across, frustratingly vague when he wished to avoid answering a question, and marvelously entertaining in either case. By 1943, his last season with the Braves, Casey was fifty-three years old with a third of a century of professional baseball behind him. With

Casey as the new manager of the Braves, 1938.

an ever expanding abundance of life experiences to draw upon, an astonishing memory for faces and events, and a colorful and earthy vocabulary, Casey increasingly moved from point A to point B not on a straight path, but rather via a series of convoluted historical detours that butchered grammar, slaughtered names, and often left listeners believing that Stengel was speaking in tongues.

"He had a lot of people to communicate to," explained Johnny Sain, who pitched for Stengel in Boston in 1942 and then later joined him on the Yankees. "He would say, 'that big guy' or 'the left-hander' because he was more concerned with the points he was making than the names."

Some observers figured Casey knew what he was doing. It was as if a veteran bus driver had decided, on a lark, to drive from Los Angeles to San Francisco by way of Baton Rouge, Beaver Dam, and Grand Rapids. Passengers trusted that he would eventually get to his destination, so the only thing to do was to just sit back and enjoy the ride.

According to longtime New York sportswriter Maury Allen, Stengelese "was mostly a public act. He doubletalked in part to diffuse pinpoint questions. If you asked him who he was going to start at second base, he'd doubletalk because he wouldn't want to decide until he made out his lineup ten minutes before the game. But he had a way of alerting the regular beat writers. If he veered off into talking about Rogers Hornsby, you knew he wanted an offensive second baseman for a high-scoring game." Conversely, if Casey "mentioned a good defensive player from years past, he wanted one for a low-scoring game."

Ray Berres, who played two seasons each in Brooklyn and Boston under Casey, was asked about Stengelese. "I don't remember that much of it in Brooklyn," said Berres, searching his memory one afternoon inside his Kenosha, Wisconsin, home. "But over in Boston he started doing a little more of it. He would hold these meetings once in a while—a players meeting before a game, say—and he would be talking about when he was managing in Toledo and this or that hadn't worked out. Then he'd be talking about something that had happened with the New York Giants when he was playing for John McGraw. Or when he'd been at Brooklyn as a player or a manager. Then he'd get back to the player or situation he was originally talking about. You could generally follow what he was saying but later on I could see where it might be hard for some people to figure out what he was getting at."

The Braves' operation was a discouragingly makeshift one, and attendance reflected that fact. During Casey's six summers at Braves Field, the team drew an average of less than four thousand a game. With America's entry in the Second

World War, the manpower shortage made the Braves' lineup problems even more acute. One year the outfield included forty-one-year-old Johnny Cooney and thirty-nine-year-old Paul Waner.

All the same, Casey liked Boston, even after a nearly fatal accident that typically had comic overtones. One rainy night in the spring of 1943, Casey was crossing Kenmore Square when he was hit by a taxi. Casey, who suffered a severely fractured right leg, was rushed to Massachusetts General Hospital. Because of a shortage of beds, he was placed in the maternity ward. While there, he received two Mother's Day cards.

Casey was released from the hospital in mid June. During his absence, the Braves had acquired Hugh Poland, a weak-hitting reserve catcher, from the Giants. Poland was behind the plate for Casey's first game back. Relegated by a cast and crutches to the bench, Stengel spent the early part of the game whistling at his catcher, hoping to draw his attention. Finally he turned to someone on the bench and asked, "Who is that fella catching?" Told that it was Hugh Poland, Casey responded, "Who's Hugh Poland?"

Stengel wasn't given much time to find out. At the end of the season, new ownership bought out his stock and pressured him to resign. Dave Egan of the *Boston Record*, the sportswriter who would go on to make life miserable for Ted Williams, displayed little compassion for Casey's predicament. "The man who did the most for baseball in Boston in 1943," he wrote, "was the motorist who ran Stengel down two days before the opening game and kept him away from the Braves for two months."

At this point it appeared that Casey's managerial career was over. For one thing he needed time to mend. His leg had been poorly set by an inexperienced doctor, resulting in a large knot, pain, and a limp, all of which would remain for the rest of his life. His wife also wanted him close by. In 1932 Edna's mother had been paralyzed,

Stengel imparts some diamond wisdom to his Braves, who never finished higher than sixth during his six seasons at the helm.

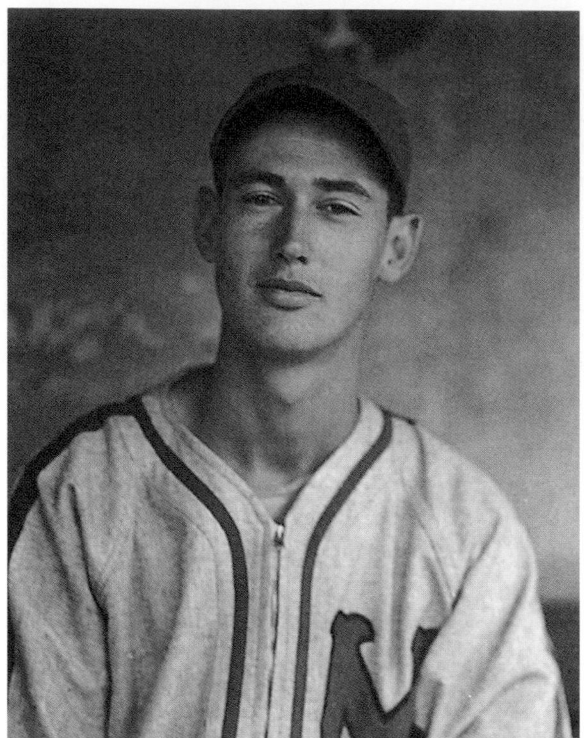

When it came to judging young talent, Casey was more right than wrong. He gave early encouragement to a skinny outfielder from San Diego named Ted Williams (left), but gave up on a lanky left-handed pitcher from Buffalo named Warren Spahn, sending him back to the minors in 1942 for refusing to pitch close to batters. Spahn won a chestful of ribbons in the Second World War and then 363 games in the majors, the most of any southpaw in history. "I said 'no guts' to a kid who wound up being a war hero and one of the best pitchers anybody ever saw," Casey later confessed. "You can't say I don't miss 'em when I miss 'em."

and her uncle killed, in a terrible auto wreck. Edna "kept the family together then," said her brother John. "Edna got my father to build an addition on the house and my mother and father moved in with Casey and Edna." Edna not only took over her mother's part of the family business, she looked after her parents until her mother passed away in 1944, followed a year later by her father. Finally, Casey didn't need the money. Thanks to savvy investments and the Lawson family's assets, he and Edna were financially secure.

So from the fall of 1943 to the following spring, he stayed home in Glendale, doing his prescribed leg exercises and sunning himself by the pool. Some minor job offers came his way, but he turned them all down—until he heard from Chicago Cubs general manager James Gallagher. Jimmy Wilson, who had been fired as the Cubs' manager, was replaced by Charlie Grimm, who had been piloting the Milwaukee Brewers of the American Association. Grimm, with a financial stake in the Brewers, needed a savvy baseball man not only on the field but in the front office. On May 6, 1944, Casey ended his brief retirement and arrived in Milwaukee.

Stengel inherited a club that had won the pennant the year before and immediately led it to a long winning streak. His success in the standings and popularity with the fans, press, and players didn't change the attitude of Bill Veeck Jr., a part-owner of the Brewers who was serving in the Marine Corps thousands of miles away in the South Pacific and thus had not been consulted. Veeck (who may have had in mind a recently conducted *Sporting News* poll of 151 sportswriters that ranked Stengel as "the funniest" of all managers) blew his stack when he found out about Casey's hiring. In a letter to his partners, Veeck listed his many objections including his opinion that "Stengel mentally is a second-division major leaguer. That is, he is entirely satisfied with a mediocre ball club as long as Stengel and his alleged wit are appreciated."

Veeck softened his objections when the Brewers once again won the pennant. Casey later became good friends with Veeck, but in the fall of 1944, he knew that he stood a good chance of getting fired when Veeck returned from the war, which was starting to wind down. Stengel decided it would look better on his resume if he resigned instead. "All I have to say is that I decided to help out Grimm and his buddy Bill," he said upon leaving. "I think I did a good job for both of them. Now I can leave with no regrets, and Veeck has a perfectly free hand in selecting my successor. Old Case will be in the game next year, but I am certain it will not be here."

Instead it was Kansas City, Casey's old stomping grounds, where a longtime friend, Yankees farm director George Weiss, had signed him to manage the Blues. Stengel couldn't do much with the team, which finished seventh in the 1945 American Association race. Still, he was willing to stick with the club while waiting for another big-league position to open up.

But then another friend, Oakland Oaks owner Cookie de Vicenzo, sold his team and recommended Casey to the new owner, Clarence "Brick" Laws. The Oaks belonged to the Pacific Coast League, a stable and prosperous circuit that had long been considered a third major league. In fact, two of its member cities, Los Angeles and San Francisco, would receive big-league franchises when Casey's old employers, the Dodgers and Giants, abandoned New York a dozen years later. Playing in Oakland meant a relatively short commute from his home in Glendale, a situation that pleased Edna, who was worn out from years of travel to Toledo, Brooklyn,

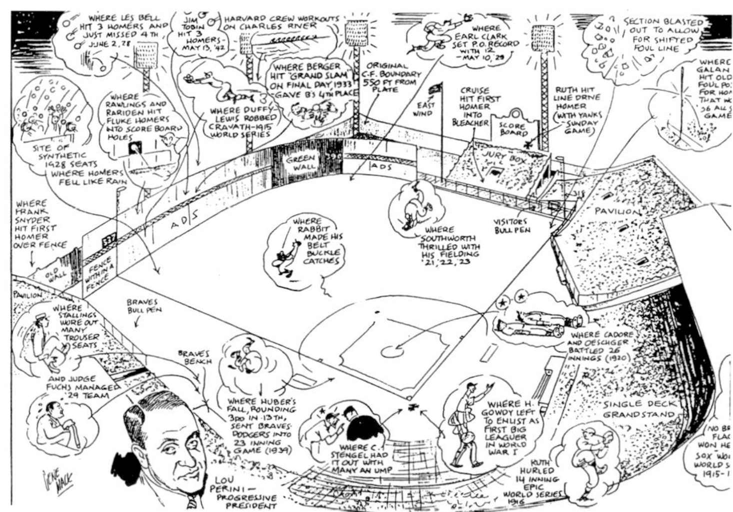

The sight of Stengel jawing with umpires became so common during six long, losing seasons in Boston that cartoonist Gene Mack later included it in his drawing of Braves Field.

Heavy-hitting but iron-gloved Max West was the kind of one-dimensional player that brought out the wit—and sarcasm—in Stengel. Once when the clumsy outfielder almost knocked himself out by crashing into a wall, Casey commented, "You got a great pair of hands, Max."

Ernie Lombardi won his second batting title while playing his only season with Stengel's Braves, hitting .330 in 1942. The lumbering, banana-nosed catcher got little respect despite a .306 average over seventeen seasons; he wound up working in a gas station when he left the game and was dead nine years before he was inducted into the Hall of Fame in 1986.

The war prompted the Braves to sign aging Paul Waner to play the outfield. Waner, who had won four batting titles during his fifteen seasons in Pittsburgh, collected the 3,000th base hit of his illustrious career playing for Casey, but his best days clearly were behind him. One exhausting afternoon at Forbes Field he dove for a ball hit to short center field and then just lay there, his thirty-nine-year-old body refusing to get up from the grass. A couple of years later, when Waner was finishing up with the Yankees, a bleachers fan asked why he was in the outfield for the Bombers. "Because," he answered truthfully, "Joe DiMaggio's in the army."

With wartime travel restrictions forcing clubs to conduct spring training in the north, the Braves opened camp at exclusive Choate School in Connecticut. A photographer posed the Ol' Perfesser lecturing several students. Listening are (from left to right) Tony Cuccinello, Phil Masi, Manuel Salvo, Lefty Gomez, and Jim Tobin.

Casey suffered a broken leg when he was hit by a Boston cab driver just prior to the 1943 season opener.

Let go by the Braves after the 1943 season, Casey spent the offseason in Glendale engaged in such leisure activities as picking grapefruit.

Milwaukee, and other far-flung corners of the baseball universe. Casey could see no immediate major-league jobs on the horizon, so he accepted the offer.

One of the things that appealed to him in Oakland, Casey liked to say, was the close proximity of the Bay Bridge. "Every manager wants to throw himself off a bridge sooner or later," he observed, "and it's very nice for an old man to know he doesn't have to walk fifty miles to find one."

Stengel felt few suicidal tendencies in Oakland. In three seasons he led the Oaks into the finals of the four-team play-offs twice and in 1948, fielding a lineup the press dubbed "the Nine Old Men," won the pennant and the championship. It was the team's first title since 1927 and made Casey a folk hero in Oakland. It was true that Casey coaxed maximum mileage out of big-league retreads like Ernie Lombardi, Ripper Collins, Nick Etten, Jim Tobin, and Cookie Lavagetto, but he also patiently developed young talent like infielder Billy Martin and knuckleball pitcher Gene Bearden.

Casey's West Coast success came at a time when the proud and staid New York Yankees were undergoing an identity crisis. The highly successful Joe McCarthy era had ended in the middle of the 1945 season with the manager's resignation over a personality clash with new owner Larry MacPhail, a flamboyant self-promoter whose interference and combativeness turned off everybody he dealt with. In 1946 MacPhail went through two more managers, Bill Dickey and Johnny Neun, before hiring Bucky Harris, who won a world championship in 1947. Beset by personal problems, MacPhail sold his interest in the team to his silent partners, Dan Topping and Del Webb. George Weiss was made general manager, and one of Weiss's first major moves was to fire Harris for daring to finish third in 1948.

Casey Stengel's Minor League Record

		As player:					*As manager:*			
Year	Club	League	GP	BA	HR	RBI	Won	Lost	Pct. Won	Finish
1910	Kankakee	NA	59	.251	1	—	Did not manage			
1910	Maysville	BGL	69	.223	2	—	Did not manage			
1910	Kansas City	AA	3	.333	0	—	Did not manage			
1911	Aurora	Wis-Ill	121	.352	4	—	Did not manage			
1912	Montgomery	SA	136	.290	0	—	Did not manage			
1925	Worcester	EL	100	.320	10	—	70	55	.560	3
1926	Toledo	AA	88	.328	0	27	87	77	.530	4
1927	Toledo	AA	18	.176	1	3	101	67	.601	1
1928	Toledo	AA	26	.438	0	12	79	88	.473	6
1929	Toledo	AA	20	.226	0	9	67	100	.401	8
1930	Toledo	AA	Did not play				88	66	.571	3
1931	Toledo	AA	2	.375	0	0	68	100	.405	8
1944	Milwaukee	AA	Did not play				91	49	.650	1
1945	Kansas City	AA	Did not play				65	86	.430	7
1946	Oakland	PCL	Did not play				111	72	.607	2
1947	Oakland	PCL	Did not play				96	90	.516	4
1948	Oakland	PCL	Did not play				114	74	.606	1
Totals	15 seasons		642	.328	18	51	1037	924	.529	

Key:
NA—Northern Association, BGL—Blue Grass League, Wis-Ill—Wisconsin-Illinois League, SA—Southern Association, EL—Eastern League, AA—American Association, PCL—Pacific Coast League

Casey was given a new Ford for bringing home a pennant for the Oakland Oaks in 1948, then feted in a parade.

Harris's dismissal was unpopular with the players, but the Yankees' choice to replace him was met with disbelief. A few years earlier when Joe McCarthy was making noise about resigning, Weiss had talked to Ed Barrow, then the Yankees' general manager, about a successor.

"I've got just the man for you," said Weiss. "Stengel."

"That clown?" replied Barrow.

That was more or less the response of Topping and Webb when Weiss once again suggested Stengel in the fall of 1948. Other names were bandied about, but for one reason or another each was deemed unsuitable. Weiss, who had known Stengel since their days in the Eastern League a quarter century earlier, continued to talk up

The nose sizes of two of Casey's favorite players on the Oakland Oaks, Ernie "The Schnozz" Lombardi and Billy Martin, had their manager shaking his head in wonderment. "Now you take Ernie Lombardi who's a big man and has a big nose and take Martin who's a little man and has a bigger nose. How do you figger it?" Later, after he'd made a little money playing with the Yankees, Martin had his nose bobbed.

his man. What finally convinced Webb was a firsthand look at the legend when he was out on the West Coast conducting business.

"I was at a party one night and Casey was among the guests," Webb later recalled. "He was in rare form. He had us standing around with our mouths open, putting on one of the best shows I've ever seen, telling stories, hopping around the room, mimicking other people."

Webb, who had made his fortune in the construction business, had an important meeting early the next morning, so he left the party to grab a couple of hours sleep. A few hours later he tumbled bleary eyed into a cab and was startled when it drove past a vacant lot filled with kids and "an old gaffer giving some instruction." The old guy, of course, was Casey, who had entertained until the wee hours of the morning and was now showing a group of boys how the major leaguers did things. If Casey cared that much about baseball, thought Webb, he must be a terrific manager.

On October 12, 1948, the Yankees held a press conference at New York's 21 Club to announce that Casey Stengel was the team's new manager. Casey was far from his usual convivial self. He appeared nervous and restrained and later admitted he knew full well the nature of the unspoken opinion of those in the room: "This bum managed nine years and never got into the first division."

Ray Berres, for one, remembered that he was thrilled when he heard the news. During his National League days, Casey had "had some good theories and he'd obeyed his convictions," the catcher said. "He'd always been a solid manager. He just didn't have the players before. In New York he could exercise his ideas."

Nick Tremark, a short and sassy outfielder who Casey had taken a liking to in Brooklyn, echoed Berres's feelings about the hiring.

"Casey was a jokester and so they never thought he was as smart as he was," said Tremark. "I was glad when he got to the Yankees. I thought, '*Now* he's got the horses.' He didn't have them in Brooklyn and he didn't have them in Boston, either. After he went to New York I said to myself, 'By God, he'll do something now.' And goddamn it, he did."

NY

☛ SIX

That Clown in Pinstripes

Casey Stengel turned fifty-nine during the 1949 baseball season, an age at which other men with his experience and resources might have been content to relax and reminisce by a roaring fire. Instead, the new manager of the New York Yankees was embarking on what would become the greatest years of his lifelong journey, years in which he would attain a fame and stature that had to surprise even him.

Physically, he was what he might himself have called "an amazin' specimen"—a severely wrinkled, slightly stooped, crab-legged old man with white, thinning hair, a rubber face, and awesome ears that, according to *Baseball Magazine*, were "about the same size, shape, and consistency as rib lamb chops." As the Yankees assembled in St. Petersburg, Florida, for spring training on March 1, 1949, those ears picked up what doubters were saying about him: *prankster . . . clown . . . loser.*

It didn't help matters when the new skipper, always at a loss when it came to remembering names, instead referred to veterans and rookies by their uniform numbers. The press was intrigued by the way he treated Gene Woodling, Jerry Coleman, and other "green peas" (Stengelese for young players) as essentially batters without positions, rotating them around the field and in and out of the lineup of spring games. Adding to the sense of confusion was the presence of three new coaches—Jim Turner, Bill Dickey, and Frankie Crosetti. Turner, an ex-Yankee, had earlier pitched for Stengel in Boston. Dickey and Crosetti, two fondly remembered members of championship squads from the glory days of Babe Ruth and Lou Gehrig, had

***Facing page:* Casey and "my assistant manager, Mr. Berra" await the arrival of a new pitcher during a 1951 game at Yankee Stadium.**

Stengel is all business as he confers with George Weiss at the beginning of spring training in 1949. After newspapers ran a widely circulated shot of Casey gazing into a crystal ball, one front-office executive moaned, "My God, we've hired a clown!"

been brought in by the front office primarily to provide a visible link to Yankees tradition, a mystique that many thought was threatened by Casey's hiring. One such person was Arthur Daley of *The New York Times.* "I've never seen such a bewildered guy in my life," the writer confided to Joe DiMaggio one day in the locker room. "He doesn't seem to know what it's all about." DiMaggio agreed. "That's the impression I have and the rest of the fellows feel the same," he admitted.

DiMaggio, along with Tommy Henrich, Johnny Lindell, and a half-dozen others, were part of the Yankees' old guard who were accustomed to the quieter and more dignified ways of Joe McCarthy and Bucky Harris. One veteran, shortstop Phil Rizzuto, had an axe to grind. Several years earlier Rizzuto had been a pip-squeak high schooler with visions of playing for the Dodgers, then managed by Stengel. After watching Rizzuto work out one day at Ebbets Field, Casey dismissed him as being too small. When Rizzuto argued, Stengel shooed him away. "Go on, get outta here. Go get a shoebox." Rizzuto instead signed with the Yankees and became an integral member of the 1941, 1943, and 1947 championship teams. The 5-foot-6 "Scooter" ultimately came to appreciate that baseball was big business. But he never forgave Casey for the callous manner in which he had dismissed his own boyhood dream.

For his part Casey expressed nothing but delight with his new charges—whatever their names might be. "I never had so many good players before. I'm with a lot of real pros. When I think of some of those other teams I had, I was wondering whether I was managing a baseball team or a golf course. You know what I mean—one pro to a club."

The Yankees' clubhouse was chock full of pros, the most famous of whom was DiMaggio. The graceful and aloof center fielder was the very personification of Yankees class. At thirty-four, he was starting his eleventh season in New York. Despite having lost three years to the army during World War II, he had already won two batting crowns and three Most Valuable Player Awards, and he had led the Yankees into seven World Series, all but one a winning affair. DiMaggio was coming off a typically productive year in 1948—a league-leading 39 homers and 155 RBI despite playing on a painful heel. The press had long ago dubbed him "the Yankee Clipper," but teammates called him Dago, an irreverent but affectionate nickname that he himself used. Casey, wary of seeming too chummy with the man who eight years earlier had captivated the country with his 56-game hitting streak, initially called him Mr. DiMaggio. The relationship between Stengel and his superstar would always be a tense and strained one. But as Casey once observed, "So what if he doesn't talk to me? I'll get by and so will he. DiMaggio doesn't get paid to talk to me, and I don't either."

Of greater concern when the Yankees broke camp was DiMaggio's right heel, which was acting up again after an operation to remove a bone spur the previous November. The pain, similar to stepping on tacks, was agonizing, and finally DiMaggio reported to Johns Hopkins Hospital in Baltimore for treatment. Nobody, not even DiMaggio, knew when he would be able to play again.

DiMaggio's absence meant that Stengel didn't have to deal with the burden of unrealistically high expectations. In a preseason poll of sportswriters, only six picked New York to win the pennant. Another 198 selected either Boston or Cleveland. Both

March 1, 1949: Casey meets his new team for the first time in Florida.

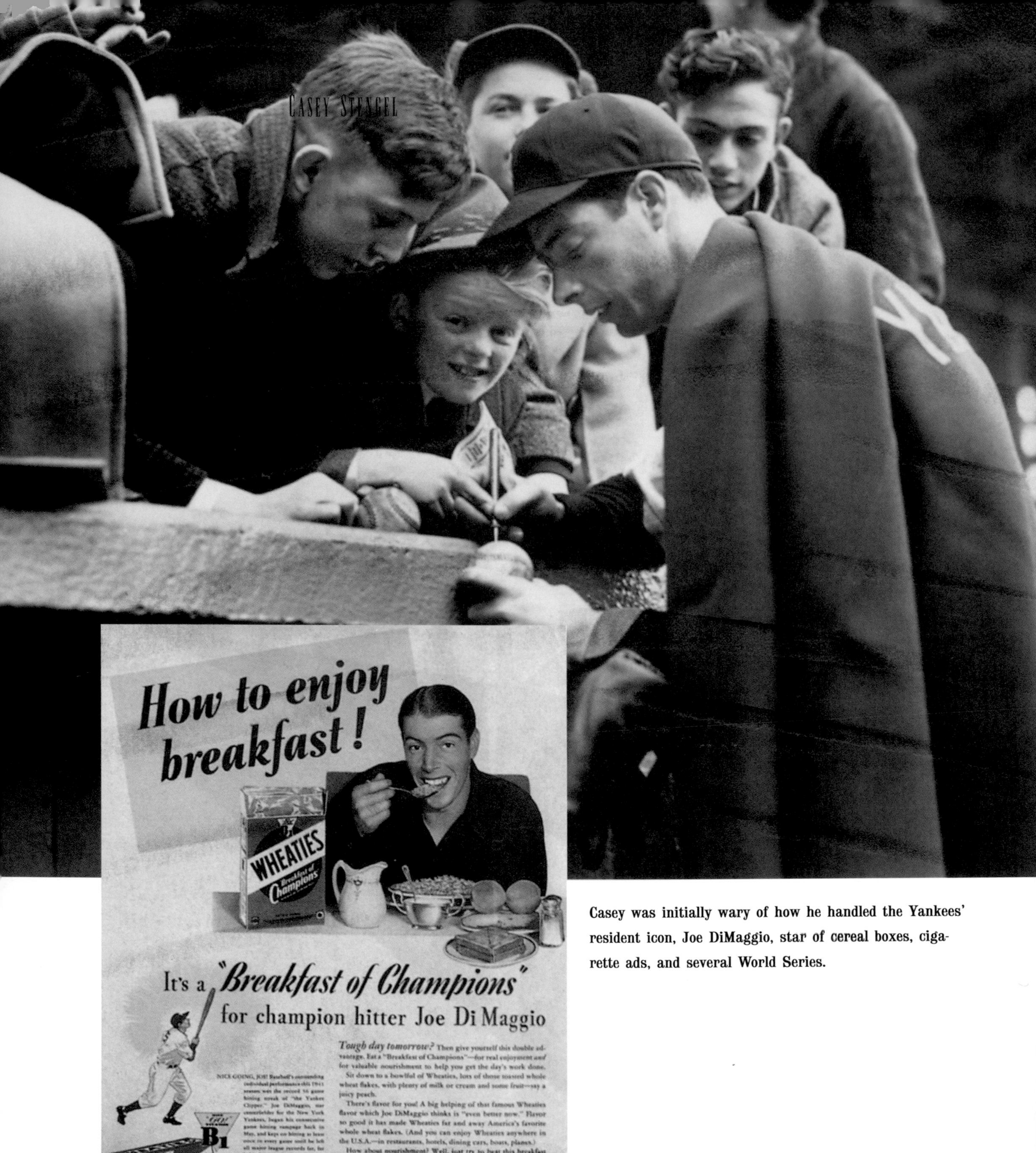

Casey was initially wary of how he handled the Yankees' resident icon, Joe DiMaggio, star of cereal boxes, cigarette ads, and several World Series.

Another member of the old guard, former shortstop Frankie Crosetti (seen here before the start of the 1938 World Series at Wrigley Field), was hired as a coach to provide a visible link to Yankees tradition, one of the club's greatest assets. Crosetti wore Yankees pinstripes for thirty-seven seasons as a player and a coach, cashing twenty-two World Series checks.

were strong clubs that had finished the previous season tied in the standings. The Indians had won the special one-game play-off, then dusted off the Boston Braves in the World Series. The Yankees were considered to be in a transitional stage—maybe, some suggested, even a second-division club, based on DiMaggio's cloudy future and Stengel's past managerial record. "Is the Yankee Empire Crumbling?" asked *Look* magazine on the cover of its April 24 issue. The solemn task of keeping the Yankees competitive meant that Casey's usual antics and mugging were missing that first summer in New York.

"Casey was serious," said Henrich, whose home-run bat carried the team in the early stages of the season. "He knew that this was his chance. Casey the clown didn't exist with the Yankees in '49."

But Casey the diamond strategist was alive and well. In May, by which time injuries were beginning to take their toll on the first-place Yanks, Harold Rosenthal wrote in the *New York Herald-Tribune* that the Yankees' new skipper was "two-platooning" his outfielders. Rosenthal had borrowed a phrase from football—where the traditional two-way, sixty-minute "iron man" was being replaced by offensive and defensive specialists—to give a name to a system that had been used irregularly for the last half century.

By 1949 it was already pretty well accepted that a right-handed batter often enjoys greater success against a left-handed pitcher than someone who swings from the left side of the plate. This is because curveballs and sliders from a southpaw break away, rather than toward, a right-handed batter, making them easier to hit. The same holds true for a left-handed batter facing a right-handed pitcher. Managers such as Ned Hanlon, Hughie Jennings, Tris Speaker, and John McGraw had previously demonstrated the potential of platooning, albeit on a limited basis. However, for a long time small rosters and tradition had mitigated against managers regularly making substitutions at more than one or two positions.

Casey had always been a firm disciple of platooning, experiencing firsthand the way playing the righty-lefty percentages had extended his own career with the Giants. Ripper Collins remembered that one season in the Pacific Coast League (where teams played a schedule of nearly 200 games because of the favorable weather), Casey had played two first basemen—one lefty, one righty—in about 170 games each for the Oakland Oaks. One was always being yanked for the other.

Stengel, not looking to rock the boat too much in his first American League season, initially planned to be more cautious with the Yankees. Early on he was content to field a more or less set lineup, substituting here and there. However, injuries soon forced him into the wholesale juggling of personnel. The meat of his batting order—DiMaggio, Henrich, and Yogi Berra (the young catcher who missed six

Joe Page and Stengel wait out a rain delay. The burly reliever had his last great season in 1949, winning thirteen games and saving twenty-seven more.

weeks down the stretch with a broken thumb)—started just 17 games together that summer.

The only daily performers were Rizzuto and second baseman Jerry Coleman, two acrobatic glove men who also knew "how to execute" (as Casey liked to say) at bat and on the bases. Otherwise, players moved in and out of the lineup at an unprecedented pace. Against right-handed pitchers, Stengel played Bobby Brown at third base and Cliff Mapes and Gene Woodling in the outfield. All three were left-handed hitters. When a southpaw was on the mound, Casey installed three right-handed hitters: Billy Johnson at third and Johnny Lindell and Hank Bauer in the outfield. First base also was a revolving door, with Casey employing seven different men at the position, including Henrich to keep his bat in the lineup. Somehow the Yankees managed to keep pace with the heavy-hitting Red Sox, who were now being managed by a familiar face—Joe McCarthy.

> **"There's not much of a secret to platooning. You put a right-hand hitter against a left-hand pitcher and a left-hand hitter against a right-hand pitcher and on cloudy days you use a fastball pitcher."**

McCarthy, who had seen DiMaggio deliver for him time

It's October 1, 1949, and Ted Williams dejectedly returns to his position after watching Johnny Lindell's home run sail into the left-field seats at Yankee Stadium. The round-tripper gave New York a 5-4 victory and pulled the Yankees into a first-place tie with Boston. The following afternoon, in the final game of the season, the Yankees won again, prompting Casey to dance a little victory jig over his first pennant.

and again when they shared the same uniform, could only join Stengel in nodding his head over the injured star's performance when he finally joined the team on June 28 for an important series in Boston. At the time the Red Sox had won 10 of 11 games and were threatening to run away from the pack. Casey, deferring to DiMaggio's stature, had allowed him to decide when he would be ready to play again. DiMaggio had missed the Yankees' first 65 games, but in a three-game sweep of the Red Sox, he slammed four home runs and drove in nine runs, all of them coming at key moments. It was an emotional lift to DiMaggio's beleaguered teammates as well as a reminder of just who the straw that stirred the Yankees' drink really was.

Not that Casey didn't get credit from some quarters for the Yankees' tenacity as the season stretched on and injuries (a total of seventy-four various disabilities, according to the team's publicist) continued to wreak havoc. "It was hard to believe, but Casey would take a guy out of the lineup and the substitute would do better than the original," said trainer Gus Mauch. "He moved players around, he switched positions, he did everything, and everything seemed to work." "If Casey pulls this one out, he's a Houdini," Bill Dickey said of New York's pennant possibilities.

Casey pulled whatever rabbits he could find out of his hat. In late August when Henrich crashed into a wall at Chicago while chasing a ball hit off Fred Sanford, Stengel jogged out to check on his fallen outfielder. "Don't get up," he instructed

Bar patrons intently watch the 1949 World Series between the Yankees and Dodgers, the first fall classic to reach a large television audience. At the time half of all receiving sets were in New York. In the decade to come the tube would play a big part in advancing and expanding the legend of the Ol' Perfesser.

Henrich, who had fractured two of his vertebrae in the crash. "Take it very easy." Just as Henrich was beginning to feel all warm and fuzzy over his manager's obvious concern for his well-being, Casey added: "Lie down and give me a little more time to get someone warmed up and get this clown out of here."

Fortunately for Casey, the pitching staff remained basically healthy. He had inherited a solid trio of starters in Vic Raschi, who finished with a 21-10 record; Allie Reynolds (17-6); and Ed Lopat (15-10), a frustratingly unhittable junkball pitcher who Ted Williams always referred to as "that fuckin' Lopat." Tommy Byrne, a scatter-armed fastballer converted into a starter, rounded out the rotation. Byrne enjoyed his first of two consecutive 15-win seasons despite chronic wildness. He walked an incredible 179 batters in 196 innings, which made his catchers complain that they had to work the equivalent of a game and a half whenever he pitched.

Casey's greatest weapon came out of the bull pen in the person of Joe Page, an imposing left-hander who was as fast and lively off the mound as on it. Two years earlier he had led the loop with 14 relief wins and 17 saves before pitching five innings of one-hit ball against the Dodgers in the seventh game of the World Series to give the Yankees their last championship. His nightclubbing had resulted in a poor 1948 season, which probably cost the Yankees the pennant. But under Casey he had the last great season of his career, appearing in 60 games, all in relief. The thirty-one-year-old workhorse won 13 games, saved 27—8 more than any other *team* in the majors—and rang up a glittery 2.60 ERA. Unlike other managers, Casey was apt to use his stopper at any time during the game, whenever he needed to quell a rally.

The season boiled down to a two-game set between the Yankees and Red Sox. Boston, which had swept three games in New York a few days earlier to knock the Yankees into second, came to the Bronx with a one-game lead, needing only one win to clinch the pennant.

On Saturday, October 1, the Sox got to Reynolds early. The score was 2-0 in favor of Boston with the bases loaded and one out in the top of the third when Casey gave his starter the hook. He waved in Page, who made his manager look like less than a genius by walking in two more runs. But Page calmed down, retiring the side without any further damage. Over the next six innings, he surrendered just one more hit, giving his teammates a chance to climb back into the game.

Tommy Henrich was known as the Yankees' "Old Reliable" during his eleven years with the club. He lived up to his clutch reputation in Stengel's inaugural season with the Yankees, swatting 16 home runs in the first 65 games of the 1949 campaign before being slowed by injuries. Henrich, who hit a ninth-inning home run to win Casey's first game as a Yankee 3-2 over Washington, also won Stengel's first World Series game 1-0 with a ninth-inning shot off Brooklyn's Don Newcombe (pictured here). Stengel's assessment of his pleasant, clean-living outfielder was: "He's a fine judge of a fly ball. He fields grounders like an infielder. He never makes a wrong throw, and if he comes back to the hotel at three in the morning when we're on the road and says he's been sitting up with a sick friend, he's been sitting up with a sick friend."

Broadcaster Curt Gowdy with Ted Williams. When the Yankees beat the Dodgers in the '49 World Series, Gowdy took his father into the clubhouse to meet Stengel. Afterwards he asked how he liked him. "Mr. Stengel is very friendly," said the senior Gowdy. "But I'll be damned if I knew what he was talking about."

They did. They scored a pair of runs in the fourth off 25-game winner Mel Parnell, tied the game with two more in the fifth, then sailed home on Johnny Lindell's home run off Joe Dobson in the bottom of the eighth. The 5-4 triumph set the stage for the winner-take-all season finale on Sunday afternoon.

This time the Yankees seized a 1-0 lead in the first inning off 23-game winner Ellis Kinder and nursed it all the way to the eighth inning when they exploded for four additional runs. Three of them came on Jerry Coleman's two-out double to right, a bloop hit down the foul line that had Ted Williams still cursing forty years later: "Oh, God, that cheap hit, that cheap goddamn hit," he told author David Halberstam.

The padding was needed as the Bosox roared back with three runs in the top of the ninth. With one out, DiMaggio, whose legs were cramping up, allowed Bobby Doerr's drive to go over his head for a run-scoring triple. DiMaggio then did something that Casey may have wished to do himself but lacked the nerve. He called time and waved for a replacement. Stengel sent in a substitute, then watched Vic Raschi close out the game and one hell of an exciting season.

The Yankees were physically drained but emotionally pumped when the World Series against the Dodgers opened three days later in front of 66,224 at Yankee Stadium. Brooklyn, which had compiled the same 97-57 record as the Yankees, wasn't going to war with popguns. These were the Dodgers of Reese, Furillo, Hodges, Snider, Newcombe, Campanella, Robinson, Roe, and Erskine, later to be immortalized by Roger Kahn as "the

"That fella runs splendid but he needs help at the plate which coming from the country chasing rabbits all winter give him strong legs although he broke one falling out of a tree which shows you can't tell and when a curveball comes he waves at it and if pitchers don't throw curves you have no pitching staff so how is a manager going to know whether to tell boys to fall out of trees and break legs so he can run fast even if he can't hit a curveball?"

Edward "Whitey" Ford in 1950, a year in which the brash rookie off the streets of Queens won his first nine decisions. Ford, who named his pet poodle after Casey, rang up a .690 winning percentage in a career that ended in 1967. He had a sneaky fastball and a slow curveball. In a pinch he would resort to his "magic elixir" of turpentine, baby oil, and rosin to doctor the ball. His infielders were instructed not to oil their gloves, which helped keep the rest of the ball dry.

Boys of Summer." Casey, realizing his crew needed no pep talk after what they had been through, prepared the Yankees very simply. "Go get 'em!" he said.

Despite Brooklyn's firepower, winning the Series proved to be considerably easier than winning the pennant. The opener was a classic duel between two hard-bitten hurlers, with Reynolds besting Don Newcombe, 1-0, behind Tommy Henrich's leadoff home run in the bottom of the ninth. The Dodgers reversed the tables the following afternoon, Preacher Roe blanking the Yanks 1-0 on Gil Hodges's second-inning single. But from the third game on, the Yankees never trailed on the scoreboard. They swept the next three games, 4-3, 6-4, and 10-6, to make Casey the manager of a championship team his first year in pinstripes. His feelings were a blend of elation, relief, and vindication. "Babe, I won one," he said to an old friend, ex-Dodger Babe Herman, back in Glendale. "I won one."

With the championship under his belt, the cocky and bellicose Casey Stengel from National League days reappeared in the spring of 1950. Although he had won

Big John Mize, who had split his four home run titles evenly between the Giants and Cardinals, came over to the Yankees at the tail end of the 1949 season and was a key ingredient in Stengel's five straight championships. In 1950 the thirty-seven-year-old first sacker slammed 25 home runs in half a season, including this go-ahead blast against the first-place Tigers at Briggs Stadium that had his teammates jumping out of the dugout.

it all his first time out, Casey found respect hard to come by. The argument—even among some Yankees—was that the team was so good, *anybody* could manage it to a title. Over the coming years, Stengel would have to contend with accusations that he was a "push-button" manager or that his coaches did the real work. As New York marched to another pennant in 1950, overtaking Detroit and preseason favorite Boston in the last couple of weeks, old-line Yankees like DiMaggio and Rizzuto remained mystified by Casey's success. "Joe D and I—we could never figure out why he did this or did that," confessed Rizzuto. "Joe used to say, 'How can this guy win?'"

The answer was by doing more of the same. Billy Johnson had been the Yankees' regular third baseman during his first four seasons with New York. After Casey's arrival, however, he found himself just another interchangeable part in Stengel's seemingly madcap shuffling. According to Johnson, Casey "believed a right-handed hitter like me couldn't hit a right-handed pitcher as well as a left-handed batter could. To prove it, one day we needed a pinch hitter, and instead of choosing a right-handed .300 hitter, he picked pitcher Tommy Byrne, who batted left-handed. Byrne was a good hitter, but he made an out. The writers, who loved Casey because he gave them great quotes, questioned Casey on his move the next day and he responded, 'If Byrne got a hit, you'd say I was the smartest manager in the world. But he didn't get a hit, so now you're saying I'm the dumbest.'"

Jerry Coleman was a Marine combat pilot in World War II and again during the Korean War, but between tours of duty he was Stengel's principal second baseman. Coleman was a clutch .263 hitter over nine seasons in New York, winning MVP honors in the 1950 World Series. "He's only a one-for-four hitter," it was said of Coleman, "but that one hit will beat you."

Aging but generally healthy again, DiMaggio earned the $100,000 the Yankees paid him in 1950, batting .301 with 32 homers, 122 RBI, and a league-leading .585 slugging percentage, while playing 137 games in center field. However, most of his production came in the final two months of the season when he took out his cold rage against Casey on opposing pitchers.

Casey had earned the icon's disdain when he dropped DiMaggio from his traditional fourth spot in the order to fifth, moving John Mize—the powerful first sacker obtained the previous August from the Giants—into the cleanup slot. Then Casey actually benched the slumping DiMaggio for several games in August, giving his thirty-five-year-old star a "rest" that he didn't want. Earlier Casey had suggested DiMaggio learn how to play first base—a tactical move that DiMaggio and some other observers considered to be another sign of Stengel's propensity for over-

The Yankees celebrate a second straight pennant on September 29, 1950, having just learned that Cleveland has eliminated Detroit from the race.

managing. A proud man, DiMaggio felt awkward at the new position. But he swallowed his pride, kept his mouth shut, and played one game there before a spate of new injuries returned him to where most people figured he belonged, center field in Yankee Stadium.

The DiMaggio experiment aside, most moves made by Stengel in 1950 could be safely categorized as smart. Mize hit 25 home runs in only 90 games while rookie Ed "Whitey" Ford, a street-wise twenty-one-year-old left-hander from New York, won nine of ten decisions. When a knee injury forced Tommy Henrich to quit in August, George Weiss got Johnny Hopp—then the second-leading batter in the National League—from Pittsburgh. And when Joe Page suddenly lost his effectiveness, Weiss picked up Tom Ferrick, a veteran reliever from the Athletics. The Red Sox may have had the most awesome starting lineup in the game—they scored 1,027 runs and hit .302 as a team, figures no club since has approached—but once again it was Casey's patchwork crew of veterans, youngsters, and late-season pickups winning another improbable pennant.

The Yankees faced Philadelphia in the World Series. The youthful, upstart Phillies, who had won their first pennant in thirty-five years on Dick Sisler's tenth-inning home run against the Dodgers on the last day of the season, were nicknamed "the Whiz Kids." For the second straight October, the Yankees opened postseason play with a 1-0 triumph. This time 21-game winner Vic Raschi outdueled surprise starter Jim Konstanty, the National League's Most Valuable Player who had won 16 games and saved 22 others, all in relief, for manager Eddie Sawyer. The only run of the game came in the top of the fourth, Jerry Coleman driving in Bobby Brown with a sacrifice fly. The second game was another low-scoring affair in Philadelphia, Allie

Reynolds and 20-game winner Robin Roberts matching fastball for fastball. After nine innings both pitchers had surrendered only one run each. Then DiMaggio, leading off the top of the tenth, settled matters with a home run into the upper left-field stands.

Up by two games, Stengel next threw Eddie Lopat against Ken Heintzelman before a crowd of 64,505 at Yankee Stadium. The Phillies' journeyman pitcher, just a week shy of celebrating his thirty-fifth birthday, surprised everybody by carrying a 2-1 lead into the eighth. Heintzelman retired the first two batters, then walked the bases full. Konstanty came on to face Bobby Brown, who Casey sent in to bat for Hank Bauer. Brown hit one to Granny Hamner at short, who bobbled it as Coleman scampered home with the tying run.

Hamner tried to make up for his miscue by leading off with a double in the top of the ninth. A sacrifice and a walk put runners on the corners with only one out. But Tom Ferrick, who had started the inning in relief of Lopat, got out of the jam when Joe Collins—who Casey had used all season as Johnny Mize's "legs" at first—grabbed a grounder and gunned down Hamner at the plate.

In the bottom of the ninth, the Yanks pulled out their third straight one-run victory. With two outs, Woodling and Rizzuto singled. This brought up Coleman, the eventual Most Valuable Player of the Series, who slapped Russ Meyer's pitch into left center for his second game-winning hit in three afternoons.

Whitey Ford wrapped up the championship the next day with a 5-2 win. The most notable moments occurred in the ninth when Gene Woodling lost a fly ball in the sun, allowing two Phillies to score. With Reynolds warmed up in the bull pen,

The heart of the Philadelphia Phillies' lineup—from left, Willie Jones, Del Ennis, Andy Seminick, and Dick Sisler—took aim on the favored Yankees in the 1950 World Series. Stengel won his second straight championship in a four-game sweep. "You knew by the way they carried themselves that they were a class act," said Seminick. "They looked like champions."

Casey went to the mound to take the ball from Ford—an unpopular decision with the crowd, which badly wanted to see the youngster finish his first World Series game. As he walked back to the dugout, Casey reacted to the boos by pantomiming Woodling dropping a fly ball, a demeaning bit of slapstick that perhaps only someone who was one out away from clinching another title would be brave enough to attempt. Woodling, who was constantly arguing with his manager about playing time, took it in stride. "The reporters said we disliked each other," he once said of Stengel. "But he made me money, so how could I hate him?"

Empowered by two straight championships and a new contract, Casey prevailed upon ownership to start an instructional school for talented farmhands. The school, which lasted two to three weeks each spring before the veterans reported to camp, was an immediate success and was quickly emulated by other major league teams. Casey enjoyed it because it gave him a chance to do what he loved best: teach and talk. From that first class in February 1951, infielder Gil McDougald, pitcher Tom Morgan, and a young phenom named Mickey Mantle made the parent club.

Joe Collins was a left-handed power hitter who alternated between first base and the outfield for ten seasons in a Yankees uniform. Like other players whose careers were extended and bank accounts fattened by Stengel's platooning, he generally had good things to say about his manager. Not that Casey cared one way or the other. The secret to managing, he professed, was "to keep the five guys who hate you away from the five guys who are undecided."

Casey and Edna had decided from the beginning that they would not have children, so young players became surrogate sons to Stengel. "He loved talking to the younger players," Ralph Houk, a third-string catcher and a future Yankees manager, once told Maury Allen.

> That was his way of including them. I was sitting on a train one day and he comes up to me. "Hey, catcher"—he always called me "catcher"—"what do you think of the hit-and-run play?" I was just a kid then and I didn't want to disagree with him and we didn't use it much, so I told him it wasn't worth a shit. "You're fulla shit and I'll tell you why," he begins, and starts telling me how McGraw thought it was a great play and now he does thirty minutes on McGraw and the Giants and the hit-and-run play. A week later he sees me again. "Hey, catcher." Now I'm ready for him. Sure enough, he asks me about the hit-and-run play and I'm smiling and saying what a great play it is and all of a sudden he starts hollering, "Now wait a minute, for chrissakes, it's a horseshit play and if you listen I'll tell you why." Damned if he didn't do thirty minutes on how McGraw hated it.

Although all youngsters were worthy of getting their ear bent by Casey, Mickey Mantle represented something much larger to the old man. Every manager, if he sticks around long enough, dreams of leaving behind a living legacy—raw material fashioned by his own hands into a superplayer. In that sense Mantle was six feet and 195 pounds of promising clay for Casey to run his gnarled fingers over.

At nineteen, the blond-haired kid from Commerce, Oklahoma, was a marvel. He was as fast as a comet, once flying from home to first in three seconds, and could crunch the ball a country mile from either side of the plate. Yankees scout Tom Greenwade signed the switch-hitting shortstop after watching him blast two balls into a river during a high-school game. Casey, who was instrumental in getting Mantle a $7,500 contract ($2,500 more than the minimum) at the end of spring training, thought he had another Ty Cobb—with Babe Ruth's power! He talked George Weiss into letting him bring the kid up to the big time instead of farming him out. Mantle was moved to the outfield, where he became the heir apparent to DiMaggio.

Casey and his prize rookie, Mickey Mantle, in 1951.

"Casey became almost like a father to me," recalled Mantle, whose own father died after his first big-league season. "He always called me 'my boy.' He would say, 'That's my boy there,' you know. That's how close we became. He loved to brag to the press about me. He would tell them that I was going to be the next Babe Ruth, Lou Gehrig, and Joe DiMaggio all rolled into one."

Casey was eager to impart his years of baseball knowledge. Once, before an exhibition game at Ebbets Field, he took his prized rookie out to right field to show him how to play the angles.

"If the ball's hit at all good, it'll hit the wall or screen, so you might as well play shallow and catch the balls that aren't hit too good," he instructed. "Also, if you're not too close to the wall, the carom will come back to you and you can hold the batter to a single. If you're too close to the wall, the ball will bounce over your head."

Mantle was flabbergasted by this attention to detail. "Did you play out here?" he asked.

"Hell, yes," said Stengel. "I was a good outfielder, too."

The next day Casey told reporters, "The kid from Oklahoma thinks I was born at the age of sixty-two and started managing immediately."

By mid May the kid from Oklahoma was hitting .308, but then he went into a tailspin, striking out far too often and getting down on himself. On July 14, Casey

It's ironic that Bill Veeck Jr., the man who objected to Casey's hiring to manage Milwaukee's American Association team in 1945 because he was a clown, is best remembered for sending a midget, Eddie Gaedel, to bat in a 1951 game. Casey, of course, had an opinion on the subject. "Midgets are smart," he said. "Smart and slick as eels. You know why? It's because they're not able to do much with those short fingers. You understand? Not being able to do anything with their fingers, what do they do? They develop their brain power."

sent him to the Yankees' Triple-A farm club in Kansas City to regain his batting eye and self-confidence. One reporter asked if Mantle was through. "You wish you were through like that kid's through," Casey snapped back. Mantle was depressed enough to seriously consider quitting, but a tongue-lashing from his father, who called him a coward and a quitter, straightened out his backbone. He went on a tear and was recalled to the Yankees for the stretch drive.

Mantle, batting in the leadoff position, wound up hitting a less-than-sizzling .267 (which was still four points better than DiMaggio). Another of Casey's young favorites, Billy Martin, was sent back to Kansas City for seasoning. Mantle and Martin would have to wait just a little bit longer before becoming major contributors to the history of the Yankees. Meanwhile, in 1951 it was an odd-looking St. Louis youngster who had the biggest impact on Casey's pursuit of a third straight pennant.

His name was Lawrence Peter Berra, but everybody just called him Yogi.

"Yogi wouldn't hurt a fly," Gene Woodling said of the occasional outfielder who Casey made into his first-string catcher. "For the public, Yogi built an image of being a dumb, funny guy. He did make those absurd nonsensical statements he was famous for—I'd say, 'Jesus, Yogi, what are you talking about?'—but he was a serious player. He wasn't dumb."

"I enjoyed winning pennants," said Gene Woodling, a combative outfielder known as "The Rock." Woodling was a .284 hitter over seventeen seasons, including six as a Yankee. He admitted that publicity and fame were not important to him. "I just liked getting a sizable paycheck and realizing I didn't have to work for a living." Although he feuded often with Stengel, he closed out his career in 1962 playing for him with the New York Mets.

Berra didn't really sit around reading comic books—or at least not as many as writers or his roommate, Bobby Brown, would have the public believe—but he was an original character all the same. Like Casey, Yogi was garrulous and homely with a penchant for delivering in pressure situations, which was one reason, perhaps, that the two got along so well. In fact, Casey got to calling Berra "my assistant manager," a tribute to the young catcher's field leadership.

His blabbermouthing could drive batters to distraction. A typical home plate exchange might go like this:

YOGI: Have a good dinner last night?
TED WILLIAMS: The food is all bad here in New York.
YOGI: If you leave a tip, the food gets better.
TED WILLIAMS: Shut up, you ugly bastard.
YOGI: Done any good fishing lately?

Berra's so-called "Yogi-isms" were as widely chuckled over as Casey's Stengelese. "Bill is learning me all his experiences," Berra said of his tutor, Bill Dickey. "You can observe a lot by watching." Thanks to Dickey, Berra rapidly developed into a fine defensive catcher. He was already a clutch batsman with an almost unearthly ability to hit bad pitches. Berra had had a tremendous season in 1950, batting .322 with 28 homers and 124 ribbies while catching a club record of 148 games. Rizzuto, however, had been selected the American League's Most Valuable Player. In 1951, as the Yankees outdistanced the preseason favorite, Cleveland, Berra hit .294 and topped the team in home runs (27) and RBI (88) as well as runs, hits, and slugging. This time he was voted the most valuable player, his first of three such awards in five years.

In the World Series, Berra and the rest of the Bronx Bombers were opposed by what appeared to be a team of destiny. On August 11, the New York Giants had trailed the Dodgers by 13½ games. But then Leo Durocher's outfit won 39 of their last 47 games to finish in a dead heat with Brooklyn. A three-game play-off followed, with New York capturing the first 3-1 and dropping the second 10-0. In the decisive game, the Dodgers had a 4-1 advantage going into the bottom of the ninth. Today even fans with only a mild interest in baseball history can relate what happened next. The Giants rallied for four runs,

Two parks to which Casey contributed his share of history, Yankee Stadium (foreground) and the Polo Grounds, were separated by the Harlem River. They also were the sites of the 1951 World Series.

The Giants gave the Yankees fits in the '51 Series, Monte Irvin stealing home to key a 5-1 first-game victory and Eddie Stanky kicking the ball out of Phil Rizzuto's glove to spark a 6-2 win in game three.

After going hitless in his first dozen at-bats against the Giants, DiMaggio led the Yankees' comeback with six hits and five runs batted in the final three games, all Yankees victories. The barrage included this fifth-inning blast off Sal Maglie in the fourth game, the last home run of his career.

the last three coming home on the most famous round-tripper ever hit, Bobby Thomson's low drive into the left-field stands off snake-bit Ralph Branca.

The Series started on October 4, the day after Thomson hit his "shot heard 'round the world." The Giants were still on an emotional high and hammered the Yanks 5-1 at Yankee Stadium. Left fielder Monte Irvin went four for four and stole home in the opening frame off Allie Reynolds, who six days earlier had pitched his second no-hitter of the season to clinch the pennant.

The next afternoon Eddie Lopat went all the way in a five-hit, 3-1 victory over 23-game winner Larry Jensen. The Yankees suffered a huge loss, however, when Mantle, wrenching his knee chasing a fly ball in right field, was lost for the Series. With play moved to the Polo Grounds for game three, the Giants put on a spirited display for their fans. In the fifth inning Berra nailed Eddie Stanky on an aborted hit-and-run play, but the Giants' second baseman kicked the ball out of Rizzuto's glove. This opened the door to five unearned runs off Vic Raschi that buried the visitors, 6-2.

Unexpectedly down two games to one to the upstart Giants, Casey held a clubhouse meeting. "Are you going to let those garbage collectors steal your money?" he fumed.

A day of rain allowed Stengel to start Reynolds, who rode a two-run homer by DiMaggio—the last of his career—to a complete-game, 6-2 victory that squared the

Series. Game five was a 13-1 laugher, thanks to a grand slam by Gil McDougald (who under Casey's platooning system alternated between second and third base) and Lopat's five-hitter.

The Giants, one loss away from elimination, regrouped for game six at Yankee Stadium. The Yankees broke open a 1-1 tie on Bauer's two-out, bases-loaded triple off Dave Koslo in the sixth. There the matter stood until the ninth when the first three batters singled to fill the bases.

Casey walked out to the mound to replace right-hander Johnny Sain, the former Braves standout who had pitched two innings in relief of the starter, Raschi. Irvin, the cleanup hitter, and then Thomson, both right-handed batters, were due up. But Casey went against conventional wisdom and brought in Bob Kuzava, a lefty making his first World Series appearance.

Even Kuzava had his doubts. "This guy has got to be crazy to bring me in here," he thought. Irvin and Thomson both flied deep to left, each bringing in a run. With the score now 4-3, a runner on second and another right-hander, Sal Yvers, at the plate, Casey stuck with Kuzava. Yvers hit the ball hard, but Bauer grabbed it a few inches off the grass in right field to nail down Casey's third straight championship.

As the Kuzava incident illustrates, Casey didn't play the percentages religiously. He relied on instinct and intuition, blowing the dust off several decades of accumulated anecdotal evidence to come up with moves that, on the surface, didn't seem to make sense.

On December 11, 1951, Joe DiMaggio, in the company of his manager and Yankees co-owner Dan Topping, announced his retirement after 13 seasons. "He quit because he wasn't Joe DiMaggio anymore," explained his brother Tom.

"Casey had a super memory," said Jesse Gonder, who played briefly for Stengel with the Yankees and, later, with the New York Mets. "If you were a right-handed hitter but couldn't hit off a certain left-handed pitcher, Casey would remember. He would also remember that a left-handed hitter had hit well off that pitcher six or seven years ago. That's why he'd make the change. Or when he'd pinch-hit a weaker hitter against a particular pitcher, people would say it was crazy. But Casey knew that this hitter had more success against that pitcher than a stronger hitter. He was amazing that way."

The cornerstones of Stengel's platoon system were execution and versatility. Players were drilled on the fundamentals until they became second nature. This was important, not only because a player would typically

Allie "Chief" Reynolds was one of the game's toughest competitors while pitching for six championship teams in New York. Reynolds, part Creek Indian, was 7-2 with four saves and a 2.79 ERA in fifteen World Series games. In 1951 he went 20-6, led the circuit with a 2.06 ERA, 160 strikeouts, and six shutouts, and became the first American League pitcher to throw two no-hitters in a season. The second one, against Boston, clinched Stengel's third straight pennant. The following year he won the deciding World Series game against Brooklyn in relief. Remarked Casey: "Reynolds is two ways great, which is starting and relieving, which no one can do like him." He was a competitor to the end. When Reynolds was dying of cancer in 1995, his son noticed that he was still winding up and throwing pitches in his sleep.

Charlie Silvera was one of twelve men to play on the Yankees' five consecutive World Series winners between 1949 and 1953. "I didn't hang around all those years because I was Casey's illegitimate son," said the seldom-used backup catcher, who filled in admirably for Yogi Berra in the late stages of the 1949 pennant race. Although he only twice played more than 20 games in a season during his nine years with the Yankees, he cashed seven World Series checks.

Phil Rizzuto hurdles Cleveland's Bobby Avila in 1951 en route to completing another double play. Rizzuto, no fan of Stengel to begin with, left the Yankees with a bitter taste in his mouth. Casey released the loyal veteran shortstop in August 1956 to make room on the roster for a more valuable commodity—a proven left-handed hitting outfielder, Enos Slaughter.

Eddie Lopat—born Edmund Walter Lopatynski in New York City—was given the more manageable name of "The Junkman" by a journalist friend, a tribute to his variety of off-speed pitches. "When Lopat was pitching," said Yogi Berra, "I didn't need my catcher's mitt. A Kleenex did fine."

In 1946 Alfredo Manuel Pesano was a skinny, big-mouthed kid from Berkeley, California, when he first caught Casey's attention as a seventeen-year-old tryout for the Oakland Acorns. By 1952 he was the old man's surrogate son, with Casey even coming to his aid during a brawl with the Browns' Clint Courtney. On June 15, 1957, Martin was traded to Kansas City, causing a split with his mentor. "Casey didn't fight hard enough to keep me and that hurt," Martin later explained. "I didn't talk to him for five years." Finally, Martin approached Casey at the winter meetings when he had taken over the Mets. "I looked over and he was surrounded by sportswriters and I thought, 'I won't be able to live with myself if he dies before I can talk to him again.' I went over like nothing happened, said, 'Hi, Casey,' and he looked at me, winked, and said to the writers, 'Let me tell you about this here fella, he caught a fly ball for me. . . .' We never mentioned it again."

find himself at several different positions during the course of a season, but also because Casey believed the proper execution of routine plays would ultimately account for the razor-thin difference in the final standings. Stengel's first four pennant winners finished in front by one, three, five, and two games, respectively. Referring to Al Lopez, whose clubs in Cleveland and then Chicago always gave Stengel's teams a run for their money, he'd say, "Lopez will win 90 games and we'll win 90 games. If we can win two more with good [outfield] relays, we'll win the pennant."

Casey once described his philosophy like this: "If you've got a number of good men setting around on the bench you'll do yourself a favor playing them, because every time one of my front players got hurt I noticed the fella I stuck in his place would bust out with hits. Then just about the time he slowed down he'd oblige me by stepping in a hole and another fella would take his place and hit. I decided I'd never count on one player taking care of one position for an entire season. If you've got two or three men who can't play anyplace else pretty soon you're gonna run out of room for pitchers, and that's why you've got to have players who can do more than one thing."

Many players didn't care for platooning, but they had no choice but to learn to accept it. Once Hank Bauer was pulled out of the order in favor of Gene Woodling—this despite the fact that Bauer had already banged out three hits in the game. Both players complained. Afterward, Stengel called them into his office. He lit into Bauer first.

"I don't give a good goddamn what you call me," he said. "You can call me a crazy old man, and maybe I am. But it's my team and I'm going to run it my way.

"Now I'm going to tell you why I pulled you. You got your three hits, right? So let me tell you something, Mr. Bauer. You're not a 1.000 hitter. And you're not a .500 hitter. In fact, Mr. Bauer, you're not even a .333 hitter. So you had your three hits for the day and that's all it was going to be. That was your quota. I didn't think you had any more hits in you."

Then Casey turned on Woodling. "The same goes for you. So forget all this old-man crap and play your position and do whatever the hell I tell you."

No matter how much players mumbled and grumbled about the machinations, they were usually whistling a happy tune come October. In 12 seasons at the helm of the Yankees, Casey would steer the team into 10 World Series. The practically annual postseason check was "an important part of our pay," recollected Phil Rizzuto.

Stengel often paid more attention to his hunches than percentages. In the seventh inning of the seventh game of the '52 World Series, he brought in Bob Kuzava (right) to relieve Vic Raschi with the bases loaded, one out, and New York ahead 4-2. Kuzava was not a control pitcher, but he retired the Dodgers the rest of the way without a hit to close out Casey's fourth straight championship.

The key moment of the seventh game of the 1952 Series was Billy Martin's knee-high grab of Jackie Robinson's pop-up with two out, the bases loaded, and the Yankees' infield seemingly paralyzed. It was the kind of pressure-packed, heads-up play that Casey never tired of talking about.

The 1952 champions. Only Joe McCarthy's 1936-39 Yankees had ever won four World Series in a row.

Stengel, already the highest paid manager in history, signed a new two-year contract for a reported $70,000 a year after the '52 Series.

"Receiving $5,627 after we beat the Dodgers [in 1949] meant I could stay at home with my family that winter and not have to find a job."

When it came to dividing the spoils, every player benefited, from front-line stars to the last guy on the roster. Charlie Silvera, a backup catcher who played as little as seven games in an entire season, managed to stick around for nine years with the Yankees. He cashed seven World Series checks totaling $46,389 despite appearing in just one postseason game. That extra money, coming at a time when a player could buy a new three-bedroom house for about $10,000, wasn't too far from what he made in regular-season salary during the same period.

No amount of money could induce Joe DiMaggio to return for a fourteenth season in 1952. Despairing over "his vanishing gifts," reported friend and writer Jimmy Cannon, the great DiMaggio turned his back on a $100,000 contract and retired.

His absence influenced baseball prognosticators. It seems almost impossible to believe today, but in Casey's first four years with New York, the Yankees were never once the favorite to win the pennant. As teams headed north from spring training in April 1952, the thrice-burned experts continued to tout the Indians as the team to beat. Stengel, meanwhile, was on a mission. He was chasing history. Only John McGraw and Joe McCarthy had ever managed teams to four pennants in a row. Only McCarthy had ever won four straight World Series.

Although McCarthy's 1936–39 champions had been a powerhouse, the squad with which Casey sought to tie the record was filled with holes. With the Korean War dragging on, pitcher Tom Morgan and starting infielders Jerry Coleman and Bobby

It was great to be old and a Yankee. Casey regularly cut a rug with Edna, and even appeared on Ralph Edwards' popular *This Is Your Life* television program in November 1952.

Brown joined Whitey Ford in military uniform. In addition, the ace of the staff, Eddie Lopat, injured his shoulder. Lopat, the winner of twenty-one games in 1951 (plus two more in the World Series), missed a chunk of the season and wound up with only ten victories.

Casey opened the 1953 season by shaking hands with President Dwight Eisenhower at Griffith Stadium, then watched his team bow to the Senators in extra innings on Mickey Vernon's home run.

Casey plugged the holes in admirable fashion. He made Gil McDougald, who'd spent his rookie season bouncing between second and third base, the everyday third baseman and installed feisty Billy Martin at second base. Mantle moved from right to center field and rang up a .311 batting average with 23 home runs and 87 runs batted in, a taste of even better seasons to come. And Allie Reynolds emerged as the new ace in Lopat's absence, going 20-8 with a league-low 2.06 ERA. Thirteen other pitchers contributed at least one win to the Yankees' final total of 95, which was good enough to bring New York home two games ahead of the Indians and reserve a spot in the World Series against Brooklyn.

The Dodgers and Yankees put on a classic subway Series, with both teams alternating wins until the final game. Behind Duke Snider's hot bat, Brooklyn won games one, three, and five, with the Yankees rebounding to grab games two, four, and six to stave off elimination. The decisive seventh game, played October 7 at Ebbets Field, saw Lopat go up against Joe Black in front of 33,195 Brooklyn faithfuls who were positive that this was the year their team would finally win the World Series.

Black, a rookie who had gone 15-2 during the season, had won the opener 4-2 on a six-hitter. He'd pitched another strong game in the fourth contest, giving up just one run in seven innings, but Reynolds had been better, pitching a four-hitter and striking out ten in a 2-0 triumph. On this afternoon Black surrendered single runs in the fourth, fifth, and sixth innings before being relieved by Preacher Roe. Lopat, meanwhile, was pulled after loading the bases with nobody out in the fourth. Stengel brought in Reynolds, who had already won game four and saved game six, and he was able to get out of the inning with only one run scored.

Both teams scored again to make it 4-2 New York at the bottom of the seventh. With Raschi now relieving Reynolds, the Dodgers loaded the bases on a single and a pair of walks. Snider, who had already tied Babe Ruth's record with four home runs in the Series, was next up, to be followed by Jackie Robinson.

In a phrase that Yogi Berra would later make famous, it was "déjà vu all over again." As he had in a similar situation the previous October against the Giants,

If Casey was feeling any pressure going after a fifth straight championship, he wasn't showing it. During a lengthy rain delay he clowned around for a bored photographer.

"Stop feeding him peanuts," was Casey's directive regarding the team's constant teasing of Yogi Berra, who was "a peculiar fellow with amazing ability," as Casey once said. Stengel's faith in the ungainly looking backstop paid off with three MVP awards, a record 75 World Series games, and 313 career home runs (a record for catchers until broken by Johnny Bench). "So I'm ugly," the Yankees' Yoo-Hoo man once shot back at some bench jockeys. "So what? I never saw anyone hit with his face." After seeing Berra hit an important home run, Casey told him, "I think you look like Tyrone Power."

The Ol' Perfesser faced the Dodgers for the third time in five years in the 1953 World Series. Jackie Robinson, who actually was a college graduate, put on cap and robe and hoped to teach his Brooklyn teammates something about winning. But once again the Yankees prevailed, this time in six games.

Casey ignored the percentages and brought in Bob Kuzava. Once again this was Kuzava's first appearance in the Series, and once again he came through, getting Snider and Robinson to pop up to end the threat. As if conspiring to add a dramatic flourish to the final out of the inning, Kuzava, Berra, and the entire Yankees infield stood frozen as Robinson's weak fly came tumbling out of the hazy sky. For a single tantalizing second, it appeared that the ball might actually fall among the fielders as the tying and go-ahead runs crossed the plate. But then Billy Martin came charging in from second base, his cap flying off as he crossed the mound to nab it at knee level. Kuzava went on to retire the side in the eighth and ninth innings to sew up Casey's fourth straight title.

Casey couldn't help but toot his own horn a little. "You know," he said, "John McGraw was a great man in New York and he won a lot of pennants. But Stengel is in town now, and he's won a lot of pennants, too."

A fifth followed with comparative ease. The Yankees, led by 18-game winner Whitey Ford, back from the army, charged through the regular season. An 18-game winning streak, one shy of the league mark, propelled them to a final 99-52 mark and put them back in the World Series against the Dodgers.

This time around the heroes included Eddie Lopat. Casey always liked pitchers

Five in a row! Casey accepts a floral tribute to commemorate the unprecedented feat of winning five straight championships.

Second baseman and batting champion Bobby Avila (left) and heavy-hitting third baseman Al Rosen helped lead the Indians to a league-record 111 victories in 1954. Cleveland, second-place finishers from 1951 to 1953, finally beat out Stengel's Yankees for the pennant, but were swept in the World Series by the Giants.

who, in his parlance, "threw ground balls"—that is, pitchers who induced batters to hit grounders, especially with men on base. A double play was "two-thirds of an inning," he said more times than anyone could count. In 1953 Lopat threw enough grounders to post a 16-4 record and to lead all pitchers in winning percentage (.800) and earned run average (2.43). The competitive hurler was looking to avenge his poor showing in the 1952 World Series when he had twice been chased out early.

After the Yankees won the curtain raiser by a 9-5 score, Lopat took the ball for game two. The Bombers were down by a run until Martin's solo home run in the seventh tied it at two runs apiece. Mantle's two-run blast in the eighth established a 4-2 lead as the Brooklyn half of the ninth began. The Dodgers had the tying runs on base with two out and the ever dangerous Duke Snider at the plate when Casey made his way to the mound.

"I got the big guy and the little guy ready," said Stengel, referring to Reynolds and Ford warming up. "Now you're sure you're all right?"

"Case," said Lopat, "how long have I been pitching for you?"

"Five years."

"Have I ever lied to you?"

"No."

"Well," said Lopat, "you don't think I'm going to start now, do you?"

One of Casey's virtues was his confidence in those men who had delivered for him in the past. "Okay, Mr. Lopat," he said, and with that he walked back to the dugout and watched his veteran junkballer retire Snider to give the Yanks a 2-0 Series lead.

Casey's best friend and emotional anchor continued to be Edna, who handled fan mail and business decisions with equal aplomb.

Brooklyn won the next two games, 3-2 and 7-3, but the comeback only served to set up their fatalistic fans for yet another letdown. The next two afternoons the Yankees bombed the Dodgers 11-7 and then squeaked out a 4-3 verdict to end the suffering. The normally light-hitting Billy Martin was the catalyst, batting .500 with a record-tying 12 hits and knocking home the Series-winning run with a single in the bottom of the ninth. With that, Stengel's New York Yankees, winners of an unprecedented five consecutive world championships, had become a team for the ages.

Casey showed no signs of wanting to abandon the limelight as he approached the traditional retirement age of sixty-five. At the annual dinner of the New York chapter of the Baseball Writers Association he donned swami headgear to entertain Dodgers president Walter O'Malley (left) and manager Walt Alston.

NY
NEW YORK

SEVEN

Most People My Age Are Dead

After hitting a slight bump in the pennant road in 1954, the Yankees continued to dominate the standings for the second half of Stengel's reign. By the mid fifties such old favorites as Lopat, Reynolds, Raschi, Woodling, and Rizzuto were giving way to fresh faces like Tony Kubek, Elston Howard, Bob Grim, Bob Turley, and Bobby Richardson. These newest Yankees joined with the nucleus of established stars and players to keep the tradition of excellence going. From 1955 to 1960, New York would win five more pennants, missing out only in 1959. The Yankees were considered so far ahead of the pack that the rest of the American League was referred to as "the Sorry Seven."

If it was true that rooting for the Yankees in the 1950s was like rooting for that other coldly efficient monopoly, United States Steel, it was equally true that during this period people across the country grew enamored of the grandfatherly fellow whose funny looks and fractured speech were so at odds with the Yankees' bloodless corporate image.

Greatly aiding Casey's visibility was the rise of television, which was bringing the miracle of major-league ball into millions of far-flung American homes for the first time. The Yankees were staples of sports programming from April to October, particularly on the extremely popular *Game of the Week* broadcasts, for which they often were one of the featured teams. At one point two-thirds of all television sets in the country were tuning to the network game on Saturday afternoons, providing a showcase not only for such stars as Mantle, Berra, and Ford, but also for their rub-

...Facing page: **Stengel in 1960, his last season with the Yankees.**

In the fifties Casey's familiar face graced the covers of several national magazines, including *Time* and *Newsweek*.

ber-faced, gravel-voiced skipper. The club's success guaranteed maximum exposure for the ubiquitous "Ol' Perfesser," who managed in a record 63 World Series games from 1949 to 1960, as well as 10 All-Star games: 1950, 1951, 1952, 1953, 1954, 1956, 1957, 1958, and 1959 (a year the leagues played two games).

It was hard to find media types who didn't like Casey. As a public figure, he put on a great show—winking, mugging, double-talking. Privately, he was indisputably a man's man, smoking, cussing, and drinking in a world that was still a male preserve. He was tireless and entertaining. "If you had a bottle of bourbon with you," said Curt Gowdy, "Casey would go on until four in the morning."

Gowdy, then a broadcaster in New York, remembered sitting at the bar one time with Casey. Beers were ordered. Before Gowdy could take more than couple of sips, Casey had drained his mug and ordered another.

"Casey, I've never seen anyone drink beer as fast as you do," the astounded broadcaster said.

"Well, it's always been that way since my accident," Casey explained.

"What accident?"

"Somebody knocked my glass over."

Casey was in his mid sixties, but his one passion remained baseball. Outside of Edna, he had no other real interests in life. Ask him something about the squeeze play and he would jump up and rearrange the furniture, chairs representing bases while nightstands and wastebaskets took the place of infielders. One writer remembered walking into a hotel lobby just in time to see the aged manager of the New York Yankees conclude a story by sliding across the carpet and into a potted plant.

Casey was an original character and a natural entertainer, and like any sea-

Hank Bauer, seen here rubbing the hair of Bob Turley, was a product of East St. Louis, Illinois, and not the best ballplayer in the family. His brother Herm, who was killed in World War II, was. Bauer fought on Iwo Jima as a Marine, then went on to play fourteen big-league seasons in gung-ho style, all but the last two with New York. In 1955 he announced that he was going to "whack that platoon thing out of whack." He hit 20 homers, then batted .429 against the Dodgers in the World Series. Eleven years later Bauer managed the Baltimore Orioles to a world championship.

Gil Hodges swung a big bat for Brooklyn, hitting four home runs in a 1950 game and driving in a hundred or more runs for seven consecutive seasons, 1949 to 1955. He went hitless in 21 at-bats in the 1952 Series, causing Brooklyn fans to light candles and bombard him with homemade batting remedies, but he rebounded to knock in both runs in the Dodgers' seventh-game win over the hated Yankees in the '55 Series. After sixteen seasons with the Dodgers the gentle first baseman played two seasons with the Mets, where he hit the final nine of his 370 lifetime home runs. In 1969 he accomplished the incredible, managing the 100-to-1 underdog Mets to a World Series victory over Baltimore. Hodges died of a heart attack at spring training in 1972.

Sandy Amoros makes his game-saving catch of Yogi Berra's line drive in the sixth inning of the final game of the 1955 Series. About thirty minutes later, jubilant Brooklyn fans pour out of the stands to celebrate Johnny Podres's masterful 2-0 win that delivered Brooklyn's first—and last—championship.

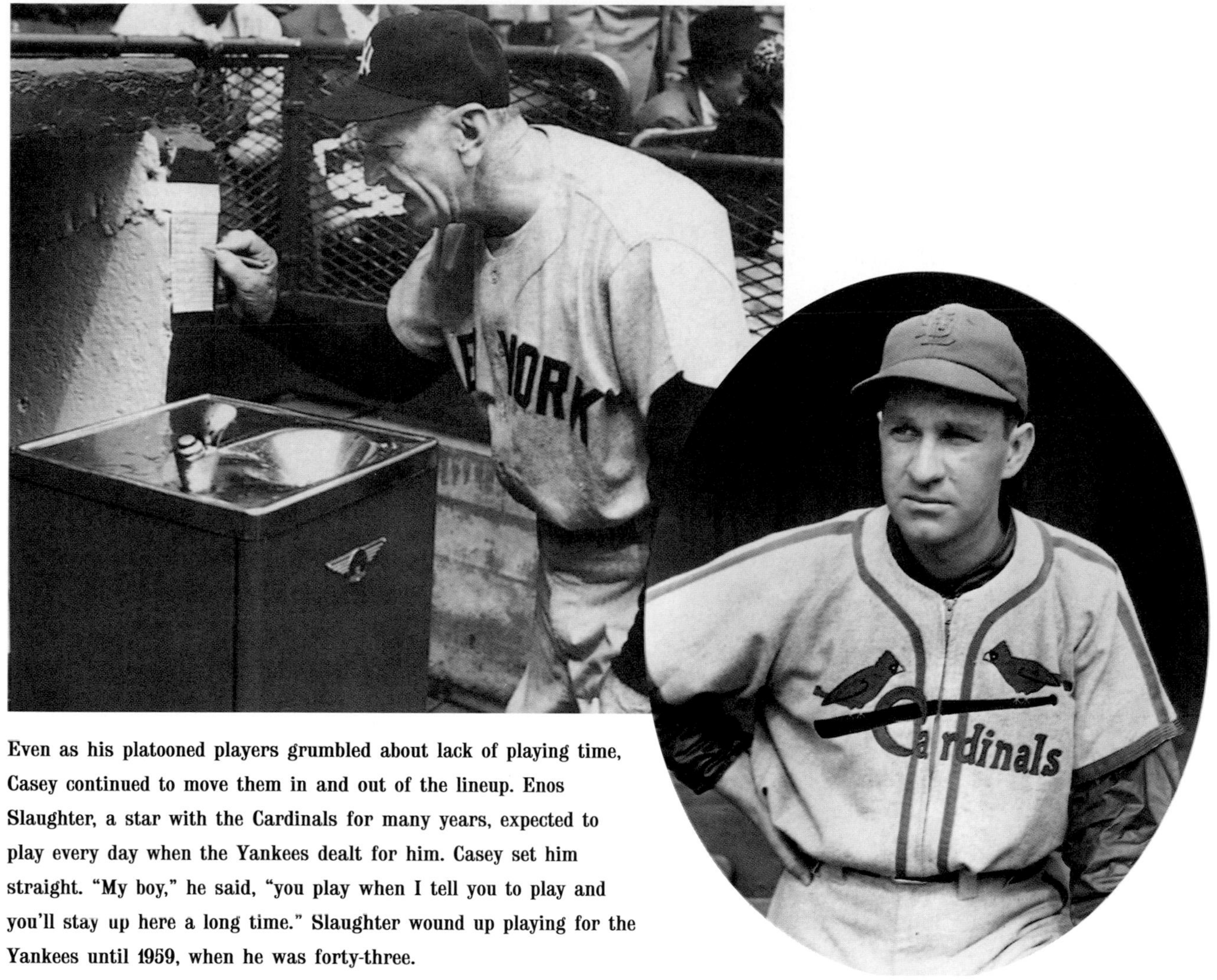

Even as his platooned players grumbled about lack of playing time, Casey continued to move them in and out of the lineup. Enos Slaughter, a star with the Cardinals for many years, expected to play every day when the Yankees dealt for him. Casey set him straight. "My boy," he said, "you play when I tell you to play and you'll stay up here a long time." Slaughter wound up playing for the Yankees until 1959, when he was forty-three.

soned performer he knew how to play to the crowd. "Stengel always seems to be addressing a vast banquet audience from an invisible dais," wrote columnist Jimmy Cannon. As an American League infielder in the 1950s, Whitey Herzog observed Stengel's shenanigans and proclaimed him "the best public-relations man who ever lived." This appraisal was shared by longtime American League umpire John "Red" Flaherty, who referred to a widely circulated photograph of Casey heatedly arguing a call. In the picture Casey appears ready to punch Flaherty in the jaw, but the fury and clenched fist were calculated for effect, said Flaherty. "Nobody was holding him back. Casey knew exactly what he was doing all the time."

Profiles in such popular national magazines as *Look*, *Life*, *Sports Illustrated*, and *Saturday Evening Post* helped build the Stengel legend by rehashing the sparrow-in-the-cap and dropped-grapefruit stories. Beat writers continually added new tales. There was the time Casey waved in a relief pitcher. "But I'm not tired," the starter protested. "Well, I'm tired of you," said Casey. On another occasion a Yankees fan serving in the military sent a letter criticizing Stengel's managing. Casey sent him a telegram: "If you're so damned smart, let me see you get out of the army." Listening once to several young Yankees playing Twenty Questions in the clubhouse after a

Mickey Mantle gets crowned by his manager after his Triple Crown season of 1956. One long home run at Chicago's Comiskey Park had Casey marveling that "Seats were flyin' around for five minutes!" Certain things would irritate Casey, The Mick once recalled, "but trying too hard or getting angry at sitting on the bench were not among them."

loss, he barked, "I'll give you the perfect question for it. Which one of you clowns won't be here tomorrow?"

And so on and so on. Some still thought he was undignified and overrated, but he was considered newsworthy enough to be placed on the covers of both *Time* and *Newsweek.* The publicity certainly didn't hurt business at the Glendale Valley National Bank, which the Lawson family helped establish in 1957. Casey, who invested $50,000 in the enterprise, was made a vice president and a member of the board of directors. On his large mahogany desk was a sign: "Stengelese Spoken Here."

The most memorable display of Stengelese took place not inside a dugout or a bank office, but inside the august chambers of the United States Senate. On July 9, 1958, Casey, Mickey Mantle, Ted Williams, and Stan Musial testified before the Senate Subcommittee on Antitrust and Monopoly. The hearing was being held on a bill exempting professional baseball, football, hockey, and basketball from antitrust restrictions. Casey's seven thousand words of testimony have to be read verbatim and in their entirety to get the full effect, so they are included as an appendix to this book. However, the flavor of it can be gleamed from his response to the first question put to him by the subcommittee chairman. "Mr. Stengel," said Senator Estes Kefauver, "you are the manager of the New York Yankees. Will you give us very briefly your background and views about this legislation?"

"Well," Casey began, "I started in profes-

"When I don't win, I'm good and mad at night. But if you think you're going to do better just by being serious all the time and never telling any stories or doing any kidding around—why, you're a little mistaken. Some people could never understand that."

sional ball in 1910. I have been in professional ball, I would say, for forty-eight years. I have been employed by numerous ball clubs in the majors and in the minor leagues. I started in the minors with Kansas City. I played as low as Class D ball, which was at Shelbyville, Kentucky, and also Class C ball and Class A ball, and I have advanced in baseball as a ballplayer. I had many years that I was not so successful as a ballplayer, as it is a game of skill. And then I was no doubt discharged by baseball in which I had to go back to the minor leagues as a manager, and after being in the minor leagues as a manager, I became a major-league manager in several cities and was discharged, we call it 'discharged,' because there is no question I had to leave."

As laughter rippled through the room, Casey picked up speed. "And I returned to the minor leagues at Milwaukee, Kansas City, and Oakland, California, and then returned to the major leagues. In the last ten years, naturally, in major-league baseball with the New York Yankees, the New York Yankees have had tremendous success, and while I am not a ballplayer who does the work, I have no doubt worked for a ball club that is very capable in the office. . . .

". . . I have been up and down the ladder. I know there are some things in baseball, thirty-five to fifty years ago, that are better now than they were in those days. In those days, my goodness, you could not transfer a ball club in the minor leagues. Class D, Class C ball, Class A ball.

"How could you transfer a ball club when you did not have a highway? How could you transfer a ball club when the railroad then would take you to a town, you got off and then you had to wait and sit up five hours to go to another ball club? How could you run baseball then without night ball? You had to have night ball to improve the proceeds, to pay larger salaries, and I went to work, the first year I received $135 a month. I thought that was amazing. I had to put away enough money to go to dental college. I found out it was not better in dentistry. I stayed in baseball.

Stengelese: A Selected Glossary

Appliances: modern, oversized gloves
Butcher boy: the act of swinging down on a pitch
Clerk: a mediocre ballplayer
Green pea: rookie
He ain't no Ned in the Third Reader, ya know: description of someone who's been around
He could make a living: a player with talent or potential
He could squeeze your eyebrows off: a player who is tough as nails
Jelly leg: a batter with a bad case of nerves
Lobs: batters who fail to hit with men on base (from LOB, box score shorthand for "left on base")
Milkshake drinker: someone who doesn't carouse
Plumber: a poor fielder kept in the lineup because of his bat
Putsie-downsie: a weak hitter with a half-hearted swing
Road apple: a bad player
Sugar plum: rookie
Taking it on the big bill: fielding a ball hit to the outfield on the big, easy hop instead of charging it
Throwing ground balls: the art of pitching the ball low to induce double plays
Whiskey slick, Whisker slick: a playboy
Whommy: a whammy or a hex on the opposition
Worm killer: a ball thrown low to the ground

"Any other questions you would like to ask me?"

There were several more questions, and many of Casey's rambling answers were met with laughter from the three hundred people in attendance. After forty-five minutes he was excused, but excerpts from his remarkable performance appeared on radio and television programs across the country and were reprinted in hundreds of newspapers. "He talked for a long time," the next witness, Mickey Mantle, later recalled, "but I don't think anybody really understood what he said."

After five straight championships, the Yankees finally encountered a slip in the standings. "If I don't win the pennant this year," Casey said in the spring of 1954, "they oughta commence firing the manager." A doubleheader loss to the Indians on September 12 sealed the Yankees' fate. Although they'd won 103 games, their most ever under Stengel's hand, they finished a distant second. Cleveland won an astounding 111 games, establishing an American League record that still stands. That the Indians were subsequently swept in the World Series by the Giants didn't salve Casey's pain; he was pulling for his friend Al Lopez to win.

Don Larsen's crewcut gets a congratulatory pat after his perfect game. Meanwhile, some enterprising soul came out with a commemorative plate that cost souvenir seekers three dollars.

The year 1955 was historic for the Yankees. That summer the club fielded its first black player, a large and soft-spoken line-drive hitter named Elston Howard.

Most observers thought the move was long overdue. Jackie Robinson had broken the majors' color line in 1947, but even as scores of talented Negro players entered both leagues in Robinson's wake, the Yankees continued to drag their feet. The front office kept silent on the issue of integration, though most observers figured the team shied away from fielding a black player because it didn't want to offend its white, middle-class customer base. As attendance continued to drop during the 1950s and the neighborhood surrounding Yankee Stadium changed complexion, the team seriously considered desegregating. Civil rights activists picketed the park, urging a change in the club's lily white roster. However, owners Del Webb and Dan Topping and general manager George Weiss were united in their belief that the first black Yankee had to have a certain image. This was the reason a promising first baseman, Vic Power, was never brought up to the big club. Power, who signed with the Yankees in 1950, hit .349 in Class AAA in 1953, but his showboating and nondeferential nature worked against him ever appearing in pinstripes. Instead, he was traded to the Philadelphia Athletics, where he began a productive twelve-year stay in the major leagues.

There's no doubt that Casey, a man born in the nineteeth century and raised in Jim Crow America, bought into the racial stereotypes of the time. Like a good number of his contemporaries in and out of baseball, he freely used words like "coon," "eight ball," and "jungle bunny." His reaction when he found out that Howard ran like a man carrying a freezer on his back was often repeated. "Well, they finally get me a nigger," he observed, "I get the only one who can't run."

Stengel could be a vicious and inventive bench jockey. After all, he had been a platooned player under McGraw, and hazing was one of the responsibilities of some-

The 1957 World Series turned on a smudge of shoe polish. With the Yankees up two games to one and leading the fourth game by a run in the bottom of the tenth inning, pinch hitter Nippy Jones claimed that a Tommy Byrne pitch had hit him. Jones persuaded umpire Augie Donatelli by showing him a smudge of polish on the ball, proof that it had nicked his foot. That opened the gates to a three-run rally that won the game and knotted the Series, which the Braves went on to win in seven games.

During the 1950s the Yankees practically ran a shuttle to and from Kansas City, acquiring such players as pitcher Ralph Terry (left) and third baseman Clete Boyer.

body riding the pine. Hazing, with its heavy emphasis on ethnic and racial stereotypes, was an integral part of the game during Casey's half century as player and manager. As distasteful as the name-calling was, most players learned to tolerate it. When somebody would rag Al Lopez as being "a low-down Mexican," Lopez would thoughtfully remind his antagonist, "You know I'm a highborn Spaniard." A more sensitive player, like Jewish star Hank Greenberg of the Tigers, sometimes let the slurs upset him to the point that they directly affected his performance—which was precisely the objective.

On July 9, 1958, Stengelese entered a new dimension with Casey's much-publicized testimony before the U.S. Senate.

Roy Campanella Jr., son of the Dodgers' gifted black catcher, remembered one World Series where he sat so close to the field that he could "hear the racist remarks coming from the opposing dugout that were directed at my father, Jackie Robinson, and the other black Dodgers. . . . Casey Stengel is so beloved that it may surprise some people that he was particularly insulting to blacks; he was a racist who used the word 'nigger' as if he thought it were appropriate."

One would reasonably assume that Elston Howard resented his manager. Far from it. Howard, whose powerful bat had Stengel moving him from first base to the outfield to behind the plate, understood there was a considerable difference between words and actions. "I never felt any prejudice around Casey," he said. "He'd scream at Newcombe and Robinson and Campanella during the World Series, but I never heard him scream racial things. He screamed at Reese and Hodges and Snider, too. . . . He always bragged about me, called me his three-way platoon, and treated me with kindness and respect. I never saw any signs of bigotry. . . ."

Elston Howard.

In the heat of battle, Casey was no different from most other managers. Minnie Minoso, who joined the White Sox in 1951,

Tony Kubek, a gangly Milwaukee boy with a crew cut and ready smile, was the American League Rookie of the Year in 1957. Stengel had Kubek playing as many as seven positions, including five in a single World Series game. "He liked to be cute that way," said Kubek, a career .266 hitter who left the Yankees after nine seasons to enter broadcasting.

remembered how Philadelphia manager Jimmie Dykes "used to call me every name in the book—'you black nigger so-and-so.'" Afterwards, Dykes would see him in the hotel and greet him, "Hello, Mr. Minoso." "I think all he was trying to do at the ballpark was to get my attention away from the game," said Minoso—an explanation that could be used to defend Casey's similar agitating of the thin-skinned Robinson.

It's difficult gauging Stengel's racial attitude. Were his comments intended to intimidate and entertain, or did they reveal a deeper animus? It's worth noting that Minoso said nobody on the Yankees, Stengel included, ever directed racial epithets at him. Indeed, he considered Casey "a great sportsman." And Minoso probably was unaware that Stengel had barnstormed against Negro leaguers often in the teens and twenties, apparently without incident. Elston Howard remembered that when he first joined the Yankees, he was refused service in restaurants in Kansas City and Chicago "until Stengel raised hell." On these occasions Casey explained the situation quite simply: "We came as a ball club and Elston Howard is part of the ball club. If he can't be accommodated, we'll leave."

By the early 1960s Casey was more sensitive to the burgeoning civil rights movement and chose his words a bit more carefully. But even during the 1950s, his public comments involving race can be viewed as being more acidic or comedic than malicious. There was the time, for instance, when Allie Reynolds, who was part Creek Indian, struck out Jackie Robinson three times in a World Series game. "Before that black son-of-a-bitch accuses us of being prejudiced," said Casey, "he should learn how to hit an Indian."

> **"I commenced winning pennants as soon as I got here, but I did not commence getting any younger."**

Robinson and the rest of the long-suffering borough of Brooklyn finally got their revenge in the 1955 World Series. The Yankees seized the first two games, and it appeared that the Dodgers—losers of the '41, '47, '49, '52, and '53 Series to the Yanks—would once again have to "wait 'til next year." No team had ever come back from losing the first two games to win the Series. But Brooklyn swept the next three games at Ebbets Field. The Yanks finally cooled off the Dodgers when Whitey Ford, the American League's leader with 18 victories, won his second game of the Series with a 5-1 gem.

Casey figured he had the edge as both teams suited up for game seven at Yankee Stadium. He had never lost a World Series in five tries; moreover, his teams had twice prevailed in previous game sevens.

This October the stardust, for once, fell on Brooklyn. Johnny Podres, possessor of a mediocre 9-10 record, pitched a masterful eight-hitter to shut down the Bombers 2-0. The Bums' beloved first baseman, Gil Hodges, drove in both runs. But it was a nifty bit of platooning that turned unheralded Sandy Amoros into as big a hero as Podres or Hodges. In the bottom of the sixth, with Brooklyn clinging to its two-run lead, Alston switched Jim Gilliam from left field to second base and installed Amoros in left. With Billy Martin and Gil McDougald on base and nobody out, Yogi Berra lined a Podres pitch into the left-field corner. It looked to be a sure extra-base hit, but Amoros raced over and snared the drive, then wheeled and threw the ball into the infield to double up McDougald. Amoros's defensive gem was the turning point, giving Brooklyn its first—and only—world championship before the team left for Los Angeles three years later.

Ryne Duren came to New York from Kansas City in 1958 and immediately led the loop in saves with twenty. His fastball was as wild and unpredictable as he was. "He takes a drink or ten," Casey said of his alcoholic reliever, "comes in with those coke bottles, throws one on the screen and scares the shit out of 'em."

It also made Stengel a losing World Series manager for the first time. He quickly remedied that in 1956, guiding the Yankees to a seventh pennant in eight years with a come-from-behind World Series win over the Dodgers.

The big stories of 1956 were Mickey Mantle's season-long brilliance and Don Larsen's two hours of perfection. At twenty-four, Mantle had the kind of year that had every boy in America wanting to "be like Mickey." He hit .353, edging past Ted Williams for the batting championship by beating out several bunts in the last days of the season. He clouted 52 home runs and knocked in 130 runs to earn batting's mythical Triple Crown and the Most Valuable Player Award. Despite having to wrap his ailing legs before each game, he was swift enough to chase down drives to the deepest parts of center field and to steal 10 bases, a modest total that nonetheless was exceeded by only six American Leaguers.

Larsen was an unlikely candidate for immortality, though the big right-handed pitcher could drink at the same championship level as Mantle. One early morning in the spring of 1956, Larsen had fallen asleep at the wheel, bouncing his car off a telephone pole and then a bakery truck. Stengel immediately took care of damage control, double-talking reporters and persuading Yankees brass not to get rid of

Casey reads congratulatory telegrams from around the country after the Yankees rallied from a 3-1 deficit to win the 1958 World Series over Milwaukee.

him. Larsen was eternally grateful to Casey. His way of paying Casey back was not to cut out the boozing—he wasn't *that* grateful—but to compile an 11-5 record as a starter and reliever.

After the Yanks dropped the opening game of the World Series to Brooklyn, 6-3, Casey chose Larsen to start game two. He didn't make it out of the second inning, blowing a six-run lead as the Dodgers rolled to a 13-8 victory. The Yankees fought back with 5-3 and 6-2 wins to square the Series. In the fifth game, played October 8 at Yankee Stadium, Casey decided to take a chance on Larsen. Larsen responded by setting the Dodgers down in order, inning after inning. Mantle aided the cause, cracking a home run in the fourth to stake Larsen to a 1-0 lead and then preserving the no-hitter with a sterling outfield catch in the fifth. Hank Bauer's RBI single in the sixth added an insurance run. The score was 2-0 when Brooklyn batted in the top of the ninth.

"I knew I had a no-hitter going for me in the seventh inning, but I didn't think too much about it until then," Larsen admitted later. "When the Dodgers came to bat in the ninth inning, I was so weak in the knees, I thought I was going to faint."

The jitters had set in about the seventh inning. Larsen had talked openly about what was going on in the dugout between innings, but Casey and the rest of the team had avoided saying anything. Superstition. Now, jogging onto the field to start the ninth, Yogi Berra tapped Larsen in the seat of the pants and said, "Go out there and let's get the first batter."

That happened to be Carl Furillo, one of baseball's finest clutch hitters. Larsen mumbled a little prayer to himself: "Please help me get through this."

Furillo flied to Bauer in right. *One out.* Roy Campanella hit a slow roller to Billy Martin, who gunned to Joe Collins. *Two outs.* That brought up pinch-hitter Dale Mitchell. The stone-faced, tobacco-chewing pickup from Cleveland stood as the sole obstacle between Larsen and immortality. This was to be the final at-bat of Mitchell's 11-year career, over which he had stroked the ball at a .312 clip and struck out once about every 34 at-bats. He figured to be one tough nut.

Larsen worked the count to two balls, two strikes. "Well," he said to no one in particular, "here goes nothing." Mitchell impassively watched the pitch sail past him. Most observers thought it was high and outside. But soon-to-retire umpire Babe Pinelli, perhaps nervous over the prospect of losing the first World Series perfect game on the last pitch he would ever call, hastily shot his right arm into the cool autumn air to signal strike three. Afterward somebody actually asked Casey if this was the best game Larsen had ever pitched. "So far," he said.

The following day Jackie Robinson's single with two outs in the tenth inning broke up a scoreless duel between Bob Turley and Clem Labine. But the Yanks went on to take the Series, routing the Dodgers in the seventh game 9-0 behind Berra's pair of two-run homers and Johnny Kucks's three-hitter. After a two-year hiatus, the Bronx Bombers were back on top of the world.

Frank "The Yankee Killer" Lary leaves the field after beating New York in the first game of a 1959 doubleheader in Detroit. Lary, who retired owning a 28-13 record against New York, was just one of many American League pitchers to have success against Stengel's team that summer. To the alarm of fans and the front office, the Yankees uncharacteristically finished third, just four games above .500.

Stengel's Yankees, the gods of baseball, had the Big Apple all to themselves after the Dodgers and Giants left for the West Coast following the 1957 season, a year in which Casey captured his eighth pennant in nine years. The media coverage became even more suffocating and the players even more insufferable.

Joe Falls of the *Detroit Times* dreaded the ordeal of entering the Yankees' locker room after a game, particularly when trying to get a quote from the main man, Mantle.

"I'd approach his locker carefully," he remembered, "not because he was Mickey Mantle but because he was surrounded by a lot of those bold, brazen Yankees, who made fun of everyone who came around. Billy Martin. Whitey Ford. Clete Boyer. They thought nothing of making others feel inferior with their biting ways. It was always a big laugh for them to make someone look ridiculous.

"I always felt Mantle was different, that he had a caring they did not know or even understand. But he was their teammate—the number-one player on the team—and he knew they looked up to him, and so he performed for them. He could get sarcastic, too, but it never seemed natural to him."

Mantle loved the nightlife. He was usually accompanied on his nocturnal rounds by Ford and, until he was traded in the middle of the 1957 season after an infamous altercation at the Copacabana nightclub, Billy Martin. Larsen also was an occasional companion. In fact, Mantle later maintained that Larsen was hung over the day he pitched his perfect game. Stengel enjoyed a few triple old-fashioneds himself, so he generally did little to rein in the rounders on the team. His philosophy had always been that as long as a man delivered on the field, what he did and where he went in his off hours was his own business.

"Stengel never said anything about my drinking or anyone else's," maintained Ryne Duren, a dangerously wild reliever and chronic alcoholic who hid his bloodshot eyes behind dark, coke-bottle lenses. "Years later, Casey would tell me that he knew there was a lot of drinking on the Yankees, but he thought it useless to ask players if they had problems. 'They might admit to having a couple of drinks,' he

Members of Chicago's Sacred Heart Grade School's baseball team turned out in force to meet Mickey Mantle at Comiskey Park in 1959. If they truly wanted to "be like Mickey" they would have had to work alcohol abuse and philandering into their routine. The lifestyles of players like Mantle, Whitey Ford, and Ryne Duren helped convince management that the sixty-nine-year-old manager had lost control of the team.

If not for Al Lopez, Casey may have won twelve straight pennants. Only Lopez's '54 Indians and '59 White Sox were able to capture a flag during Stengel's amazing tenure, though his teams were swept in the World Series each time. Although the big prize escaped him, Lopez—who had caught for Casey in Brooklyn and Boston—was a fine manager, accumulating 1,410 wins in seventeen seasons in Cleveland and Chicago and earning a spot in the Hall of Fame.

said, 'but what they wouldn't tell me is that they were as big as pisspots.'"

However, the conservative Yankees' brass grew concerned. The worst incident occurred May 15, 1957, when several players and their wives celebrated Billy Martin's birthday. After dinner at Danny's Hideaway, they decided to catch the ten o'clock show at the Copacabana. Sammy Davis Jr. was performing, which prompted some racial slurs from the drunken members of a bowling league. Several Yankees told the bowlers to watch their language. One word led to another, and soon there was a fight inside the cloakroom. The fallout from the rumble was that Hank Bauer was sued for punching out a fellow and Martin was traded to Kansas City by George Weiss, who had long considered the brash infielder a bad influence on Mantle. It took years for Martin to get over the hurt, especially his anger at Casey for not doing more to prevent the trade.

The apparent lack of discipline affected Casey's status with the image-conscious front office. Weiss even hired snoops to keep tabs on his star players. Once on a road trip to Detroit, a private detective trailed Mantle and Ford. The fellow picked up the scent as the players left the lobby of the Statler Hotel, where the team was staying, and followed at a safe distance as the two players walked into the promising night air on Bagley Street. He saw them duck into an establishment, whereupon he reported his findings to Stengel.

"I followed him, he went into this place, he had a milk shake," the informant said. "The place was an ice cream parlor."

Stengel was incredulous but pleased—until he discovered the detective had mistakenly followed the Yankees' choirboy shortstop, Tony Kubek.

Losing the 1957 World Series to the Milwaukee Braves in seven games also affected ownership's feelings about Casey continuing to manage. Ex-Yankees farmhand Lew Burdette had won three games, two of them by shutout. The Milwaukee media jumped on a remark allegedly made by Casey that the city was "bush" and

Roger Maris accepts a Gold Glove Award from New York broadcaster Mel Allen. The moody right fielder, whose hair would fall out while overtaking Babe Ruth's hallowed single-season home run record in 1961, was one of Casey's steadiest and favorite players. "I never had any trouble with him," Maris said of his manager. "If you played ball hard, kept your mouth shut, and hustled, he never said much to you."

proudly proclaimed the home of the Braves "Bushville." A public relations official was actually the culprit, but it didn't matter. Milwaukee fans, many of whom remembered the pennant Casey had delivered as a minor-league manager during the war, roundly booed him. Casey blew them kisses.

That was more than his players were receiving. Entering the 1958 season, the last year on his latest two-year contract, Casey was being scrutinized by players and owners. He would turn sixty-eight during the summer, and there was considerable speculation that he might soon be "retired." Players were grumbling that he was increasingly caustic and impatient. On occasion, he fell asleep on the bench, whereupon some of the more mean-spirited members of the team would wake him by loudly banging a bat on the dugout steps. There also was a headline-grabbing incident when, during a train ride after the Yankees clinched the pennant, first-base coach Ralph Houk smacked Ryne Duren in the face, opening a cut above the drunken pitcher's eye. Dan Topping was all for letting Stengel go after the season. But Weiss and Del Webb thought it more practical to continue to groom Houk, who had earned glowing reviews as a minor-league manager in Denver, as Casey's eventual successor.

In early August the Yankees, sparked by Cy Young Award winner Bob Turley, led

Casey and Edna share a toast on Casey's seventieth birthday, July 30, 1960.

the Sorry Seven by an unheard-of 17 games. They faltered, but still finished comfortably on top. It was Casey's ninth pennant, tying the league record held by Joe McCarthy. After that, it was back to Bushville to meet the Braves.

This time Casey really pulled one out of his hat. Down three games to one, the Yankees stormed back to take the Series in seven games. The hero was the stocky Turley, who shut out the Braves 7-0 in game five, saved New York's 10-inning, 4-3 win in game six, then pitched six and two-thirds innings of outstanding relief in the finale to get credit for the 6-2 victory that produced Casey's seventh—and last—championship.

Casey and the man who would replace him as manager, Ralph Houk. The former third-string catcher would win pennants his first three years as well as back-to-back championships in 1961 and 1962.

The win also created a terrific quandary for the front office. There was no way a manager as popular as Stengel could be let go after he had just won the World Series. Still, the opinion was that he would have to step down soon. The compromise was to offer another two-year contract—$85,000 for 1959, $90,000 for 1960—after which Stengel could be graciously retired. Nobody spelled this out to Casey, but he was wise to the inner machinations of big-league baseball. He had to know that his number would be up soon.

The number that most concerned him at the start of 1959 was ten. That was how many pennants John McGraw and Joe McCarthy had each won in their managerial careers. Casey badly wanted to be ranked either ahead or even with them.

The year 1959 was a wash, though. Injuries and old age caught up with the team. To the shock of the baseball world, the Yankees actually fell into the basement in May. The White Sox, now managed by Al Lopez, took the flag. New York finished third at 79-75, a mere four games over .500. It was the worst record for a Yankees squad since 1925 and had many howling for Casey's scalp.

After the season Weiss swung yet another in a long series of trades with the Kansas City Athletics, a perennial also-ran that was often called New York's farm club. It was a justifiable charge. Kansas City owner Arnold Johnson and Dan Topping were close friends and business associates while Athletics general manager Parke Carroll had once worked for his counterpart in New York, Weiss. From 1955 to 1960, the two teams made seventeen separate deals, with the Yankees getting such quality players as pitchers Ralph Terry, Bobby Shantz, Art Ditmar, and Ryne Duren,

The unexpected slugging star of Casey's last World Series was Bobby Richardson. The Yankees' slender second baseman, who spent his entire twelve-year career in pinstripes, had driven in just twenty-six runs during the 1960 season, but he exploded for a record dozen RBI against Pittsburgh. Curiously, Richardson would go another seventeen World Series games before knocking in his next run.

third baseman Clete Boyer, and outfielders Bob Cerv, Enos Slaughter, Hector Lopez, and Roger Maris, without giving up much in return.

Maris was a quiet, businesslike twenty-five-year-old outfielder whose left-handed, upper-cut swing was made to order for Yankee Stadium's short right-field porch. Stengel was ecstatic with the acquisition, batting him third in the order, ahead of Mantle. Together the "M & M Boys" demolished American League pitching. Mantle led the circuit with 40 home runs while Maris was right behind him with 39. Maris also knocked in a league-high 112 runs and patrolled right field with authority, winning his first of two consecutive Most Valuable Player Awards.

Maris, of course, would become famous for his 61 home runs the following summer (Mantle would chip in with 54 of his own), but Casey was enamored with his all-around ability. "I give him one point for speed," he said. "I do this because he can run fast. I give him another point because he can slide fast. Then I give him a point because he can bunt. I also give him a point because he can field, very good around the fences, even on top of the fences. Next, I give him a point because he can throw. . . . So I add up my points and I've got five for him even before I come to his hitting. I would say this is a good man."

Doctors basically said the same thing of Casey when he submitted to a thorough physical examination in May. He had been having chest pains—brought on, perhaps, by excessive drinking—but after a couple of weeks in a New York hospital, he was proclaimed fit to return to the rigors of another pennant race. "They examined all my organs," he explained. "Some of them are quite remarkable and others are not so good. A lot of museums are bidding for them." On July 30 he turned seventy with the observation that "Most people my age are dead at the present time."

After leaving the hospital, Casey swore off drinking for the remainder of the season, which climaxed with a 15-game winning streak that gave him the birthday gift he most coveted: a record-tying tenth pennant. His opponent in the World Series was Pittsburgh. The Pirates, whose 95 wins were just two fewer than New York's, were nonetheless big underdogs. This despite the presence of a solid pitching staff and proven performers like second baseman Bill Mazeroski, shortstop and batting champion Dick Groat, and right fielder Roberto Clemente (who would go on to capture four silver bats himself).

Twenty-game winner Vernon Law, aided by relief ace Elroy Face, led the Pirates past Art Ditmar in the opener 6-4 but New York's bats soon began to assert themselves. The Yankees, who would set postseason records for runs, hits, extra-base hits, and batting average, humiliated the Pirates by scores of 16-3 and 10-0 in the next two games. However, the Pirates rebounded to win game four 3-2 behind Law and Face. The following afternoon Face picked up his third save of the Series, closing out Harvey Haddix's 5-2 win. The Series shifted to Forbes Field, where the Yankees needed to sweep both games to claim the championship. They got halfway there when Whitey Ford blanked the Bucs 12-0 for his second shutout of the Series.

This made it Bob Turley versus Vernon Law on October 13, 1960, in what evolved into one of the most dramatic seventh games ever. The Bucs chased Turley in the second inning, building a 4-0 lead on Rocky Nelson's two-run homer and Bill Virdon's two-run single. The Yankees crept back on Bill Skowron's solo blast in the fifth, then exploded in the sixth with Mantle's run-scoring single and Berra's three-run homer off Face.

The Yanks added two more runs in the eighth to pad their lead to 7-4. They might have had even more had Stengel not gone against his usual policy of pulling out all the stops to sustain a rally. With runners on second and third and two out, he allowed Bobby Shantz, who had pitched five innings of relief at that point, to bat for himself. Shantz flied to right to end the inning.

In the bottom of the inning, Shantz surrendered a leadoff single to pinch-hitter Gino Cimoli. Then came the turning point of the game and of the Series. Virdon hit a grounder to shortstop. As Tony Kubek moved to field the ball, it caromed wickedly off a pebble and struck him in the throat. This was a particularly bad hop, knocking Kubek out of the game and placing Cimoli on second and Virdon on first.

After Dick Groat slapped a single to score Cimoli, Casey waved in Jim Coates from the bull pen. A bunt moved the runners to second and third with one out. Coates retired Nelson on a shallow fly, the runners holding, but then Clemente nar-

Bill Mazeroski jubilantly concludes his tour of the bases after smacking his famous World Series-winning home run. "We've beaten the Yankees," he recalled thinking as he stepped on home plate. "We've beaten the great Yankees." Mazeroski's blast had also sealed Casey's fate.

rowly beat out an infield chopper to plate Virdon. This brought up catcher Hal Smith, who belted a three-run homer to cap the five-run comeback.

Down 9-7, the Yanks stormed back in the top of the ninth. Bob Friend, in relief of Face, gave up singles to Bobby Richardson and Dale Long before leaving in favor of Harvey Haddix. Roger Maris was retired, but Mantle responded with a single to right to make it 9-8. With runners on first and third, Berra brought in the tying run with a ground ball. Haddix finally stopped the rally by getting Skowron to ground into a force out, Groat to Mazeroski.

"When we trotted off the field for our turn at bat," recalled Mazeroski, "I was thinking, 'I'd like to hit a home run and win it all!' The time before, in the seventh inning, I had gone for the long ball and I overswung. I grounded into a double play. This time, I kept saying to myself, 'Don't overswing. Just meet the ball.'"

The twenty-four-year-old Mazeroski, arguably the finest fielding second baseman ever, could shift the ball from glove to throwing hand so quickly he was known as "No Touch." With just 11 home runs during the season, Casey was banking that the nickname also applied to his bat. Ralph Terry, a former Yankee who'd compiled an undistinguished record with Kansas City before being reacquired by New York midway through the 1959 season, was on the mound.

"I thought I'd be more nervous this time," said Mazeroski, "but I wasn't a bit. I wanted a homer, but I didn't want to overswing. I was guessing all the way. As Terry wound up, I was saying to myself, 'Fastball! Fastball!' That's what I wanted.

"The first one was a high slider. The next one was down a little, but still high—a fastball right into my power."

Mazeroski wrapped his bat around Terry's speedball and sent it sailing toward the ivy-covered brick wall in left. Yogi Berra stood and watched the ball climb over his head and disappear, then jogged off the field. Just like that, the Pirates—outhit .338 to .256 and outscored 55 to 27 by the Yankees—were improbable world champs.

"A moment after I hit that ball," Mazeroski continued, "a shiver ran down my back. We always felt we could pull it out—even after the Yankees tied it up in the ninth—but I didn't think I'd be the guy to do it."

Neither did the Yankees. They couldn't shake the feeling that the better team had lost. Elroy Face, for one, was having none of that kind of talk. As the Steel City went wild, celebrating its first championship in thirty-five years, he appeared in the Yankees' dressing room. Several of the disconsolate players looked up.

"Fuck you guys," said Face.

Five days later, at a press conference held at Le Salon Bleu inside the tony Savoy Hilton Hotel, the Yankees' brass essentially said the same thing to their aged skipper. There had been a good deal of muttering and second-guessing in the wake of the Yankees' disappointing defeat. Why had Stengel held out Whitey Ford until game three, preventing his most reliable pitcher from starting the crucial seventh contest? That was just one of many moves that had been increasingly criticized over the past several years. Some painted Stengel as a senile, bitter, out-of-touch old man. He was said to be heaping the blame on Terry for losing the Series, although Terry always maintained that this wasn't so. "He was great," the traumatized pitcher said. "He sensed I felt guilty as hell and he was enough of a pro not to make it worse."

As the knot of reporters and cameramen waited for Dan Topping to take the lectern, they debated Casey's fate. His record in pinstripes could be looked at in two ways. The long view showed ten pennants in twelve years, including seven world championships. The three World Series he did lose all went to the limit of seven games. The short view, however, revealed only two world titles in the last seven seasons, and even then the Yankees had had to scramble back from two-game deficits to pull them out. It was a classic case of "what have you done for us lately" coupled to Dan Topping's longstanding disenchantment with a garrulous old man whose fame had outstripped that of the team and its owners.

Stengel announces that he's through with the Yankees. Listening intently in the front row is one of Casey's most vociferous detractors, lawyer-turned-sportscaster Howard Cosell.

"Casey Stengel has been, and deservedly so, the highest paid manager in baseball history," Topping began in a thin, nervous voice. "Casey has been—and is—a great manager. He is being well rewarded with $160,000 to do with as he pleases."

"Do you mean he's through—resigned?" a reporter shouted.

"Now wait a minute, for chrissakes, and I'll tell ya," exploded Casey, who had been sitting, dutifully quiet, nursing a glass of bourbon. "Now I wasn't fired," he said, commandeering the microphones. "I was paid up in full."

"The Associated Press has a bulletin, Casey," a writer yelled. "It says you were fired. What about it?"

"What do I care what the AP says," he responded. "Their opinion ain't gonna send me into any fainting spell. Anyway, what about the UP?" Laughter filled the room. With this Casey commenced explaining, and the Yankees' plan for a carefully orchestrated press conference fell to pieces.

"Mr. Webb and Mr. Topping have started a program for the Yankees," he said. "They needed a solution as to when to discharge a man on account of age. My services are no longer required by this club and I told them if this was their idea not to worry about me."

A reporter asked if he had been fired.

"Resigned, fired, quit, discharged, use whatever you damn please," he said. "I don't care. You don't see me crying about it."

"What will you do now?"

"Have another drink, that's what." Then the stooped and floppy-eared septuagenerian led a pack of reporters to the bar, where he ordered another bourbon with soda.

"I'll never make the mistake of being seventy again," he said.

Mets

EIGHT

An Amazin' Exit

Casey Stengel's final season with the Yankees also was the last year the major leagues operated under their traditional 16-team, 154-game format. In 1961 the American League placed expansion teams in Los Angeles and Washington, the latter replacing the Senators, who had moved to Minneapolis to become the Minnesota Twins. The next season the National League followed suit, adding teams in Houston and New York. Both leagues increased their schedules to 162 games. By the end of the decade there would be two more franchise shifts (the Milwaukee Braves to Atlanta, the Kansas City Athletics to Oakland), four new franchises (in San Diego, Montreal, Seattle, and Kansas City), and four six-team divisions with playoffs instead of only two eight-team leagues with a single postseason tournament.

The catalyst for baseball's most ambitious decade was New York Mayor Robert Wagner's rebuffed attempts to secure a National League team to replace the departed Dodgers and Giants. In 1959 the mayor's point man on the project, attorney Bill Shea, joined forces with Branch Rickey, the architect of championship teams in St. Louis and Brooklyn and one of the most forceful front-office men the game had ever seen. The two announced their intention to create a third major league. It would be called the Continental League. Wealthy investors in several cities had been lined up to bankroll franchises.

"There are enough good players around right now to staff a new league," said

Facing page: **The Mets had Casey reaching for the water bottle from the very start.**

Casey and the Mets were feted in a ticker-tape parade that wound up on the steps of city hall. They had yet to play a game.

The enthusiasm surrounding the Mets seemed to have carried over to four of their original players. From left: outfielder Frank Thomas, first baseman Gii Hodges, third baseman Don Zimmer, and pitcher Roger Craig. "Our first Mets game was April 10, 1962," their manager recalled. "And it was our best game. It was rained out."

The 1962 season was filled with episodes like this one against the Phillies: Frank Thomas (25) retreats to third base, only to find Charlie Neal occupying the bag. "They've shown me ways to lose I never knew existed," said Casey.

Shea. "You can't tell me that a nation of 160 million can't produce 200 more big-league ballplayers."

Major-league owners not only respected Rickey's involvement, but were also reluctant to have Congress reexamine the issue of baseball's exemption from antitrust laws. In the spring of 1960, they shocked the sporting world by announcing that they had reached a compromise with Shea and Rickey. The upstart league would be dissolved, having never played a game or signed a player, and in return, the majors would take in four of the Continental League's franchises by 1962. One of those franchises, of course, was in New York. On October 17, 1960, the day before Stengel was cut loose by the Yankees, the National League officially granted a franchise to the Metropolitan Baseball Club of New York. Joan Whitney Payson, a chubby and cheerful blue blood who had grown up rooting for John McGraw's Giants, was an early investor and soon took control of the club.

When Rickey demanded too much money and power to run the new franchise, the Metropolitan Baseball Club turned to George Weiss. The Yankees had dismissed their sixty-six-year-old general manager just two weeks after firing Stengel. The Yankees agreed to pay Weiss $35,000 annually for the next five years on the condition that he did not become the general manager of another big-league club. Weiss got around this clause by being named president of the expansion team. In short order the new ball club acquired a playing site (the decrepit Polo Grounds, after the Yankees refused to share Yankee Stadium), a nickname (the Mets, although Skyliners finished a close second in a newspaper contest), and—most important—a manager.

At first Casey wasn't sure that he wanted to get back into the game. He had already turned down an offer to manage Detroit. Moreover, he was involved with the banking business and was still recuperating from a fall that had seriously injured his back. It took several months of wheedling by Weiss, a personal phone call from Joan Payson, and the offer of a $100,000 contract before Casey allowed himself to be coaxed out of Glendale.

On October 2, 1961, just two days before the Yankees were to meet the Cincinnati Reds in the World Series, the Mets held a press conference to announce that the Ol' Perfesser had returned to New York. The news upstaged the Series, which was Weiss's intent; in fact, he had purposely scheduled the conference inside the same room at the Savoy Hilton where Casey had been fired nearly one year earlier.

He was the same old Casey. "It's a great honor for me to be joining the Knickerbockers," he told the clamorous horde of writers and photographers. *Knickerbockers*? Casey seemed to have confused his new employer with Gotham's

Former Phillies great Richie Ashburn led the Mets with a .306 average in 1962. "I learned more baseball and had more fun playing one year under Casey with the Mets than in any other season in my entire career," claimed Ashburn.

franchise in the National Basketball Association. But some realized Casey had produced the name of Alexander Cartwright's famous nine from the 1840s. Younger members of the media might have supposed that the ancient Casey actually played for Cartwright.

Stengel's hiring was a public relations coup. Not only was he a proven teacher of young players, he was a tireless promoter. Both qualities were invaluable for an expansion club. "I may be able to sell tickets with my face," Casey acknowledged.

Eight days later the Mets and the other expansion team, the Houston Colt 45s (later to be renamed the Astros), held a draft of players placed in a pool by the eight existing National League clubs. New York's first choice was a thirty-one-year-old catcher, Hobie Landrith, a veteran of 12 big-league seasons. Landrith had hit .239 in limited action with San Francisco in 1961, but Casey considered him essential. "You gotta have a catcher," he explained, "or you're going to have a lot of passed balls."

By the end of the session New York had paid a total of $1.8 million for the rights to twenty-two players. For trivia lovers, here are the names of these original Mets, the nucleus of a team destined to become the losingest team in the twentieth century: pitchers Jay Hook, Bob Miller, Craig Anderson, Roger Craig, Ray Daviault, Al Jackson, and Sherman Jones; infielders Don Zimmer, Ed Bouchee, Sammy Drake, Gil Hodges, Felix Mantilla, and Elio Chacon; outfielders Lee Walls, Gus Bell, Joe Christopher, Jim Hickman, John DeMerit, and Bobby Gene Smith; and catchers Chris Cannizarro, Clarence Coleman, and Hobie Landrith. (Technically speaking, *the* original Met was former Boston infielder Ted Lepcio, a free agent who signed a contract on October 25, 1961, and was subsequently cut on the last day of spring training.)

Weiss's strategy in fielding a team differed from Houston's, an organization committed to building with younger veterans and farmhands. Weiss felt New York fans wanted recognizable names like Hodges, Bell, and Craig. All were older veterans whose best years, unfortunately, were behind them. Casey's own preference was "the youth of America." However, as had been the case when both men were with the Yankees, Weiss had the final word in matters of player personnel and trades. As the Mets prepared to gather in St.

"You couldn't play on my Amazin' Mets without having held some kind of record, like one fella held the world's international all-time record for a pitcher getting hit on the ankles."

The Mets drew exceptionally well at the Polo Grounds for home dates against San Francisco and Los Angeles, two clubs viewed as turncoats.

Petersburg in early 1962, the former architect of the Yankees' dynasty continued to wheel and deal for established players. Milwaukee slugger Frank Thomas and former two-time batting champion Richie Ashburn would become bright spots. Backstop Joe Ginsberg and outfielder Neil Chrisley, journeymen from the American League, quickly disappeared from the roster. Johnny Antonelli and Billy Loes, a pair of popular pitchers from the glory days of the Giants and Dodgers, simply retired rather than report.

"You can make a living with this here new club," Casey told his troops at the start of camp. "There ain't nobody got a job won and there ain't nobody can't win one if he shows me he wants to play on my ball club. The owners put a lot of money in here and they want to see how fast you can get better." It wasn't nearly fast enough. "Look at that guy," he marveled one day. "He can't hit, he can't run, and he can't throw. Of course, that's why they gave him to us."

The Mets, hoping to attract disgruntled Dodgers and Giants fans, had a familiar look. Their blue and orange uniforms combined the colors of the old Giants and Dodgers and emulated the Yankees' famous pinstripes. They played at the Polo Grounds, empty since the end of the 1957 season, while waiting for a new stadium to be built in Flushing. Big Jim Thompson, the longtime stadium manager of Yankee Stadium, was hired to get the old park in shape. Red Ruffing was brought on as pitching coach, and another ex-Yankee, Gus Mauch, was hired as trainer. Former Brooklyn infielder Cookie Lavagetto coached third base.

Weiss and Casey both wanted to stick it to their crosstown rivals whenever possible. On March 22 the Yankees played the Mets for the first time. It was just an exhibition game, but Casey fielded his first team and used his best pitchers. When the Mets won 4-3 in ten innings, it became front-page news in the New York dailies and prompted noisy parties at watering holes in St. Petersburg and New York. The mood inside Joe DiMaggio's favorite spot, Toots Shor's, was particularly festive. "It's like

Los Angeles sold old Brooklyn favorite Duke Snider to the Mets in 1963, where he received a hero's welcome from old Dodgers fans. "Being sold was humiliating enough," he admitted some time later, "but being sold to the Mets was the ultimate humiliation. They were the worst team in baseball. Without Casey there, I would have gone nuts. He used to call me 'Kid,' which at my age, thirty-seven, was nice of him. I learned Stengelese that summer and listened to him talk about the '49, '52, '53 World Series, but never about the '55 Series when we Dodgers won over the Yanks."

New Year's Eve in this joint," Shor shouted over the phone to Stengel. The Mets racked up a credible 12-15 exhibition record, moving some to predict as high as a seventh-place finish for the newcomers.

The tone of the Mets' season was set when, the day before the opener in St. Louis, sixteen players—including starting pitcher Roger Craig—got stuck in a hotel elevator. They escaped, only to be crushed, 11-4. Gil Hodges hit the Mets' first home run in the game. A more telling event, third baseman Don Zimmer fielded the first ground ball hit his way and heaved it over Hodges' head.

It didn't matter. New York awaited them with a ticker-tape parade down Broadway that climaxed with the mayor giving Casey the key to the city. On a cold, dreary Friday the thirteenth, the Mets played their first home game in front of 12,477 damp fans. Pittsburgh won that day, 4-3, and continued to win, reeling off 10 straight victories to open the campaign. Meanwhile, the Mets dropped their first nine games. As hard as it was for Casey to believe, in just eleven days his team was already nine and a half games out of first. And there were still more than five months left in the schedule.

The Mets finally won on April 23 at Pittsburgh, beating the Pirates, 9-1. In May Stengel's group of cast-offs came to life, beating Milwaukee in a doubleheader to cap an 11-7 spurt that put them in eighth place with a 12-19 record. That turned out to be the high point of the year. Bad weather and flight delays caused the team to stagger into its Houston hotel at eight-thirty the next morning. Even Casey, who had been up for hours talking, talking, talking, found himself drained. "If anybody comes looking for me," he wearily instructed the traveling secretary, "tell 'em I'm being embalmed."

The Mets lost that night, precipitating a 17-game losing streak that permanently planted them in last place. The losing continued for the rest of the summer. "Going to the ballpark," said Frank Thomas, "you wondered how you would lose that day. We'd lose on errors, balks, throws to the wrong base, bad base-running, every conceivable way."

Marvelous Marv Throneberry.

Richie Ashburn, who came over from the Cubs for a reported $100,000, hit .306 in 135 games then retired to enter the broadcast booth, later took time to recall that season of ineptitude.

"When I went down to spring training I knew it was going to be a tough year," he said, "but I didn't think it would be that tough because I was surrounded by a lot of players who were pretty good. Gil Hodges, Gus Bell, Frank Thomas. They could do some damage.

"We didn't have much pitching, obviously. Our defense wasn't very good, but we did not have a bad hitting team, believe it or not. Up until '86, when the Mets won the World Series, the '62 Mets had the team record for most home runs. We did score some runs in the Polo Grounds, but we were always playing behind. The one team we beat pretty well that year was Cincinnati. I don't know why, but we did. That was Fred Hutchinson's team, with Frank Robinson and Vada Pinson.

"I'll tell you, it was a bunch of good guys. Usually on a losing team you have dissension. We didn't have any of that. We were miserable sometimes, but we didn't take it out on anybody, and we didn't blame each other. I give Casey a lot of credit for that. Stengel was a guy who deflected all the criticism you would have with that kind of team."

Stengel was the ringmaster of this circus, appealing to his writers and to the youth of America to support his Amazin' Mets. Both responded in a big way. The indulgent media (notably the influential Dick Young of the *New York Daily News*) considered the team a refreshing alternative to the stuffy Yankees, while the "new breed" of fans (as Young dubbed them) came to the Polo Grounds to cheer, rather than jeer, their lovable losers.

There was a counterculture zaniness to their enthusiasm. They rocked the park with chants of "Let's go, Mets," wildly cheered even mild displays of competence,

The '62 Mets: A New Low

When somebody asked Casey Stengel at the beginning of the Mets' inaugural season where he thought the team would finish, he answered, "We'll finish in Chicago." And they did, losing for the 120th time on the final day of the schedule at Wrigley Field. No big-league team this century has ever lost more games. Needless to say, the Mets placed tenth in a ten-team league, the first of four consecutive last-place finishes. For the record, here's how the disaster known as the '62 Mets unfolded, day by amazing day.

Date	Opponent	Result	Record
April 11	at St. Louis	L, 11-4	0-1
April 13	Pittsburgh	L, 4-3	0-2
April 14	Pittsburgh	L, 6-2	0-3
April 15	Pittsburgh	L, 7-2	0-4
April 17	Houston	L, 5-2 (11)	0-5
April 18	St. Louis	L, 15-5	0-6
April 19	St. Louis	L, 9-4	0-7
April 21	at Pittsburgh	L, 8-4	0-8
April 22	at Pittsburgh	L, 4-3	0-9
April 23	at Pittsburgh	W, 9-1	1-9
April 24	at Cincinnati	L, 7-3	1-10
April 25	at Cincinnati	L, 7-1	1-11
April 27	Philadelphia	L, 11-9	1-12
April 28	Philadelphia	W, 8-6	2-12
April 29	Philadelphia	W, 8-0	3-12
	Philadelphia	L, 10-2	3-13
May 1	Cincinnati	L, 8-2	3-14
May 4	at Philadelphia	L, 6-5	3-15
May 5	at Philadelphia	L, 2-1	3-16
May 6	at Philadelphia	W, 7-5 (12)	4-16
May 8	at Chicago	W, 3-1	5-16
May 11	Milwaukee	L, 8-5	5-17
May 12	Milwaukee	W, 3-2	6-17
	Milwaukee	W, 8-7	7-17
May 13	Milwaukee	L, 3-2	7-18
May 15	Chicago	W, 6-5 (13)	8-18
May 16	Chicago	W, 6-5 (11)	9-18
May 18	at Milwaukee	L, 5-2	9-19
May 19	at Milwaukee	W, 6-5	10-19
May 20	at Milwaukee	W, 7-6	11-19
	at Milwaukee	W, 9-6	12-19
May 21	at Houston	L, 3-2	12-20
May 22	at Houston	L, 3-2	12-21
May 23	at Los Angeles	L, 3-1	12-22
May 24	at Los Angeles	L, 4-2	12-23
May 25	at Los Angeles	L, 17-8	12-24
May 26	at San Francisco	L, 7-6 (10)	12-25
May 27	at San Francisco	L, 7-1	12-26
	at San Francisco	L, 6-5	12-27
May 30	Los Angeles	L, 13-6	12-28
	Los Angeles	L, 6-5	12-29
May 31	Los Angeles	L, 6-3	12-30
June 1	San Francisco	L, 9-6	12-31
June 2	San Francisco	L, 10-1	12-32
	San Francisco	L, 6-4	12-33
June 3	San Francisco	L, 6-1	12-34
June 6	at Philadelphia	L, 2-0	12-35
	at Philadelphia	L, 2-1	12-36
June 8	at Chicago	W, 4-3	13-36
	at Chicago	L, 3-2	13-37
June 9	at Chicago	W, 11-6	14-37
June 10	at Chicago	W, 2-1	15-37
	at Chicago	L, 5-4 (10)	15-38
June 11	at Houston	W, 3-1	16-38
June 12	at Houston	L, 3-2	16-39
June 14	at Houston	L, 10-2	16-40
June 15	Chicago	L, 5-1	16-41
June 16	Chicago	L, 6-3	16-42
June 17	Chicago	L, 8-7	16-43
	Chicago	L, 4-3	16-44
June 18	Milwaukee	L, 7-1	16-45
June 19	Milwaukee	W, 6-5	17-45
June 20	Milwaukee	L, 9-4	17-46
	Milwaukee	L, 3-2	17-47
June 22	Houston	W, 2-0	18-47
	Houston	L, 16-3	18-48
June 23	Houston	W, 13-2	19-48
June 25	at Pittsburgh	L, 13-3	19-49
June 26	at Pittsburgh	L, 5-2	19-50
June 27	at Pittsburgh	L, 6-5 (10)	19-51
June 28	at Los Angeles	L, 5-4 (13)	19-52
June 29	at Los Angeles	W, 10-4	20-52

June 30	at Los Angeles	L, 5-0	20-53
July 1	at Los Angeles	L, 5-1	20-54
July 2	at San Francisco	W, 8-5	21-54
July 3	at San Francisco	L, 10-1	21-55
July 4	at San Francisco	L, 11-4	21-56
	at San Francisco	L, 10-3	21-57
July 6	St. Louis	W, 10-3	22-57
July 7	St. Louis	W, 5-4	23-57
	St. Louis	L, 3-2	23-58
July 8	St. Louis	L, 15-1	23-59
July 12	Los Angeles	L, 3-0	23-60
July 13	Los Angeles	L, 5-4	23-61
July 14	Los Angeles	L, 17-3	23-62
July 15	San Francisco	W, 5-3	24-62
	San Francisco	L, 9-8	24-63
July 16	San Francisco	L, 3-2	24-64
July 19	Pittsburgh	L, 5-1	24-65
	Pittsburgh	L, 7-6 (10)	24-66
July 20	at Cincinnati	L, 3-1	24-67
July 21	at Cincinnati	L, 5-3	24-68
July 22	at Cincinnati	L, 11-4	24-69
	at Cincinnati	L, 4-3	24-70
July 24	at Milwaukee	L, 5-4 (12)	24-71
July 25	at Milwaukee	L, 11-5	24-72
July 26	at Milwaukee	L, 6-1	24-73
July 27	at St. Louis	W, 1-0	25-73
	at St. Louis	L, 6-5	25-74
July 28	at St. Louis	W, 9-8	26-74
July 29	at St. Louis	L, 6-5	26-75
	at St. Louis	L, 5-1	26-76
August 1	Philadelphia	L, 11-9	26-77
August 2	Philadelphia	L, 9-4	26-78
August 3	Cincinnati	L, 8-6	26-79
August 4	Cincinnati	W, 9-1	27-79
	Cincinnati	W, 3-2 (14)	28-79
August 5	Cincinnati	W, 5-2	29-79
	Cincinnati	L, 6-3	29-80
August 6	at Los Angeles	L, 2-1	29-81
August 7	at Los Angeles	L, 7-5	29-82
August 8	at San Francisco	W, 5-2	30-82
August 9	at San Francisco	L, 7-1	30-83
August 10	at Cincinnati	L, 8-4	30-84
August 11	at Cincinnati	L, 2-1	30-85
August 12	at Cincinnati	L, 8-4	30-86
August 14	Philadelphia	L, 3-1	30-87
August 15	Philadelphia	L, 9-3	30-88
	Philadelphia	L, 8-7 (13)	30-89
August 18	St. Louis	L, 7-4	30-90
	St. Louis	L, 10-0	30-91
August 19	St. Louis	L, 10-5	30-92
August 20	Pittsburgh	L, 2-0	30-93
	Pittsburgh	L, 6-3	30-94
August 21	Pittsburgh	L, 8-6	30-95
	Pittsburgh	W, 5-4	31-95
August 22	San Francisco	W, 5-4	32-95
August 23	San Francisco	L, 2-1 (10)	32-96
August 24	Los Angeles	W, 6-3	33-96
August 25	Los Angeles	L, 8-2	33-97
August 26	Los Angeles	L, 16-5	33-98
August 28	at Philadelphia	W, 2-0	34-98
	at Philadelphia	L, 10-1	34-99
August 29	at Philadelphia	L, 3-2 (10)	34-100
August 30	at Philadelphia	L, 8-7	34-101
August 31	at St. Louis	L, 4-2	34-102
Sept. 1	at St. Louis	L, 10-5	34-103
Sept. 2	at St. Louis	W, 4-3	35-103
Sept. 3	at Pittsburgh	L, 2-0	35-104
	at Pittsburgh	L, 5-4	35-105
Sept. 4	at Pittsburgh	L, 5-1	35-106
Sept. 7	at Houston	L, 4-2	35-107
Sept. 8	at Houston	L, 4-3	35-108
	at Houston	L, 6-5 (10)	35-109
Sept. 9	at Houston	T, 7-7	35-109
Sept. 10	Milwaukee	L, 5-2	35-110
Sept. 14	Cincinnati	W, 10-9	36-110
Sept. 15	Cincinnati	L, 9-6	36-111
Sept. 16	Cincinnati	W, 8-2	37-111
Sept. 18	Houston	L, 6-2	37-112
	Houston	L, 8-6	37-113
Sept. 20	Houston	L, 7-2	37-114
	Houston	L, 5-4 (12)	37-115
Sept. 21	Chicago	W, 4-1	38-115
Sept. 22	Chicago	L, 9-2	38-116
Sept. 23	Chicago	W, 2-1	39-116
Sept. 25	at Milwaukee	L, 7-3	39-117
Sept. 26	at Milwaukee	L, 6-3	39-118
Sept. 28	at Chicago	L, 3-2	39-119
Sept. 29	at Chicago	W, 2-1	40-119
Sept. 30	at Chicago	L, 5-1	40-120

Casey became a major cult figure at the Polo Grounds, with the new breed of fans clamoring for autographs and turning bedsheets into signs of affection.

and hung out their adoration for all the world to see on bed sheet banners. "I've been a Mets fan all my life," said one. "To err is human, to forgive is a Mets fan" and "The Mets ain't first / 'Tis sad but true / But dear old Mets / We love you," said other signs. Initially, anybody unfurling a banner was escorted out of the park, but the press raised such a stink about the policy that George Weiss caved in and let the fans have their fun. By the following year the club was holding a special Banner Day, allowing fans to parade around the field before the game with their homemade signs.

Casey remained eminently quotable, even as the losses mounted. He observed that "the only thing worse than a Mets game is a Mets doubleheader." One day he climbed into a cab with some writers, headed for the park. "Are you fellows players?" the cabbie asked. "No," responded Casey. "Neither are my players players." Another time a smart aleck interrupted a press conference to ask about Don Zimmer, who was in the midst of an 0-for-34 slump. "That Zimmer's the guts of your club, isn't he?"

"Why, he's beyond that," responded Casey. "He's much more. He's the perdotious quotient of the qualificatilus. He's the lower intestine."

This was an apt analogy, for the Mets were indeed the lower intestine of the National League. That summer they had losing streaks of 17, 13, 11, and 9 games. On twenty-three occasions the opposing team scored 10 or more runs; five times an opponent scored 15 or more runs. Roger Craig lost 24 games, Al Jackson 20, and Jay Hook 19. Craig Anderson won both games of a twin bill against Milwaukee, then dropped 16 straight. Despite Frank

"I love signing autographs. I'll sign anything but veal cutlets. My ballpoint pen slips on veal cutlets."

Ralph Kiner always remembered the first time he had Casey on his postgame show for an interview. "I knew that Casey talked and talked," said Kiner, "and I wondered about getting him off the show. But he quit right at the moment he was supposed to. Then he got up and walked away and tore the whole set down. He was still hooked up to the lavaliere."

Thomas's 34 home runs, the Mets were shut out 10 times (including a no-hitter by the Dodgers' Sandy Koufax June 30) and scored a single run in 32 other games. Only Houston (which finished eighth) scored fewer runs. Casey watched helplessly as his team allowed the most runs, banged out the fewest hits, and committed the most errors of any club in the majors. The Amazin' Mets wound up with a 40-120 record, which placed them 60½ games behind first-place San Francisco and 18 games behind ninth-place Chicago. "I've been in this game a hundred years," he admitted, "but I see new ways to lose I never knew existed before."

The player who best personified the team's ineptitude was Marvin Eugene Throneberry, a twenty-nine-year-old product of Collierville, Tennessee, whose initials were MET. The chunky first baseman with a bald, freckled head and jawful of chewing tobacco had played parts of three seasons with the Yankees, where he had acquired the nickname "Marvelous Marv." To those who questioned his ability, he could always retort that he had played for Casey's 1958 champions (he had struck out in his only World Series appearance). The Yankees had shipped him to Kansas City, which in turn sent him to Baltimore. On May 9, 1962, the Orioles sold him to the Mets for an estimated $40,000.

Mets fans got their money's worth in entertainment. Every ball, whether airborne or on the ground, was an adventure to Throneberry, who also displayed a discouraging propensity for killing rallies with strikeouts and bad baserunning. In a game against Chicago, the notoriously immobile Throneberry stood in the baseline, got in the way of the runner, and was called for interference. That helped the Cubs to a four-run inning. In the bottom of the frame, Throneberry looked to redeem himself with a blast to right field. Two runs scored as he chugged into third with a triple. Before he could catch his breath, however, the umpire called him out for failing to touch first base. Casey came out to argue the call, but he was intercepted by coach Cookie Lavagetto. "Don't argue too much, Case," he said. "I think he missed second base, too."

Whether it was dropping a pop-up or grounding into a rally-killing double play, Marvelous Marv was a lightning rod for disaster. Fans ate it up. "Cranberry, Strawberry, we love Throneberry," they chanted. Throneberry led all first basemen in errors with 17, despite playing only 97 games at the position. On September 2 the Mets celebrated his birthday with a rare victory in St. Louis. In the clubhouse Casey reportedly told him, "We was gonna get ya a cake, but we figured you'd drop it."

The following season Stengel placed Throneberry in the outfield, where his fielding reached slapstick proportions. He recalled a ball hit directly at him in his first game there. "I saw that ball coming and I said to myself, 'Oh God, what do I do now?'" He slipped and wound up sliding several feet through the wet grass on the

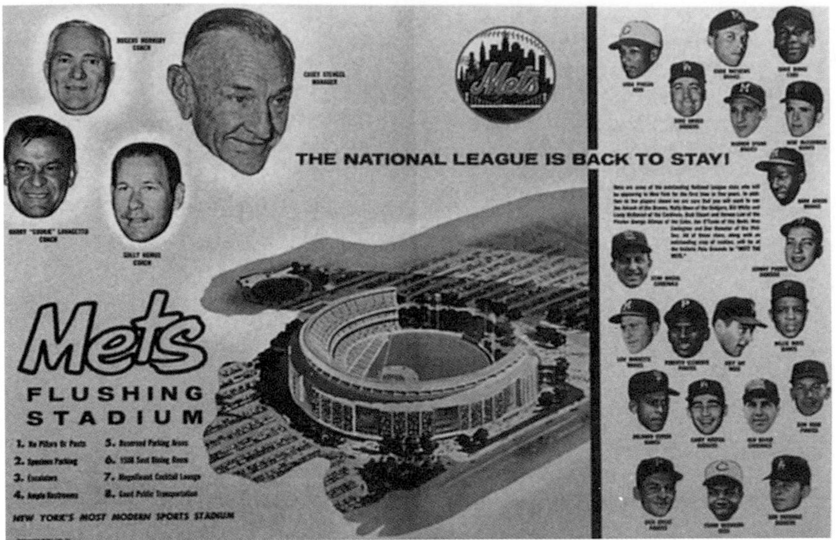

The Mets moved into their new home, 55,300-seat Shea Stadium in Flushing, in 1964. "Lovely, just lovely," said Casey. "The place is lovelier than my team."

seat of his pants. The center fielder, rushing over to help, stood there and laughed. Casey wasn't amused. Not much later, Marvelous Marv was cut by the Mets—gone, but far from forgotten.

The Mets opened the 1963 season by getting shut out by the Cardinals, 7-0. It promised to be another long summer at the Polo Grounds. Stengel not only didn't have the horses, the players he was putting out there were candidates for the glue factory. "We're still frauds," he said. "We're cheating the public." The Mets lost their first eight games en route to a final total of 111. They batted a woeful .219, scored an average of three runs a game, and were shut out 30 times. Their fielding remained consistently atrocious. For the second year in a row, they committed 210 errors (the most since the 1948 Phillies). They also tied their all-time record for lowest team fielding percentage (.967). The pitching was marginally better, with Al Jackson accounting for 13 of the team's 51 victories. Roger Craig dropped 22 games, including 18 straight, becoming the first pitcher to lead his league in losses two years in a row.

Rather than dim enthusiasm, the Mets' day-in, day-out sad-sack performance boosted attendance to nearly 1.1 million, just a tad less than the almighty Yankees. The Mets were a commercial, if not competitive, success. Toy manufacturers released dolls outfitted in Mets uniforms, publishers cranked out books detailing the travails of the team, and record companies came out with musical tributes. When President John F. Kennedy visited West Berlin that year, he was greeted by a sign that said, "Let's Go Mets." An off-Broadway revue, *Put It in Writing*, included this production number devoted to America's favorite losers:

That was quite an exhibition you gave the crowd today
Three triples and a home run and a snappy double play
You played it like a champion, there isn't any doubt
Well, from now on, Buster—CUT IT OUT!

On this here club we're happiest when other teams outscore us
Frankly kid, the more we lose, the more the fans adore us

When you run for a ball, run right into the stands
    Don't forget, you're a Met
When a grounder arrives, let it slip through your hands
    Don't forget, you're a Met
When the ump says, "You're out!" never put up a fight
Just turn and say politely, "Why, you're perfectly right!"
Playing Little League ball is what your contract demands
Don't forget, you're a Met!

Casey listens to the matron of the Amazin' Mets, Joan Payson.

Not everybody was enamored of the Mets' image as a laughingstock or with their manager. Jackie Robinson, broadcaster Howard Cosell, and some disgruntled players like Ed Bouchee openly criticized Stengel. He was accused of being senile and of frequently falling asleep on the bench. "Casey Stengel shouldn't have been managing that team," Bouchee said. A veteran first baseman of six National League seasons when he was acquired by the Mets, Bouchee told Danny Peary in *We Played the Game*:

> He was worthless. Worthless! A manager who falls asleep on the bench every day—and this is no exaggeration—should not be managing in the majors....He was there for no other reason than to attract fans. How could he play Gil Hodges, a one-legged first baseman who you had to shoot up with Novocaine, just because he had a name in the New York area and would draw people? How can you play a cripple? I was the guy that should have been playing first base. Gil knew. I told him, "You shouldn't be playing, Gil. Shit! You can hardly walk." And he agreed. At the beginning of the season I pinch-hit five times. I hit two home runs and a single. I drove in seven runs. I started the next game against Pittsburgh and went 2 for 4, with a home run. I went 1 for 4 in the next game against Pittsburgh. I never played again! So don't give me no bullshit about Stengel being a good manager. It's all politics.

In 1964 Casey moaned that the team would finish "thirtieth," a number he arrived at by adding the Mets' two previous tenth-place finishes. The prospects for a healthier gate, however, were excellent, as the Mets moved into their new home, Shea Stadium. The park, christened April 17, 1964, with a 5-4 defeat to the Pirates, had been built adjacent to the New York World's Fair, which also opened that spring. Freeways, special trains, and subway lines fed the area surrounding the park. The fans at Shea were less demonstrative than the ones who had brought their bed sheets to the Polo Grounds, but management didn't care if they never made a peep. Silence could only make the hum of the turnstiles spinning that much sweeter.

That summer the last-place Mets outdrew the two-time defending world champion Yankees, 1.7 million to 1.3 million. Ralph Houk won a third straight pennant, but Casey's part in the Mets' commercial success convinced the suddenly worried Yankees that it would help attendance if they too had a manager built along the lines of Stengel. Consequently, Houk was replaced by that other great baseball philosopher, Yogi Berra.

The Mets' 53-109 record in 1964 had Casey musing on innovative ways to move up the standings. "This here team won't go anywhere unless we spread enough of

Stengel patiently sits as makeup is dabbed on his wrinkled mug prior to the cameras rolling.

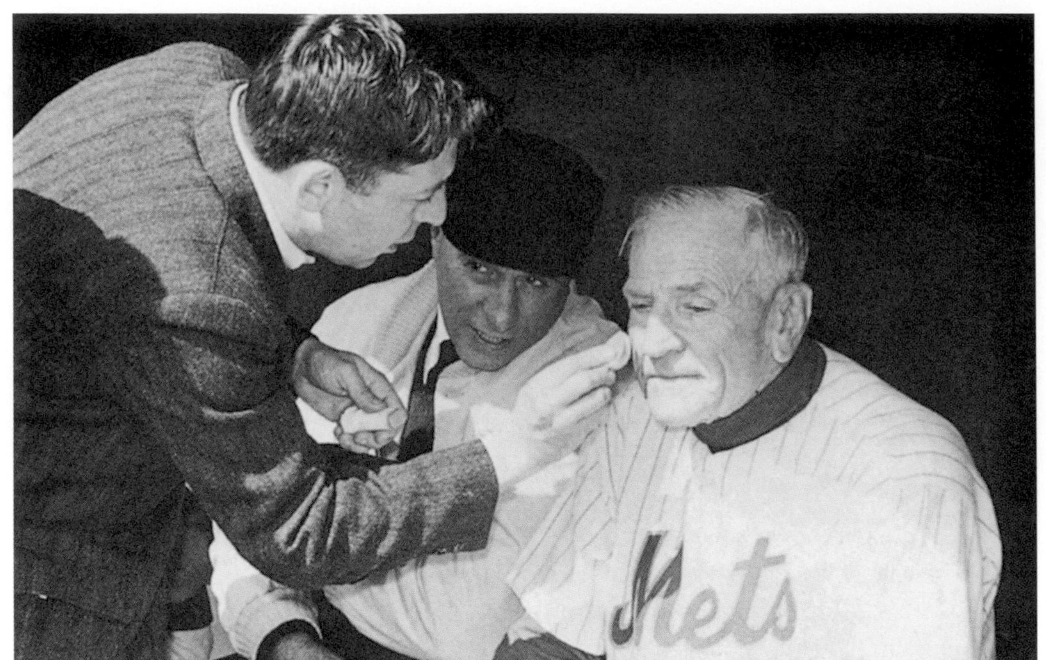

The Ol' Perfesser contemplates another last-place finish. "Players used to sit in the lobbies and talk about baseball," he mused. "Now they sit in their rooms, watch movies, and forget about baseball. A lot of them forget about it on the field, too."

Yogi Berra joined the Mets as a coach in spring 1965, after he was fired as Yankees manager following a seventh-game loss to the Cardinals in the 1964 World Series. He even tried catching again, but gave it up after just one nine-inning game behind the plate.

our players around the league and make the other teams horseshit, too."

If only he could remember their names. Tim Harkness was "Harshman." Charlie Smith was "Charlie Davis." Chris Cannizzaro was alternately called "Canzonarri," "Canzonarria," or "my catcher."

Another of Casey's catchers was Joe Pignatano, who the Mets bought from San Francisco. Pignatano reported to the park early, was outfitted in a Mets uniform, then joined Stengel on the bench. There was nobody else around, so the two talked for more than an hour. Soon a reporter stopped by, recognized Pignatano, and chatted with him for a while before asking Casey who his starting catcher was going to be for that evening's game.

"I'll catch that new kid from the Giants if he ever gets here," he said.

To add to the fun, Casey had two relief pitchers named Bob Miller. One day he called the bull pen and told Pignatano to get Nelson warmed up. "I didn't know what he was talking about," said Pignatano. "We didn't have anybody named Nelson. I told him that but he repeated he wanted 'Nelson' to warm up. So I just took a baseball and put it on the rubber and said to the guys in the bull pen, 'He wants Nelson.' Bob Miller got up immediately and grabbed the ball. 'He always calls me Nelson,' Miller said."

Casey, who turned seventy-four during the 1964 season, maintained a remarkable reservoir of energy. Maury Allen remembered accompanying him to the lounge of the Chase Hotel, where the Mets stayed when they were in town. Singer Robert Goulet interrupted his act to pay homage. Introduced as "one of the world's great heroes," the slightly embarrassed manager admitted, "He has effeminate appeal, just like me."

Casey wound up drinking with several sportswriters until five in the morning. "I'll be down for breakfast at seven," he told Allen at the elevator. "C'mon down and I'll give you a story." Two hours later Casey was seated for breakfast. His thirty-two-year-old companion didn't get up until late afternoon.

The end of the line came on August 30, 1965, when a fractured hip forced Casey to finally call it quits after some six decades in the game. Edna was there to console him.

In 1965 Casey started his fourth year at the helm. By now only four of the original Mets—Jim Hickman, Al Jackson, Joe Christopher, and Chris Cannizarro—were left. The team improved to a degree, having added promising young players like pitcher Frank "Tug" McGraw and outfielders Cleon Jones and Ron Swoboda ("Saboda"). "And we have this fine young catcher named Goossen," bragged Casey, "who is only twenty years old, who in ten years has a chance . . ." At this point Casey paused. He couldn't fathom what Greg Goossen had a chance to be. "In ten years," he continued, "he has a chance to be thirty."

The Mets continued to be a great attraction. Attendance would reach almost 1.8 million in 1965 and nearly 2 million the following season. The Yankees, by contrast, would continue to drop at the gate and in the standings. Sixth place was in store for them in 1965—their lowest placement in forty years—with only 1.2 million bothering to come out to the park. In 1966, the year the Mets finally escaped the National League cellar, the once dreaded Bronx Bombers would finish dead last.

As the Mets slowly moved up in the world, losing became less of a laughing matter to fans and management. There were subtle hints from the front office that Casey should retire, but he ignored them. After two-thirds of a century of playing ball, Casey still felt most comfortable and most useful reporting to a ballpark somewhere in the United States every day. Houston, New York, San Francisco, Cincinnati—it didn't matter where. It was the environment he enjoyed most and understood best. Even a broken wrist, suffered when he slipped on wet steps during a Mets' exhibition visit to West Point in May 1965, didn't dampen his enthusiasm for teaching.

"He would talk about game situations from forty years ago, and I was twenty at the time," said Ron Swoboda. "On a couple of occasions he caught my eye when he was going into those verbal meanders. He would talk in parables. Next thing you know he was talking about a player who was involved in a situation that applied to a situation he had been talking to you about. You realized the story was for you."

On Saturday, July 24, 1965, the Mets lost to the Phillies at Shea Stadium, 5-1. It was the last game Casey would ever manage. That evening he was drinking and spinning yarns at Toots Shor's, feeling good about the seventy-fifth birthday festivities that were to be held between games of the following day's doubleheader. There are different explanations of how Casey broke his left hip, but the most plausible is that he was drunk and simply fell. A friend took him home, but by the next morning Casey was in so much pain that he had to be taken to Roosevelt Hospital in Manhattan. The next day an artificial hip joint was installed. Any doubts that he would leave the Amazin' Mets were dispelled on August 30 when a press conference was held at the Essex House to announce his retirement. He had once said, "Nuts to being old. I'll try to manage as long as I don't have to go take a pitcher out in a wheelchair." But using a cane was just as bad, he later confessed. "I couldn't strut out to the mound to take out a pitcher. It was time to step down." Coach Wes Westrum, the interim manager in Casey's absence, was officially named his successor.

Casey would live another ten years after leaving baseball, making the transition from the Ol' Perfesser to Perfesser Emeritus with tangled syntax and good humor intact. In a nice gesture the Baseball Writers Association of America successfully petitioned the Baseball Hall of Fame to waive its customary five-year waiting period for election. The ensuing vote was unanimous.

Casey was inducted on July 25, 1966, along with one of his favorites, Ted Williams. It was a splendid Monday morning in rustic Cooperstown, New York, with some ten thousand people in attendance when he was introduced by the new commissioner of baseball, William Eckert, as "one of the greatest managers of all time and a great judge of men."

"Mr. Eckert and those distinguished notables that are sitting on the rostrum," Casey began. "I want to thank everybody. I want to thank some of the owners who were amazing to me, and those big presidents of the leagues who were kind to me when I was so obnoxious. I want to thank everybody for my first managerial experience at Worcester, which was last in the Eastern League, and where I met that fine fellow George Weiss, who ran the New Haven club and who would find out whenever I was discharged and would re-employ me. I want to thank my parents for letting me play baseball, and I'm thankful I had baseball knuckles and couldn't become a dentist.

"I got $2,100 a year when I started in the big league and lived at Broadway and

By March 1966 the Ol' Perfesser had slipped into his role as Perfesser Emeritus, offering advice to young Mets at spring training.

Ted Williams was the other inductee on the day Casey entered the Hall of Fame. Commissioner William D. Eckert is holding Casey's plaque. For the rest of his life he would proudly sign all of his correspondence, "Casey Stengel, Hall of Famer."

47th Street. And they get more money now. I chased the balls that Babe Ruth hit. We couldn't play on Sundays, that was the preacher's day to collect. But in Baltimore we played at a racetrack even, and Ruth hit one over my head and Robby said, 'You'd think you'd play back on a guy who swings like that.' So I replied, 'Who's Babe Ruth? He's a kid who just came out of that school.' But I backed up fifty feet more and called over to Hy Myers, 'Far enough?' And he said okay. And Ruth hit it way over my head just the same. And Grover Cleveland Alexander pitched in a bandbox in those days and still won thirty games. . . ."

And off he went, his raspy voice on a twenty-minute free flight that ended, "And I want to thank the tree-mendous fans. We appreciate every boys group, girls group, poem and song. And keep going to see the Mets play."

Approaching his eighties, Casey remained clear-eyed and active, faithfully following his morning regimen of pushups and other exercises. He was convivial as ever, regaling guests and strangers, a drink in one hand and a cigarette in the other, telling for the umpteenth time the story of his "rooster," Billy Martin, grabbing "Mr. Rob-a-son's" pop up in the deciding game of the 1952 World Series. "And you could

Facing page: **Casey gives his induction speech at Cooperstown: "I chased the balls that Babe Ruth hit."**

Stengel in the sitting room of his California home, a space given over to a lifetime of mementos and memories. "When I played in Brooklyn," he reminisced, "I could go to the ballpark for a nickel carfare. But now I live in Pasadena, and it costs me fifteen or sixteen dollars to take a cab to Glendale. If I was a young man, I'd study to become a cabdriver."

look it up," he would invariably say before launching into yet another story. He continued to be as demonstrative as his body would allow him to be, though his bad hip meant he could no longer end the story of his inside-the-park home run in the 1923 World Series with a flourish by sliding across the carpet. His drinking occasionally got out of hand. At four o'clock in the morning of New Year's Day, 1969, he drove his 1960 black Cadillac into a tree in Glendale and was arrested for drunk driving. The judge slapped the seventy-eight-year-old offender with a hefty $302 fine.

Anybody who wanted a comment from Casey on this or any other subject didn't have to search hard, for his phone number remained listed in the Glendale directory, as it had always been. "Call me," he'd say, "and I'll give ya all the answers." In addition to providing a quote or twenty when called upon, he was a regular sight at exhibition, World Series, All-Star games, reunions, banquets, and other public functions. One year when he was in his eighties, he went along with an Old-Timers' Day stunt that had him riding a chariot onto the field at Shea Stadium. With a bullwhip in hand, he and a driver zipped past grandstands filled with gaping fans, some of whom held up signs saying, "All Hail Casey!"

"Old-timers' weekends and airplane landings are alike," he once observed. "If you can walk away from them, they're successful."

The honors piled up. The Mets, who made him a vice president in charge of scouting on the West Coast, quickly retired his uniform number, followed by the Yankees. In 1969, as part of baseball's centennial celebration, he was named Greatest Living Manager. He followed the Mets avidly, promoted them relentlessly, and was just as astounded as everybody else when the truly amazing 1969 edition of the team not only rose from ninth place to capture a divisional title and then the pennant, but went on to whip the heavily favored Baltimore Orioles in five games in the World Series. Art Rust Jr., then a reporter for NBC, found Casey inside the jubilant Mets clubhouse. "How did they do it?" Rust asked.

"They were drinking vodka, vodka," said Casey.

"For those unfamiliar with Stengelese," Rust later explained, "that means, 'They were flying.' It had nothing to do with intoxication."

The years passed, and so did more and more of Casey's friends and loved ones. In 1974 he made his annual pilgrimage to spring training, alone and lonely. Edna was back in Glendale, having been struck down the previous fall by a stroke. At the Mets' camp a friend approached and inquired about his wife's health.

Casey made a hand gesture toward his neck. "She's no good from here up," he said. "She went crazy on me overnight." Then he turned away, his eyes moist.

"I don't like comin' here without Edna," he said weakly. "I miss her and why wouldn't ya after your whole life."

Edna, incapacitated mentally and physically, was being looked after in the Glen Oaks Convalescent Home, a short distance from their Glendale home. Casey, who by now had had his driver's license revoked, would walk the twenty or so blocks every day to spend time with her. "When I'm gone," he told his live-in assistant, June Bowlin, "don't forget to hold her hand." Edna died February 3, 1978, outliving her husband by two and a half years.

June Bowlin was a middle-aged divorcee with three children who had once been a companion for another old player, Jesse "Pop" Haines, back in Ohio. She moved in with Casey at the Lawson family's suggestion. Without the meticulous Edna around to keep the household running smoothly, Casey had lost a lot of his zest for life and just let the place go to hell. He couldn't cook, so he was eating out of cans. He didn't know how to wash or iron, so he slept in the same unkempt bed for months. Fan mail and utility bills piled up unanswered. He had been showing signs of senility for several years, but in this, the last year of his life, he was very erratic. He stayed in his room, listening to the radio and arguing with disembodied voices: "You're full of shit and I'll tell you why." He stuffed wads of bills—a thousand dollars here, five thousand there—into cubbyholes around the house including suit pockets, bureau drawers, closets, suitcases, even the fireplace. When everything was added up, the cache came to about $35,000 in cash—a relative pittance. His and Edna's estate was worth in excess of $4 million, which ultimately was divided up among their nephews and nieces.

By the middle of 1975, Casey, a practical man, realized that he was dying. He had been diagnosed with cancer of the lymph nodes. On September 15 he was driven to Glendale Memorial Hospital, crying and resisting the attempts of Bowlin and

The Dodgers helped Casey celebrate his seventy-seventh birthday with a giant cake in 1967.

By the early 1970s Billy Martin had become a successful manager in Minnesota, Detroit, and Texas, where he utilized much of what he had learned under Casey's tutelage. Martin took over the Yankees halfway through the 1975 season at the time Stengel was dying in his Glendale home. The following year Martin wore a black patch to commemorate Casey, filled his office with Stengel photos, then guided the Yankees to their first pennant in a dozen years. In 1977 he managed the Bombers to a World Series championship.

Casey lived long enough to witness something that for so many years seemed unthinkable: someone breaking Babe Ruth's all-time home run record. And by a black man yet! But he gave Hank Aaron his due. "Now this man in Atlanta is amazing," he said. "He hits the ball the best for a man of his size. But I can't say he hits the ball better than Ruth. Ruth could hit the ball so far nobody could field it. . . ."

"They've All Got Automobiles"

On October 9, 1970, the day before the World Series between the Reds and Orioles opened in Cincinnati, the Ol' Perfesser's rumination on modern youth appeared on the op-ed page of *The New York Times*:

> Let me ask you why we can't communicate with those young people and I'll tell you because there's too much fast transportation today if they want to go away from home. The only place you can get anybody to go in is an automobile.
>
> You used to be known in your neighborhood and you had a reputation, and you had the five-cent fare too. Now they want to go someplace where they can get into trouble and they've even got automobiles to get there. So they can go forty miles and disturb people in some other city if they don't want to be seen in their own town. They can even go 300 or 1,000 miles away, and sleep on the ground besides.
>
> The reason is fast transportation, and they've all got automobiles, and there's the airplane, too. There're more places to go to and you can't keep them in anymore, and how can you communicate with them 300 miles away?...
>
> But I don't mind the hair, they can wear it any way they want to as long as they don't use fast transportation to get out of their own towns. That's the thing that disappoints me when you ask if I can communicate with them. Not the hair. I wouldn't mind how long they wore it if I could find them and talk to them, and besides they didn't have wigs in those days.

Casey died September 29, 1975, and services were held at the Church of the Recessional at Forest Lawn Cemetery in Glendale.

her son to help him out of the car. "You don't have to hold me up," he snapped. "What am I, a goddamn cripple?" Then he started sobbing again. "I wish Mrs. Stengel and I had a dozen kids," he said, "and we'd put them all on the pension plan."

The cancer was inoperable. At 10:58 on the night of September 29, as Bowlin sat at his side reciting a rosary, Casey gave out a low gasp, blinked his eyes, tried to form some words on his lips, and then was gone. "Well," wrote columnist Jim Murray in the *Los Angeles Times*, "God is certainly getting an earful tonight."

Truth be told, there's not much evidence that Stengel, an existentialist at heart, believed in an afterlife. Nonetheless, a Methodist minister performed services at the Church of the Recessional at Forest Lawn Cemetery, after which Casey was laid to rest in the shade of a wall of Vermont marble. In time Edna would join him in the single grave. There is a large plaque on the wall, containing a likeness of Casey and several bits of information about the man—the dates of his birth, death, wedding, and induction at Cooperstown—so one doesn't have to look them up. At its base is a classic bit of Stengelese that, in the best tradition of the man himself, always produces a small smile.

"There comes a time in every man's life," it says, "and I've had plenty of them."

380

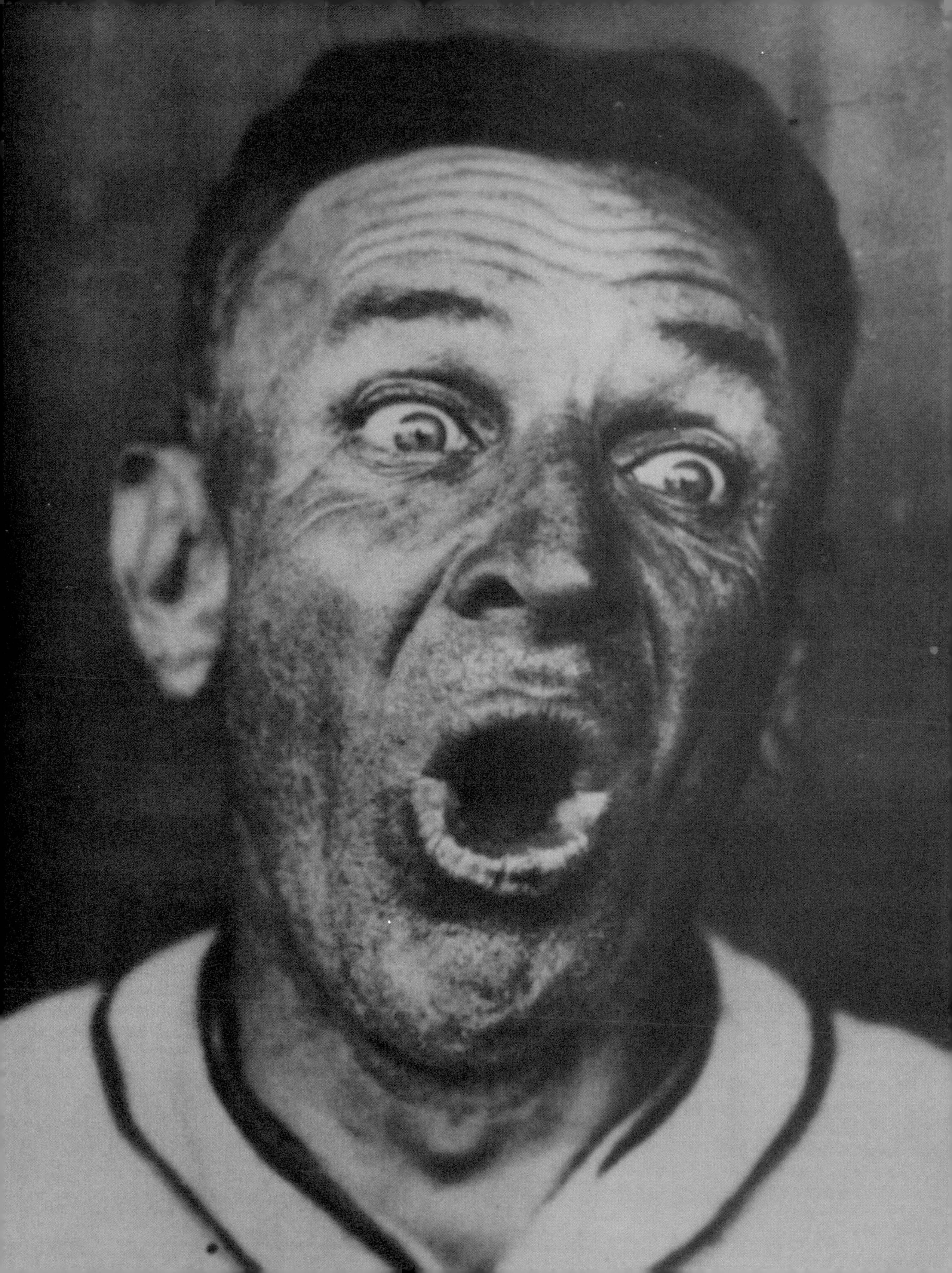

Appendix A

You Could Look It Up

Casey Stengel's Major League Playing Record

Year	Club	G	AB	R	H	2B	3B	HR	RBI	BA	SA	SB
1912	Brooklyn (NL)	17	57	9	18	1	0	1	13	.316	.386	5
1913	Brooklyn (NL)	124	438	60	119	16	8	7	43	.272	.393	19
1914	Brooklyn (NL)	126	412	55	130	13	10	4	60	.316	.425	19
1915	Brooklyn (NL)	132	459	52	109	20	12	3	50	.237	.353	5
1916	Brooklyn (NL)	127	462	66	129	27	8	8	53	.279	.424	11
1917	Brooklyn (NL)	150	549	69	141	23	12	6	73	.257	.375	18
1918	Pittsburgh (NL)	39	122	18	30	4	1	1	12	.246	.320	11
1919	Pittsburgh (NL)	89	321	38	94	10	10	4	43	.293	.424	12
1920	Philadelphia (NL)	129	445	53	130	25	6	9	50	.292	.436	7
1921	Philadelphia (NL)	24	59	7	18	3	1	0	4	.305	.390	1
	New York (NL)	18	22	4	5	1	0	0	2	.227	.273	0
1922	New York (NL)	84	250	48	92	8	10	7	48	.368	.564	4
1923	New York (NL)	75	218	39	74	11	5	5	43	.339	.505	6
1924	Boston (NL)	131	461	57	129	20	6	5	39	.280	.382	13
1925	Boston (NL)	12	13	0	1	0	0	0	2	.077	.077	0
Totals	14 Years	1277	4288	575	1219	182	89	60	535	.284	.410	131

World Series

Year	Opponent	G	AB	R	H	2B	3B	HR	RBI	BA	SA	SB
1916	Red Sox	4	11	2	4	0	0	0	0	.364	.364	0
1922	Yankees	2	5	0	2	0	0	0	0	.400	.400	0
1923	Yankees	6	12	3	5	0	0	2	4	.417	.917	0
Totals		12	20	5	11	0	0	2	4	.393	.607	0

Casey Stengel's Major League Managerial Record

		Regular Season				World Series			
Year	Club	Won	Lost	Pct. Won	Finish	Opponent	Won	Lost	Pct. Won
1934	Brooklyn (NL)	71	81	.467	6				
1935	Brooklyn (NL)	70	83	.458	5				
1936	Brooklyn (NL)	67	87	.435	7				
1938	Boston (NL)	77	75	.507	5				
1939	Boston (NL)	63	88	.417	7				
1940	Boston (NL)	65	87	.428	7				
1941	Boston (NL)	62	92	.403	7				
1942	Boston (NL)	59	89	.399	7				
1943	Boston (NL)	68	85	.439	6				
1949	New York (AL)	97	57	.630	1	Dodgers	4	1	.800
1950	New York (AL)	98	56	.636	1	Phillies	4	0	1.000
1951	New York (AL)	98	56	.636	1	Giants	4	2	.667
1952	New York (AL)	95	59	.617	1	Dodgers	4	3	.571
1953	New York (AL)	99	52	.656	1	Dodgers	4	2	.667
1954	New York (AL)	103	51	.669	2				
1955	New York (AL)	96	58	.623	1	Dodgers	3	4	.429
1956	New York (AL)	97	57	.630	1	Dodgers	4	3	.571
1957	New York (AL)	98	56	.636	1	Braves	3	4	.429
1958	New York (AL)	92	62	.597	1	Braves	4	3	.571
1959	New York (AL)	79	75	.513	3				
1960	New York (AL)	97	57	.630	1	Pirates	3	4	.429
1962	New York (NL)	40	120	.250	10				
1963	New York (NL)	51	111	.315	10				
1964	New York (NL)	53	109	.327	10				
1965	New York (NL)	31	64	.326	—				
Totals	25 years	1905	1842	.508			37	26	.587

Appendix B

Washington's Original "Great Communicator"

If there is one moment that defined Casey Stengel to the American public, it was his testimony on July 9, 1958, before the Senate Subcommittee on Antitrust and Monopoly.

It started innocently enough. "Mr. Stengel," said Senator Estes Kefauver of Tennessee, "you are the manager of the New York Yankees. Will you give us very briefly your background and views about this legislation?"

What followed were seven thousand words of vintage Stengelese, its meandering flow interrupted here and there by questions from several bemused and perplexed senators, who tried—largely in vain—to steer Casey back on course. As a public service, here is Casey's testimony, complete and unexpurgated. Take a deep breath and read on.

STENGEL: Well, I started in professional ball in 1910. I have been in professional ball, I would say, for forty-eight years. I have been employed by numerous ball clubs in the majors and in the minor leagues. I started in the minor leagues with Kansas City. I played as low as Class D ball, which was at Shelbyville, Kentucky, and also Class C ball and Class A ball, and I have advanced in baseball as a ballplayer.

I had many years that I was not so successful as a ballplayer, as it is a game of skill. And then I was no doubt discharged by baseball in which I had to go back to the minor leagues as a manager, and after being in the minor leagues as a manager, I became a major league manager in several cities and was discharged, we call it "discharged," because there is no question I had to leave. [Laughter.]

And I returned to the minor leagues at Milwaukee, Kansas City, and Oakland, California, and then returned to the major leagues. In the last ten years, naturally, in major league baseball with the New York Yankees, the New York Yankees have had tremendous success, and while I am not the ballplayer who does the work, I have no doubt worked for a ball club that is very capable in the office.

I must have splendid ownership, I must have very capable men who are in radio and television, which no doubt you know that we have mentioned the three names—you will say they are very great. We have a wonderful press that follows us. Anybody should in New York City, where you have so many million people. Our ball club has been successful because we have it, and we have the spirit of 1776. We put it into the ball field, and if you are not capable of becoming a great ballplayer since I have been in as the manager, in ten years, you are notified that if you don't produce on the ball field, the salary that you receive, we will allow you to be traded to play and give your services to other clubs.

The great proof of that was yesterday. Three of the young men that were stars and picked by the players in the American League to be in the All-Star Game were Mr. Cerv, who is at Kansas City; Mr. Jensen who was at Boston, and I might say, Mr. Triandos that caught for the Baltimore ball club, all three of those players were my members and to show you I was not such a brilliant manager they got away from me and were chosen by the players and I was fortunate enough to have them come back to play where I was successful as a manager.

If I have been in baseball for forty-eight years there must be some good in it. I was capable and strong enough at one time to do any kind of work but I came back to baseball and I have been in baseball ever since. I have been up and down the ladder. I know there are some things in baseball, thirty-five to fifty years ago, that are better now than they were in those days. In those days, my goodness, you could not transfer a ball club in the minor leagues, Class D, Class C ball, Class A ball.

How could you transfer a ball club when you did not have a highway? How could you transfer a ball club when the railroads then would take you to a town, you got off and then you had to wait and sit up five hours to go to another ball club? How could you run baseball then without night ball? You had to have night ball to improve the proceeds, to pay larger salaries, and I went to work, the first year I received $135 a month. I thought that was amazing. I had to put away enough money to go to dental college. I found out it was not better in dentistry. I stayed in baseball.

Any other questions you would like to ask me?

I want to let you know that as to the legislative end of baseball you men will have to consider that what you are here for. I am a bench manager. I will speak about anything from the playing end—in the major or minor leagues—and do everything I can to help you.

SENATOR KEFAUVER: Mr. Stengel, are you prepared to answer particularly why baseball wants this bill passed?

STENGEL: Well, I would have to say at the present time, I think that baseball has advanced in this respect for the player help. That is an amazing statement for me to make, because you can retire with an annuity at fifty and what organization in America allows you to retire at fifty and receive money?

I want to further state that I am not a ballplayer, that is, put into that pension fund committee. At my age—and I have been in baseball, well, I will say I am possibly the oldest man who is working in baseball—I would say that when they start an annuity for the ballplayers to better their conditions, it should have been done, and I think it has been done. I think it should be the way they have done it, which is a very good thing. The reason they possibly did not take the managers in at that time was because radio and television or the income to ball clubs was not large enough that you could have put in a pension plan.

Now I am not a member of the pension plan. You have young men here who are, who represent the ball clubs. They represent them as players and since I am not a member and don't receive pension from a fund which you would think, my goodness, he ought to be declared in that too, but I would say that is a great thing for the ballplayers. That is one thing I will say for the ballplayers, they have an advanced pension fund. I should think it was gained by radio and television or you could not have enough money to pay anything of that type.

Now the second thing about baseball that I think is very interesting to the public or to all of us is that it is the owner's own fault if he does not improve his club, along with the officials in the ball club and the players. Now what causes that?

If I am going to go on the road and we are a traveling ball club and you know the cost of transportation now—we travel sometimes with three pullman coaches—the New York Yankees, and remember I am just a salaried man and do not own stock in the New York Yankees, I found out that in traveling with the New York Yankees on the road and all, that it is the best, and we have broken records in Washington this year, we have broken them in every city but New York and we have lost two clubs that have gone out of the city of New York.

Of course we have had some bad weather, I would say that they are mad at us in Chicago, we fill the parks. They have come out to see some good material. I will say they are mad at us in Kansas City, but we broke their attendance record. Now on the road we only get possibly twenty-seven cents. I am not positive of these figures, as I am not an official. If you go back fifteen years or if I owned stock in the club I would give them to you.

SENATOR KEFAUVER: Mr. Stengel, I am not sure that I made my question clear. [Laughter.]

STENGEL: Yes, sir. Well that is all right. I am not sure I am going to answer yours perfectly either. [Laughter.]

SENATOR KEFAUVER: I was asking you, sir, why it is that baseball wants this bill passed.

STENGEL: I would say I would not know, but I would say the reason why they would want it passed is to keep baseball going as the highest paid ball sport that has gone into baseball and from the baseball angle, I am not going to speak of any other sport. I am not in here to argue about other sports, I am in the baseball business. It has been run cleaner than any business that was ever put out in the one hundred years at the present time. I am not speaking about television or I am not speaking about income that comes into the ball parks. You have to take that off. I don't know too much about it. I say the ballplayers have a better advancement at the present time.

SENATOR KEFAUVER: One further question, and then I will pass to the other senators. How many players do the Yankees control, Mr. Stengel?

STENGEL: Well, I will tell you: I hire the players and if they make good with me I keep them without any criticism from my ownership. I do not know how many players they own as I am not a scout and I cannot run a ball club during the daytime and be busy at night and up the next day and find out how many players that the Yankees own. If you get any official with the Yankees that is here, why he could give you the names.

SENATOR KEFAUVER: Very well. Senator Langer?

SENATOR LANGER: Mr. Stengel?

STENGEL: Yes, sir.

SENATOR LANGER: What do you think is the future of baseball? Is it going to be expanded to include more clubs than are in existence at the present time?

STENGEL: I think every chamber of commerce in the major league cities would not change a franchise, I think they will be delighted because they have a hard time to put in a convention hall or to get people to come to your city, and if it is going to be like Milwaukee or Kansas City or Baltimore, I think they would want a major league team. But if I was a chamber of commerce member and I was in a city I would not want a baseball team to leave the city as too much money is brought into your city even if you have a losing team and great if you have a winning ball team.

SENATOR LANGER: You look forward then, do you not, to, say, ten years or twenty years from now this business of baseball is going to grow larger and larger and larger?

STENGEL: Well, I should think it would. I should think it would get larger because of the fact we are drawing tremendous crowds, I believe, from overseas programs in television—that is one program I have always stuck up for. I think every ballplayer and everyone should give out anything that is overseas for the Army, free of cost and so forth. I think that every hospital should get it. I think that because of the lack of parking in so many cities that you cannot have a great ball park if you don't have parking space. If you are ancient or forty-five or fifty and have acquired enough money to go to a ball game, you cannot drive a car on a highway, which is very hard to do after forty-five, to drive on any modern highway, and if you are going to stay home you need radio and television to go along for the ball club.

SENATOR LANGER: That brings us to another question.

STENGEL: Yes, sir.

SENATOR LANGER: That is, what do you think of pay-as-you-go television?

STENGEL: Well, to tell you the truth, if I were starting in it myself I would like to be in that line of business as I did not think they would ever have television and so forth here but they have got it here now. [Laughter.]

Forty years ago you would not have had it around here yourself and you would not have cameras flying around here every five minutes but we have got them here and more of them around here than around a ball field, I will give you that little tip.

SENATOR LANGER: You believe the time is ever going to come when you will have pay-as-you-go in the World Series, which would be kept from the public unless they had pay-as-you-go television in their homes?

STENGEL: I think you have got a good argument there and it is worthy of you to say that. I am thinking myself of anybody that is hospitalized and anybody who cannot go to a ball park. I should think if they could pass that they should try to pass it. But I don't think they will be able to do it because they have gone in television so far that they reach so many outside people, you have to have a sponsor for everything else you do, go pay television and that is going to run all the big theaters out of business where you have to use pay television. All the big theaters and all the big movie companies went broke. We know that. You see that now or you would not have a place to hold a television for pay. I don't know how they would run that of course. I am not on that side of the fence. I am paid a salary—.

SENATOR LANGER: Just one further question. You do not have to answer it unless you want to. That is, is there any provision made whereby the team owners can keep a racketeer out of the baseball business?

STENGEL: Well, sir—.

SENATOR LANGER: Can the owners of the New York Yankees, for example, sell out to anyone who may want to buy the club at a big price without the consent of the other owners?

STENGEL: That is a very good thing that I will have to think about but I will give you an example. I think that is why they put in as a commissioner Judge Landis, and he said if there is a cloud on baseball I will take it off, and he took the cloud off and they have only had one scandal or if they had it is just one major league city. How can you be a ballplayer and make twenty-five ballplayers framed without it being heard? It is bound to leak, and your play will show it. I don't think, an owner possibly could do something but he can't play the game for you. It is the most honest profession I think that we have, everything today that is going on outside—.

SENATOR LANGER: Mr. Chairman, my final question. This is the Antimonopoly Committee that is sitting here.
STENGEL: Yes, sir.
SENATOR LANGER: I want to know whether you intend to keep on monopolizing the world's championship in New York City.
STENGEL: Well, I will tell you, I got a little concerned yesterday in the first three innings when I say the three players I had gotten rid of and I said when I lost nine, "What am I going to do?" and when I had a couple of my players I thought so great of that did not do so good up to the sixth inning I was more confused, but I finally had to go and call on a young man in Baltimore that we don't own and the Yankees don't own him, and he is doing pretty good, and I would actually have to tell you that I think we are more the Greta Garbo type now from success.

We are being hated I mean, from the ownership and all, we are being hated. Every sport that gets too great or one individual—but if we made twenty-seven cents and it pays to have a winner at home why would you not have a good winner in your own park if you were an owner. That is the result of baseball. An owner gets most of the money at home and it is up to him and his staff to do better or they ought to be discharged.
SENATOR LANGER: That is all, Mr. Chairman. Thank you.
SENATOR KEFAUVER: Thank you, Senator Langer. Senator O'Mahoney?
SENATOR O'MAHONEY: May I say, Mr. Stengel, that I congratulate you very much for what happened on the field at Baltimore yesterday. I was watching on television when you sent Gil McDougald up to bat for Early Wynn. I noticed with satisfaction that he got a hit, knocking Frank Malzone in with the winning run. That is good management.
STENGEL: Thank you very much. [Laughter.]
SENATOR O'MAHONEY: Did I understand you to say, Mr. Stengel, at the beginning of your statement that you have been in baseball for forty-eight years?
STENGEL: Yes, sir; the oldest man in the service.
SENATOR O'MAHONEY: How many major league teams were there in the United States when you entered baseball?
STENGEL: Well, there was in 1910—there were sixteen major league baseball teams.
SENATOR O'MAHONEY: How many are there now?
STENGEL: There are sixteen major league clubs but there was one year that they brought in the Federal League, which was brought in by Mr. Ward and Mr. Sinclair and others after a war, and it is a very odd thing to tell you that during tough times it is hard to study baseball. I have been through two or three depressions in baseball and out of it. The First World War we had good baseball in August. The Second World War we kept on and made more money because everybody was going to the services, the larger the war, the more they come to the ball park, and that was an amazing thing to me. When you were looking for tough times, why it changed for different wars.
SENATOR O'MAHONEY: How many minor leagues were there in baseball when you began?
STENGEL: Well, there were not so many at that time because of this fact: Anybody to go into baseball at that time with the educational schools that we had were small. While you were probably thoroughly educated at school—you had to be—we had only small cities that you could put a team in, and they would go defunct. Why, I remember the first year I was at Kankakee, Illinois, and a bank offered me $550 if I would let them have a little notice. I left there and took a uniform because they owed me two weeks' pay. But I either had to quit but I did not have enough money to go to dental college so I had to go with the manager down to Kentucky.

What happened there was if you got by July, that was the big date. You did not play night ball and you did not play Sundays in half of the cities on account of a Sunday observance, so in those days when things were tough, and all of it was, I mean to say, why they just closed up July 4 and there you were sitting there in the depot. You could go to work some place else but that was it. So I got out of Kankakee, Illinois, and I just go there for the visit now. [Laughter.]

I think now, do you know how many clubs they have? Anybody will start a minor league club but it is just like your small cities, the industries have left them and they have gone west to California, and I am a Missourian—Kansas City, Missouri—but I can see all those towns and everybody moving west and I know if you fly in the air you can see everything from the desert, you can see a big country over there that has got many names. Well, now why wouldn't baseball prosper out there, with that many million people?
SENATOR O'MAHONEY: Are the minor leagues suffering now?
STENGEL: I should say they are.
SENATOR O'MAHONEY: Why?
STENGEL: Do you know why? I will tell you why. I don't think anybody can support minor league ball. When they see a great official, it would be just like a great actress

or actor had come to town. If Bob Hope had come here or Greta Garbo over there, half of them would go to see Greta Garbo and half Bob Hope but if you have a very poor baseball team they are not going to watch you until you become great, and the minor leagues now with radio and television will not pay very much attention to minor league ballplayers. Softball is interesting, the parent is interested; he goes around with him. He watches his son, and he is more enthusiastic about the boy than some stranger that comes to town and wants to play in a little wooden park and with no facilities to make you be interested. You might rather stay home and see a program.

SENATOR O'MAHONEY: How many baseball players are now engaged in the activity as compared to when you came in?

STENGEL: I would say there are more, many more. Because we did not have as many cities that could support even minor league baseball in those days.

SENATOR O'MAHONEY: How many players did the sixteen major league clubs have when you came in?

STENGEL: At that time they did not have as many teams. They did not have near as many teams as below. Later on Mr. Rickey came in and started what was known as what you would say numerous clubs, you know in which I will try to pick up this college man, I will pick up that college boy or I will pick up some corner lot boy and if you picked up the corner lot boy maybe he became just as successful as the college man, which is true. He then had a number of players.

Now, too many players is a funny thing, it costs like everything. I said just like I made a talk not long ago and I told them all when they were drinking and they invited me in, I said you ought to be home. You men are not making enough money. You cannot drink like that. They said, "This is a holiday for the Shell Oil Company," and I said, "Why is it a holiday?" and they said, "We did something great for three years and we are given two days off to watch the Yankees play the White Sox," but they were mostly White Sox rooters. I said, "You are not doing right." I said, "You can't take all those drinks and all even on your holidays. You ought to be home and raising more children because big league clubs now give you a hundred thousand for a bonus to go into baseball." [Laughter.]

And by the way I don't happen to have any children but I wish Mrs. Stengel and I had eight, I would like to put them in on that bonus rule. [Laughter.]

SENATOR O'MAHONEY: What I am trying to find out, Mr. Stengel, is how many players are actively working for the major league teams now as was formerly the case?

STENGEL: You are right, I would honestly tell you they naturally have more and they are in more competition now. You have to buck now a university—anyone who wants to be a hockey player—.

SENATOR O'MAHONEY: Let's stick to baseball for a minute.

STENGEL: I stay in baseball. I say I can't name them. If you want to know you get any executive, you have got any names, bring any executive with the Yankees that is an official in the ball club and he will tell you how many players the Yankees have. And there is his jurisdiction—every ball club owner can tell you, he is an official, they have enough officials hired with me with a long pencil, too.

SENATOR O'MAHONEY: I recently saw a statement by a baseball sports writer that there were about four hundred active ballplayers in the major leagues now. Would you think that is about correct now?

STENGEL: I would say in the major leagues each club has twenty-five men which is the player limit. There are eight clubs in each league so you might say there are four hundred players in the major leagues. You mean outside of it that they own two or three hundred each individual club, isn't that what you have reference to?

SENATOR O'MAHONEY: I was coming to that, but is that the fact?

STENGEL: Well, I say that is what you would say [laughter]. If you want to find that out you get any of those executives that come in here that keep those books. I am not a bookkeeper for him. But I take the man when he comes to the big leagues. They can give it to you and each club should. That does not mean and I would like to ask you, how would you like to pay those men? That is why they go broke.

SENATOR O'MAHONEY: I am not in that business.

STENGEL: I was in that business a short time, too; it is pretty hard to make a living at it.

SENATOR O'MAHONEY: But the stories that we read in the press—

STENGEL: That is right.

SENATOR O'MAHONEY: —are to the effect that the minor leagues are suffering. There are no more major league teams now than there were when you came into baseball, and what I am trying to find out is: What are the prospects for the future growth of baseball and to what extent have the sixteen major league teams, through the farm system, obtained, by contract or agreement or understanding, control over the professional lives of the players?

STENGEL: That is right. If I was a ballplayer and I was discharged, and I saw within three years that I could not become a major league ballplayer I would go into another profession. That is the history of anything that is in business.

SENATOR O'MAHONEY: Do you think that the farm system keeps any players in the minor leagues when they ought to be in the majors?

STENGEL: I should say it would not keep any players behind or I have been telling you a falsehood. I would say it may keep a few back, but very few. There is no manager in baseball who wants to be a success without the ability of those great players and if I could pull them up to make money in a gate for my owner and for myself to be a success, I don't believe I would hold him back.

SENATOR O'MAHONEY: The fact is, is it not, Mr. Stengel, that while the population of the United States has increased tremendously during the period that you have been engaged in professional baseball, the number of major league teams has not increased; it remains the same as it was then. The number of players actually engaged by the major league teams is approximately the same as back in 1903, and there is now, through the farm system, a major league control of the professional occupation of baseball playing. Is that a correct summary?

STENGEL: Well, you have that from the standpoint of what you have been reading. You have got that down very good. [Laughter.]

But if you are a player—.

SENATOR O'MAHONEY: I am trying to get it down from your standpoint as a forty-eight-year man in baseball.

STENGEL: That is why I stayed in it. I have been discharged fifteen times and rehired; so you get rehired in baseball, and they don't want a good ballplayer leaving, and I always say a high-priced baseball player should get a high salary just like a moving-picture actor. He should not get the same thing as the twenty-fifth man on the ball club who is very fortunate he is sitting on your ball club, and I say it is very hard to have skill in baseball.

SENATOR O'MAHONEY: You are not changing the subject, are you, sir?

STENGEL: No. You asked the question and I told you that if you want to find out how minor league baseball is; it is terrible now. How can you eat on $2.50 a day when up here you can eat on $8 or better than $8? Now how can you travel in a bus all night and play ball the next night to make a living? How can you, a major league man, make it so that you can't? Is he going to fly all of them to each place?

SENATOR O'MAHONEY: I am not arguing with you, Mr. Stengel.

STENGEL: I am just saying minor league ball has outgrown itself, like every small town has outgrown itself industrially because they don't put a plant in there to keep the people working so they leave.

SENATOR O'MAHONEY: Does that mean in your judgment that the major league baseball teams necessarily have to control ball playing?

STENGEL: I think that they do. I don't think that if I was a great player and you released me in four years, I think it would be a joke if you released a man and he made one year for you and then bid for a job and then played the next year, we will say, out of Washington, he played in New York the third year, he would play in Cleveland and put himself up in a stake. I think they ought to be just as they have been.

A man who walks in and sees you get fair compensation and if you are great be sure you get it because the day you don't report and the day you don't open a season you are hurting the major league and hurting yourself somewhat, but you are not going to be handicapped in life if you are great in baseball. Every man who goes out has a better home than he had when he went in.

SENATOR O'MAHONEY: Did I understand you to say that in your own personal activity as manager, you always give a player who is to be traded advance notice?

STENGEL: I warn him that—I hold a meeting. We have an instructional school, regardless of my English, we have got an instructional school.

SENATOR O'MAHONEY: Your English is perfect and I can understand what you say, and I think I can even understand what you mean.

STENGEL: Yes, sir. You have got some very wonderful points in. I would say in an instructional school we try you out for three weeks and we clock you, just like—I mean how good are you going to be in the service; before you go out of the service we have got you listed. We know if you are handicapped in the service and we have got instructors who teach you. They don't have to listen to me if they don't like me.

I have a man like Crosetti, who never has been to a banquet; he never would. He does a big job like Art Fletcher; he teaches that boy and teaches his family; he will be there. I have a man for first base, second base, short; that is why the Yankees are ahead. We have advanced so much we can take a man over to where he can be a big league player, and if he does not, we advance him to where he can play opposition to us. I am getting concerned about opposition. I am discharging too many good ones.

SENATOR O'MAHONEY: Mr. Chairman, I think the witness is the best entertainment we have had around here for a long time and it is a great temptation to keep asking him questions but I think I had better desist. Thank you.

SENATOR KEFAUVER: Senator Carroll.

SENATOR CARROLL: Mr. Stengel, I am an old Yankee fan and I come from a city where I think we have made some contributions to your success—from Denver. I think you have many Yankee players from Denver.

The question Senator Kefauver asked you was what, in your honest opinion, with your forty-eight years of experience, is the need for this legislation in view of the fact that baseball has not been subject to antitrust laws?

STENGEL: No.

SENATOR CARROLL: It is not now subject to the antitrust laws. What do you think the need is for this legislation? I had a conference with one of the attorneys representing not only baseball but all of the sports, and I listened to your explanation to Senator Kefauver. It seemed to me it had some clarity. I asked the attorney this question: What was the need for this legislation? I wonder if you would accept his definition. He said they didn't want to be subjected to the *ipse dixit* of the federal government because they would throw a lot of damage suits on the *ad damnum* clause. He said, in the first place, the Toolson case was *sui generis*, it was *de minimus non curat lex*. Do you call that a clear expression?

STENGEL: Well, you are going to get me there for about two hours.

SENATOR CARROLL: I realize these questions which are put to you are all, I suppose, legislative and legal questions. Leaning on your experience as a manager, do you feel the farm system, the draft system, the reserve clause system, is fair to the players, to the managers, and to the public interest?

STENGEL: I think the public is taken care of, rich and poor, better at the present time than years ago. I really think that the ownership is a question of ability. I really think that the business manager is a question of ability. Some of those men are supposed to be very brilliant in their line of work, and some of them are not so brilliant, so that they have quite a bit of trouble with it when you run an operation of a club in which the ownership maybe doesn't run the club.

I would say that the players themselves—I told you, I am not in on that fund, it is a good thing. I say I should have been, to tell you the truth. But I think it is a great thing for the players.

SENATOR CARROLL: I am not talking about that fund.

STENGEL: Well, I tell you, if you are going to talk about the fund you are going to think about radio and television and pay television.

SENATOR CARROLL: I do not want to talk about radio and television, but I do want to talk about the draft clause and reserve systems.

STENGEL: Yes, sir. I would have liked to have been free four times in my life; and later on I have seen men free, and later on they make a big complaint "they wuz robbed," and if you are robbed there is always some club down the road to give you an opportunity.

SENATOR CARROLL: That was not the question I asked you, and I only asked you on your long experience—.

STENGEL: Yes, sir. I would not be in it forty-eight years if it was not all right.

SENATOR CARROLL: I understand that.

STENGEL: Well, then, why wouldn't it stay that?

SENATOR CARROLL: In your long experience —.

STENGEL: Yes.

SENATOR CARROLL: Do you feel—you have had experience through the years—

STENGEL: That is true.

SENATOR CARROLL: —with the draft system, and the reserve clause in the contracts. Do you think you could still exist under existing law without changing the law?

STENGEL: I think it is run better than it has ever been run in baseball, for every department.

SENATOR CARROLL: Then I come back to the principal question. This is the real question before this body.

STENGEL: All right.

SENATOR CARROLL: Then what is the need for legislation, if they are getting along all right?

STENGEL: I didn't ask for the legislation. [Laughter.]

SENATOR CARROLL: Your answer is a very good one, and that is the question Senator Kefauver put to you.

STENGEL: That is right.

SENATOR CARROLL: That is the question Senator O'Mahoney put.

STENGEL: Right.

SENATOR CARROLL: Are you ready to say there is no need for legislation in this field, then, insofar as baseball is concerned?

STENGEL: As far as I am concerned, from drawing a salary and from my ups and downs and being discharged, I always found out that there was somebody ready to employ you, if you were on the ball.

SENATOR CARROLL: Thank you very much, Mr. Stengel.

SENATOR KEFAUVER: Thank you very much, Mr. Stengel. We appreciate your testimony.

SENATOR LANGER: May I ask a question?

SENATOR KEFAUVER: Senator Langer has a question. Just a moment, Mr. Stengel.

SENATOR LANGER: Can you tell this committee what countries have baseball teams besides the United States, Mexico, and Japan?
STENGEL: I made a tour with the New York Yankees several years ago, and it was the most amazing tour I ever saw for a ball club, to go over where you have trouble spots. It wouldn't make any difference whether he was a Republican or a Democrat, and so forth. I know that over there we drew 250,000 to 500,000 people in the streets, in which they stood in front of the automobiles, not on the sidewalks, and those people are trying to play baseball over there with short fingers [laughter], and I say, "Why do you do it?"

But they love it. They are crazy about baseball, and they are not worried at the handicap. And I'll tell you, business industries run baseball over there, and they are now going to build a stadium that is going to be covered over for games where you don't need a tarpaulin if it rains. South America is all right, and Cuba is all right. But I don't know, I have never been down there except to Cuba, I have never been to South America, and I know that they broadcast games, and I know we have players that are playing from there.

I tell you what, I think baseball has spread, but if we are talking about anything spreading, we would be talking about soccer. You can go over in Italy, and I thought they would know DiMaggio everyplace. And my goodness, you mention soccer, you can draw fifty thousand or a hundred thousand people. Over here you have a hard time to get soccer on the field, which is a great sport, no doubt.
SENATOR LANGER: What I want to know, Mr. Stengel, is this: When the American League plays the National League in the World Series and it is advertised as the world championship—
STENGEL: Yes, sir.
SENATOR LANGER: —I want to know why you do not play Mexico or Japan or some other country and really have a world championship.
STENGEL: Well, I think you have a good argument there. I would say that a couple of clubs that I saw, it was like when I was in the Navy, I thought I couldn't get special unless they played who I wanted to play. So I would look over a team. When they got off a ship I would play them, but if they had been on land too long, my team couldn't play them. So I would play the teams at sea six months, and I would say, "You are the club I would like to play." I would like to play those countries, and I think it should be nationwide and governmentwide, too, if you could possibly get it in.
SENATOR LANGER: Do you think the day is ever going to come, perhaps five years from now or ten—
STENGEL: I would say ten years, not five.
SENATOR LANGER: —when the championship team of the United States would play the championship team of Mexico?
STENGEL: I really think it should be that way, but I don't think you will get it before ten years, because you have to build stadiums and you have to have an elimination in every country for it, and you have to have weather at the same time, or how could you play unless you would hold a team over?
SENATOR LANGER: Do you not think these owners are going to develop this matter of world championship of another country besides the United States?
STENGEL: I should think they would do that in time. I really do. I was amazed over in Japan. I couldn't understand why they would want to play baseball with short fingers and used the same size ball, and not a small size, and compete in baseball. And yet that is their great sport, and industries are backing them.
SENATOR LANGER: In other words, the owners some day, in your opinion, Mr. Stengel, are going to make a lot of money by having the champions of one country play another country and keep on with eliminations until they really have a world championship?
STENGEL: That is what I say. I think it is not named properly right now unless you can go and play all of them. You would have to do that.
SENATOR LANGER: That is all, Mr. Chairman.
SENATOR KEFAUVER: Mr. Stengel, one final question. You spoke of Judge Landis and the fact that he had rather absolute control over baseball. There was a clause in Judge Landis' contract which read:

> We, the club owners, pledge ourselves to loyally support the commissioner in his important and difficult task, and we assure him that each of us will acquiesce in his decisions even when we believe they are mistaken, and that we will not discredit the sport by criticism of him or one another.

This same clause was in Mr. Chandler's contract, but we do not understand it to be in Mr. Frick's contract. Do you think the commissioner needs to have this power over management?
STENGEL: I would say when there was a cloud over baseball, like any sport, you have to have a man that has the power to change things. Now when Landis was in, that was the situation with baseball. You were bucking race-

tracks. We don't have a tote board. We are playing baseball for admission fees. Now, we don't want a tote board in baseball. Who would? That would be great, if you have that out there, and you could go out there and, you know, use a tote board and say, "Does he get to first or won't he get to first?" and so forth.

Now, Landis was an amazing man. I will give you an example of him. It is a good thing you brought him in. I was discharged one year, and I was the president of a ball club at Worcester, Massachusetts, so I discharged myself, and I sent it in to Landis and he okayed it. Why, I was president. Then I could release my player, couldn't I? And I was the player. So I was the only player ever released by the president, and that was in Worcester, Massachusetts, so I got discharged.

SENATOR KEFAUVER: Do you think the present commissioner ought to have the same power?

STENGEL: There are sixteen men in baseball who own ball clubs. We will say that an individual can hardly make it any more unless he is wealthy. That is how it has grown. I would say the biggest thing in baseball at the present time now, and with the money that is coming in, and so forth, and with an annuity fund for the players, you can't allow the commissioner to just take everything sitting there, and take everything insofar as money is concerned, but I think he should have full jurisdiction over the player and player's habits, and the way the umpires and ball clubs should conduct their business in the daytime and right on up tight up here.

SENATOR KEFAUVER: Thank you very much, Mr. Stengel. We appreciate your presence here.

With this, Stengel left the Senate chambers, laughter trailing him out the door. Senator Kefauver next called Mickey Mantle to testify.

"Mr. Mantle," Kefauver asked, "do you have any observations with reference to the applicability of the antitrust laws to baseball?"

"My views are just about the same as Casey's," Mantle impishly replied.

"If you will redefine just what Casey's views were," the senator suggested above a fresh round of laughter, "we would be very happy."

Bibliography

Alexander, Charles C. *John McGraw.* New York: Viking, 1988.

Allen, Maury. *You Could Look It Up: The Life of Casey Stengel.* New York: Times Books, 1979.

——. *Damned Yankee: The Billy Martin Story.* New York: Times Books, 1986.

Berkow, Ira, and Jim Kaplan. *The Gospel According to Casey.* New York: St. Martin's Press, 1992.

Berra, Yogi, with Tom Horton. *Yogi: It Ain't Over.* New York: McGraw-Hill, 1989.

Breslin, Jimmy. *Can't Anybody Here Play This Game?* New York: Viking, 1963.

Carmichael, John P. "Casey Stengel—My Greatest Thrill as a Player." *Baseball Digest,* April 1950.

Caroulis, John. "Richie Ashburn Savors 50 Years of Baseball Memories." *Baseball Digest,* December 1994.

Cohen, Stanley. *Dodgers! The First 100 Years.* New York: Carol Publishing Group, 1990.

Costello, James, and Michael Santa Maria. *In the Shadows of the Diamond: Hard Times in the National Pastime.* Dubuque, Iowa: Elysian Fields Press, 1992.

Creamer, Robert W. *Stengel: His Life and Times.* New York: Simon & Schuster, 1984.

———. "Casey Stengel—an Appreciation." *Sports Illustrated,* October 13, 1975.

Curran, William. *Big Sticks: The Phenomenal Decade of Ruth, Gehrig, Cobb, and Hornsby.* New York: Morrow, 1990.

Dawidoff, Nicholas. *The Catcher Was a Spy: The Mysterious Life of Moe Berg.* New York: Pantheon, 1994.

Durso, Joseph. *Casey: The Life and Legend of Charles Dillon Stengel.* Englewood Cliffs, N.J.: Prentice-Hall, 1967.

———. *Joe DiMaggio: The Last American Knight.* Boston: Little, Brown & Co., 1995.

Falkner, David. *Great Time Coming: The Life of Jackie Robinson from Baseball to Birmingham.* New York: Simon & Schuster, 1995.

Feller, Bob, with Bill Gilbert. *Now Pitching, Bob Feller.* New York: Birch Lane Press, 1990.

Fleming, G. H. *The Dizziest Season.* New York: Morrow, 1984.

Forbes, Gordon. "Bill Terry: The Strong-Willed Giant." *Sport*, May 1965.
Ford, Edward C. ("Whitey"), with Joseph Durso and Mickey Mantle. *Whitey and Mickey: A Joint Biography of the Yankee Years.* New York: Viking, 1977.
Forker, Dom. *Sweet Seasons: Recollections of the 1955-64 New York Yankees.* Dallas: Taylor Publishing Co., 1990.
Gallen, David, ed. *The Baseball Chronicles.* New York: Galahad, 1991.
Goldstein, Richard. *Spartan Seasons: How Baseball Survived the Second World War.* New York: Macmillan, 1980.
Golenbock, Peter. *Dynasty: The New York Yankees, 1949-1964.* New York: Berkley, 1975.
Graham, Frank, Jr. *Casey Stengel: His Half Century in Baseball.* New York: John Day, 1958.
Gregory, Robert. *Diz: The Story of Dizzy Dean and Baseball During the Great Depression.* New York: Viking, 1992.
Halberstam, David. *The Summer of '49.* New York: Morrow, 1989.
Henrich, Tommy. *Five O'Clock Lightning: Ruth, Gehrig, DiMaggio, Mantle, and the Glory Years of the New York Yankees.* New York: Carol Publishing Group, 1992.
Holway, John B. *Blackball Stars: Negro League Pioneers.* Westport: Meckler, 1988.
Honig, Donald. *Baseball When the Grass Was Real.* New York: Coward, McCann & Geoghegan, 1975.
———. *Baseball Between the Lines.* New York: Coward, McCann & Geoghegan, 1976.
———. *The Man in the Dugout.* Chicago: Follett, 1977.
———. *The October Heroes.* New York: Simon & Schuster, 1979.
Howard, Elston. "Baseball's Grand Old Man." *Reader's Digest*, October 1967.
Hynd, Noel. *The Giants of the Polo Grounds.* New York: Doubleday, 1988.
Illman, Harry R. *Unholy Toledo.* San Francisco: Polemic Press, 1985.
Jacobson, Steve. "Celebrating Casey's 100th." *Newsday*, August 26, 1990.
James, Bill. *The Bill James Historical Baseball Abstract.* New York: Villard, 1986.
———. "Casey Stengel." *Sport*, December 1986.
Jennison, Christopher. *Wait 'til Next Year: The Yankees, Dodgers, and Giants, 1947-1957.* New York: Norton, 1974.
Kahn, Roger. *The Boys of Summer.* New York: Harper & Row, 1971.
———. *The Era, 1947-1957: When the Yankees, the Giants, and the Dodgers Ruled the World.* New York: Ticknor & Fields, 1993.
Koppett, Leonard. *The New York Mets: The Whole Story.* New York: Macmillan, 1970.
Kuenster, John. "What They Thought When the Pressure Was the Greatest!" *Baseball Digest*, June 1961.
Lang, Jack, and Peter Simon. *The New York Mets: Twenty-five Years of Baseball Magic.* New York: Henry Holt, 1986.
Lardner, John. "The Improbable Casey Stengel." *Sport*, December 1948.
Lardner, Ring. *Lose with a Smile.* New York: Scribner's, 1933.
Lieb, Fred. *Baseball As I Have Known It.* New York: Coward, McCann & Geoghegan, 1977.
Lieber, Leslie. "Was Casey Really So Great?" *This Week*, June 25, July 2, July 9, 1961.
Linn, Edward. "The Last Angry Man." *The Saturday Evening Post*, July 3, 1965.
Mantle, Mickey. *The Education of a Baseball Player.* New York: Simon & Schuster, 1967.
Mantle, Mickey, with Herb Gluck. *The Mick.* New York: Doubleday, 1985.
Mead, William B. *Low and Outside: Baseball in the Depression, 1930-1939.* Alexandria, Virginia: Redefinition, 1990.

Meany, Tom. "They Didn't Hire Him for Laughs." *The Saturday Evening Post*, March 12, 1949.

Miller, Douglas T., and Marion Nowak. *The Fifties: The Way We Really Were.* New York: Doubleday, 1977.

Neft, David S., and Richard M. Cohen. *The World Series: Complete Play-by-Play of Every Game, 1903-1989.* New York: St. Martin's Press, 1990.

Paxton, Harry T. "Casey the Indestructible." *The Saturday Evening Post*, April 7, 1962.

Peary, Danny. *We Played the Game: 65 Players Remember Baseball's Greatest Era, 1947-1964.* New York: Hyperion, 1994.

Ritter, Lawrence S. *The Glory of Their Times.* New York: Morrow, 1984.

———. *Lost Ballparks: A Celebration of Baseball's Legendary Fields.* New York: Viking, 1992.

Rizzuto, Phil, with Tom Horton. *The October Twelve: Five Years of New York Yankee Glory, 1949-1953.* New York: Forge, 1994.

Rust, Art, Jr., with Edna Rust. *Recollections of a Baseball Junkie.* New York: Morrow, 1985.

Shecter, Leonard. *Once Upon the Polo Grounds: The Mets That Were.* New York: Dial Press, 1970.

Smith, Curt. *Voices of the Game: The Acclaimed Chronicle of Baseball Radio and Television Broadcasting, from 1921 to the Present.* New York: Simon & Schuster, 1992.

———. *The Storytellers.* New York: Macmillan, 1995.

Stengel, Casey. "They've All Got Automobiles." *New York Times*, October 9, 1970.

Stengel, Casey, with Harry T. Paxton. *Casey at the Bat: The Story of My Life in Baseball.* New York: Random House, 1962.

Stump, Al. *Cobb: A Biography.* Chapel Hill, N.C.: Algonquin, 1994.

Thomas, Henry W. *Walter Johnson: Baseball's Big Train.* Washington, D.C.: Phenom Press, 1995.

Tygiel, Jules. *Baseball's Great Experiment: Jackie Robinson and His Legacy.* New York: Oxford University Press, 1983.

Vecsey, George. *Joy in Mudville.* New York: McCall Publishing Group, 1970.

Weinberger, Miro, and Dan Riley. *The Yankees Reader.* Boston: Houghton Mifflin, 1991.

Williams, Ted, with John Underwood. *My Turn at Bat.* New York: Simon & Schuster, 1969.

Yardley, Jonathan. *Ring: A Biography of Ring Lardner.* New York: Random House, 1977.

Index

A

Aaron, Hank, **177**
Alexander, Grover Cleveland, **29**
Allen, Maury, 82, 169
Allen, Mel, **148**
Alston, Walt, **129**
Amoros, Sandy, **134**, 143
Anderson, Craig, 164
Archer, Jimmy, 20
Ashburn, Richie, **158**, 161
Avila, Bobby, **117**, **127**

B

Babich, John, 74
Baker Bowl, **34-35**, 36-37, 76-77
Baker, Frank (Home Run), **42**
Bancroft, Dave (Beauty), 40, 55
Barnes, Jesse, **61**
Barrow, Ed, 90
Baseball Magazine, 93
Bauer, Hank, 98, 115, 119, **133**, 145, 147
Bearden, Gene, 89
Beck, Walter (Boom-Boom), 76-77
Becker, Beals, 28
Berra, Yogi, **92**, 110-111, 114, **124**-125, **133**-134, 143, 145, 151-152, 167,
Berres, Ray, 79, 82, 91
Black, Joe, 123
Bly, Nellie, 2
Bordagaray, Stanley (Frenchy), **77**, 79
Bouchee, Ed, 167
Bowlin, June, 175, 178
Boyer, Clete, **140**
Branca, Ralph, 114
Braves Field, 35, **85**
Briggs Stadium, **104**
Brooklyn Tip-Tops, **26**, 31
Broun, Heywood, 54
Brown, Bobby, 98, 106-107, 111
Burdette, Lew, 147
Burke, Jimmy, 61
Burns, George, 41
Bush, Bullet Joe, 52, 65
Byrne, Tommy, 105, 139

C

Cadore, Leon, 32
Campanella, Roy, 145
Campanella, Roy, Jr., 141
Cannizzaro, Chris, 169
Cannon, Jimmy, 135
Carey, Max, **64**, 68-69
Carper, Fern, 8
Carroll, Parke, 149
Casey at the Bat (movie), 20
Casey at the Bat (poem), 19-20
Causey, Red, 37
Central High School (Kansas City), **6-10**
Cheney, Larry, 28-29
Cimoli, Gino, 151
Clemente, Roberto, 150
Coates, Jim, 151
Cobb, Ty, 18, **24**, 65
Coleman, Jerry, 93, 98, 102, **105**-107
Collins, Joe, 107-**108**, 145
Collins, Ripper, 89, 97
Conlan, Jocko, **62**, 66
Continental League, 155
Coombs, Jack, 29
Cosell, Howard, 153
Courtney, Clint, **118**
Craig, Roger, **156**, 160, 164
Cravath, Gavvy, **34**
Crawford, Wahoo Sam, 65
Crosetti, Frankie, 93-94, **97**
Cuccinello, Tony, 81, **87**
Cunningham, Bill, 55
Cutshaw, George, 24, 32

D

Dahlen, Bill, 19, 24
Daley, Arthur, 94
Dalton, Jack, 28
Daubert, Jake, 19, 24, 28, **31**
Dean, Dizzy, 74-**76**, 78
Dean, Paul, **76**-77
Dempsey, Jack, 61
de Vicenzo, Cookie, 85
Dickey, Bill, 89, 93-94, 99
Dillon, John F., 3
DiMaggio, Joe, 94-**96**, 97-99, 105-107, 110, **114-115**, 121, 159
Ditmar, Art, 150-151
Doerr, Bobby, 102
Donatelli, Augie, **139**
Donovan, Bill, 37
Dreyfuss, Barney, 35-36
Dugan, Joe, 53
Duren, Ryne, **143**, 146, 148

E

Ebbets, Charlie, 20, 22, 25, 30-32
Ebbets Field, 20-**21**, 22, 36, 109, 123
Eckert, William, 171, **173**
Egan, Dave, 83
Eisenhower, Dwight D., **123**
Elberfeld, Norman (Kid), **18**
Ennis, Del, **107**
Etten, Nick, 89
Evers, Johnny, **20**

F

Face, Elroy, 150-152
Falls, Joe, 145-146
Farr, Jamie, 65
Federal League, **26**, 31
Ferrick, Tom, 107
Ferry, Jack, 19
Flaherty, John (Red), 135
Flaherty, Pat, 11
Fletcher, Elbie, 80-81
Ford, Edward (Whitey), **103**, 106-108, 125, 143, 150, 152
Frisch, Frank, 40, **47**, 52
Fuchs, Emil, 61
Furillo, Carl, 145

G

Gaedel, Eddie, **110**
Gallagher, James, 84
Gallico, Paul, 77
Gas House Gang, **76**-78
George V, King, **59**
Gomez, Lefty, **87**
Gonder, Jesse, 115
Goossen, Greg, 170
Goulet, Robert, 169
Gowdy, Curt, **102**, 132
Greenberg, Hank, 141
Grimes, Burleigh, 20, 32, **80**
Grimes, Charlie, 44, 74-75
Grimm, Charlie, 84-85
Groat, Dick, 150-152

H

Haddix, Harvey, 150-152
Haines, Jesse (Pop), 175
Hallahan, Bill, 25
Hamner, Granny, 107
Harkness, Tim, 169
Harris, Bucky, 89-90
Harrison, Benjamin, 2
Harzfeld, Siggy, 6, 8
Heintzelman, Ken, 107
Hendrix, Claude, **19**
Henrich, Tommy, 97, 99-**101**, 106
Herman, Babe, 103
Herring, Art, 73, 76-77
Herzog, Whitey, 135
Hickey, Tom, 66
Hodges, Gil, **133**, 143, **156**, 167
Honig, Donald, 81
Hook, Jay, 164
Hopp, Johnny, 106
Hopper, DeWitt, 19-20
Hornsby, Rogers, **35**, 43, 45, 47
Houk, Ralph, 108, 148-**149**, 167
How the Other Half Lives, 3
Howard, Elston, 138-139, **141**-142
Hoyt, Waite (Schoolboy), 52
Hughes, Ed, 77

I

Igoe, Hype, 54
Illman, Harry, 63
Irvin, Monte, **113**-115

J

Jackson, Al, 164
Jackson, Travis, **59**
Jensen, Larry, 114
Johnson, Arnold, 149
Johnson, Billy, 98, 105
Johnson, Ernie, 53
Johnson, Walter, 21-22
Johnston, Jimmy, 30
Jones, Nippy, **139**
Jones, Willie, **107**
Jordan, John, 3-5

K

Kansas City (Missouri), **2**-3, **4**-5, 6-15
Kansas City Blues, 9-11, **12**, 15
Kansas City Improved Street Sprinkling Co., 6-7
Kansas City Monarchs, **33**
Kansas City Red Sox, 8-9, **11**, 19
Kefauver, Estes, 136-138
Kelley, Frank, 25
Kelly, George, 40
Kennedy, John F., 166
Kieran, John, 77
Kinder, Ellis, 102
Kiner, Ralph, 165
King, Lee
Koenecke, Len, **79**
Konstanty, Jim, 106-107
Koslo, Dave, 115
Koufax, Sandy, 165
Kubek, Tony, **142**, 147, 151-152
Kucks, Johnny, 145
Kuzava, Bob, 115, **119**, 125

L

Labine, Clem, 145
Landis, Judge, 54, 66
Lardner, John, 72
Lardner, Ring, **64**, 68-69
Larsen, Don, **138**, 143-145
Lary, Frank, **145**
Lavagetto, Cookie, 89, 159, 165
Law, Ruth, 25, 27-**28**
Law, Vernon, 150-151
Laws, Clarence (Brick), 85
Lawson, John, 48, 58
Lawson, Larry, 57
Lederman, Harold, 14
Lepcio, Ted, 158
Lieb, Fred, 53
Lindell, Johnny, 98-99
Lombardi, Ernie, 81, **86**, 89, **91**
Look, 97
Lopat, Ed, 100, 107, 114-115, **117**, 125, 127
Lopez, Al, 81, 118, 138, 141, **147**, 149
Lose With a Smile, 69
Luderus, Fred, **34**

M

MacFayden, Danny, 81
Mack, Connie, 67
Mack, Gene, 85
MacPhail, Larry, 89
Maglie, Sal, 114
Mannix, Al, 32
Mantle, Mickey, 108-**109**, 114, 123, **124**, 127, 136, 138, 143-**146**, 147, 151-152
Maris, Roger, **148**-150, 152
Marquard, Rube, 28-30
Marr, Runt, 9
Martin, Billy, 89, **91**, 110, **118**, **120**, 123, 127, 143, 146-147, 173, **176**
Masi, Phil, **87**
Mauch, Gus, 159
Mazeroski, Bill, 150-**151**, 152
McCarthy, Joe, 90, 98-99, 121, 149
McDougald, Gil, 108, 115, 123, 143
McGraw, John, 24-25, 39-**40**, 44-47, 52-55, **58**-59, **67**, 71, 108, 149
McKechnie, Bill, 80
McNamee, Graham, **46**, 53
McTigue, Bill, 11

Meadows, Lee, 35
Merkle, Fred, **30**
Meusel, Bob, **42**, **49**, 53
Meusel, Emil (Irish), 36-37, 41, 47, **49**, 52, 65
Meusel, Van, 47-48
Meyers, John (Chief), 29
Miller, Bob, 169
Miller, Dots, 19
Miller, Otto, 24
Minoso, Minnie, 141-142
Mitchell, Dale, 145
Mize, Johnny, **104**-107
Moore, Randy, 80
Morgan, Tom, 108
Mowrey, Mike, 29
Mungo, Van Lingle, 74, 77
Murray, Jim, 178
Musial, Stan, 136
Myers, Hy, 173

N

Nelson, Rocky, 151
Neun, Johnny, 89
Newcombe, Don, 101, 103
Nichols, Charles (Kid), **12**

O

Oeschger, Joe, 55
Olson, Ivy, **5**, 29
O'Malley, Walter, **129**

P

Page, Joe, **98**, 100-101, 106
Parade, The, **4**
Parker, Dan, 72
Parmalee, Roy, **63**
Payson, Joan Whitney, 157
Peary, Danny, 167
Peckinpaugh, Roger, **42**
Pfeffer, Jack, 29, 65
Pignatano, Joe, 169
Pinelli, Babe, 145
Pipp, Wally, **42**
Podres, Johnny, 143
Poland, Hugh, 83
Polo Grounds, **48**, 50-54, 77-78, **112**, **114**, **159**, 163-164
Powell, William, 8-**9**
Power, Vic, 139
Put It in Writing, 166

Q

Quinn, Bob, 72, 80-**81**

R

Rapp, Goldie, 37
Raschi, Vic, 100, 106, 115, **119**
Rawlings, Johnny, 37, 39
Reynolds, Allie, 100, 103, 107, 114-**116**, 123, 142
Rice, Grantland, 53
Richardson, Bobby, **150**, 152
Richbourg, Lance, 37
Rickey, Branch, 155-157
Riis, Jacob, 3
Rizzuto, Phil, 94, 105, **113**-114, **117**, 119-120
Robinson, Jackie, 33, 123, **125**, 138-139, 142, 145, 173
Robinson, Wilbert, 24-25, **27**-30, 36
Rockefeller, John D., 2
Roe, Preacher, 103
Rogan, Bullet Joe, **33**
Rosen, Al, **127**
Rosenthal, Harold, 97
Rowe, Lynwood (Schoolboy), **76**
Rue, Joe, 66
Ruffing, Red, 159
Runyon, Damon, **50**-54
Ruppert, Jacob, 54
Rust, Art, Jr., 174
Ruth, Babe, 30, **32**, 41-**42**, 44, **46**, 54, 123, 177
Ryan, Rosy, 52, **61**, 65

S

Sain, Johnny, 82
Salvo, Manuel, **87**
Sanders, Isador, 13
Sanford, Fred, 99-100
Saturday Evening Post, 68-69
Sawyer, Eddie, 106
Schang, Wally, 53
Schtengal, Karl, 3
Scott, Everett, **61**, 65
Seminick, Andy, **107**
Shannon, Bill (Spike), 11
Shantz, Bobby, 151
Shay, Danny, 11
Shea Stadium, **166**
Sheetz, Willard, 11
Shore, Ernie, 30, 32
Silvera, Charlie, **116**, 121
Sisler, Dick, 106-**107**
Slaughter, Enos, **135**
Smith, Charlie, 169
Smith, Hal, 152
Smith, Ken, 59
Smith, Red, 36
Smith, Sherry, 30
Snider, Duke, **160**
Southworth, Billy, 55
Spahn, Warren, **84**
Stanky, Eddie, **113**-114
Stengel, Charles Dillon (Casey)
  acquires "Casey" nickname, 19-20
  base-stealing ability, 20, **25**
  batting ability, 21, 28
  Boston Braves managerial career, 80-**82**, **83**-84, 86-**87**
  Boston Braves playing career, 55-**56**, 57-59, 61
  Brooklyn managerial career, **70**-80
  Brooklyn playing career, **16**-21, **22**, 24-**25**, 27-**29**, 30-**31**, 32-**33**
  childhood, 1-6
  clowning, 27, 30, **41**, 75, 81, **99**, **124**, **129**
  dancing prowess, 8
  death, **178**
  dental student, **14**-15, 22
  fielding ability, 27, **29**, 37, 109
  fights, 30, **44**, 66, **118**
  high school days, 6, **7**-**8**, 9-**10**
  hit by taxi, 83-84, **87**
  humor, 32, 35, 36, 55, 75, 79, 86-88, 135-136, 153, 159, 164-165
  inducted into Baseball Hall of Fame, 171, **172**-**173**
  inside-the-park home run in 1923 World Series, **48**, 50-**51**, 52-54
  major-league debut, 19
  minor-league managerial career, 59, **61**-66, 68, 84-**90**, **91**
  minor-league playing career, **11**, 13-15, 17-18, 20, 59, **61**-66, 68
  navy duty, 32, 35
  New York Giants playing career, 37-**38**, 39-41, 42, **43**-**45**, 46-**48**, 49-**51**, 52-55
  New York Mets managerial career, **152**-171
  New York Yankees managerial career, 91-**92**, 93-**129**, **130**-153
  Philadelphia playing career, **34**-37
  Pittsburgh playing career, 32, 35-36
  platooning of as player, 28, 30, 41
  platooning as manager, 42, 97-99, 105-106, 115, 118-125

racial attitudes, 33, 138-142
salary, 22, 26, 31-32, 72, 121, 149, 157, 171
speaks Stengelese, 75, 81-82, 93, 136-138
teaching ability, 79-80, 108-110
testifies before Congress, 136-138, **141**, 183-191
trading cards, **45**
wedding, 57
Stengel, Edna (Lawson), 47-48, 52, 57-58, 60, 63, 65, 68, 80, 108, **122**, **128**, **148**, **170**, 174-**175**, 178
Stengel, Grant, 3-7, 10, 32, 35
Stengel, Jennie Jordan, **3**, 4-6
Stengel, Louis, 3-4, 6, 9, 13
Stengel, Louise, 3
Stenzel, Jake, 19
Street, Gabby, 25
Sutton, Larry, 17
Swayne Field, 66
Swoboda, Ron, 170

T

Tebeau, Al, 15
television, **100**, **122**, 131-132, **165**
Terry, Bill, **47**, 52, 71-**73**, 77-78
Terry, Ralph, **140**, 152
Thayer, Ernest, 19-20
This Is Your Life, **122**
Thomas, Frank, **156**, 161, 164-165
Thomas, Pinch, **31**
Thompson, Big Jim, 159
Thomson, Bobby, 114-115
Throneberry, Marv, **161**, 165-66
Tobin, Jim, **87**
Toledo Mud Hens, **61-63**, 65-66, 68
Topping, Dan, 89, 115, 139, 149, 152-153
Tremark, Nick, **74-75**, 91
Turley, Bob, 145, 148-149, 151-152
Turner, Jim, 93
Twain, Mark, 7

V

Veach, Bobby, **61**, 65
Veeck, Bill, Jr., 84-85, 110
Vernon, Mickey, 123
Virdon, Bill, 151

W

Wagner, Honus, **12**
Wagner, Robert, 155
Waner, Paul, **86**
Ward, Chuck, 32
Warner, Danny, 68-69
Washington Park, 20, **26**
Watson, John (Mule), 52
Webb, Del, 89-91
Weiss, George, 85, 89-91, **94**, 106, 109, 139, 147, 149-150, 157-158
West, Max, **86**
Western Dental College, **14**-15
Wheat, Zack, 19, 24, **26**,
Whitted, George (Possum), 36
Whiz Kids, 106-**107**, 108
Wilkinson, J.L., 33
Willard, Jess, 61
Williams, Cy, 34, 36
Williams, Joe, 24, 72
Williams, Ted, 83-**84**, **99**-100, **102**, 111, 136, 143, **173**
Wilson, Jimmy, 84
Wilson, Lewis (Hack), 61, **72**-77
Wolff, Charles, 3-4
Wood, Smoky Joe, 10, 30, **32**
Woodling, Gene, 93, 107, **111**, 119
World Series:
1916 (Dodgers-Red Sox), 30-**31**
1921 (Giants-Yankees), 41-**42**
1922 (Giants-Yankees), 44
1923 (Giants-Yankees), **46**, **48**, **50-51**, 52-54
1949 (Dodgers-Yankees), 102-103
1950 (Phillies-Yankees), 106-**107**, 108
1951 (Giants-Yankees), 111-**112**,
1952 (Dodgers-Yankees), **119-120**, 123, 125
1953 (Dodgers-Yankees), 127, 129
1954 (Giants-Indians), 138
1955 (Dodgers-Yankees), **134**, 142-143
1956 (Dodgers-Yankees), **138**
1957 (Braves-Yankees), **139**, 147-148
1958 (Braves-Yankees), **144**, 149
1960 (Pirates-Yankees), 150-**151**, 152
1969 (Mets-Orioles), 174

Y

Yankee Stadium, **99**, **112**
You Know Me, Al, 68
Young, Dick, 161
Youngs, Ross, 45, 52
Yvers, Sal, 115

Z

Zimmer, Don, **156**, 164
Zwilling, Eddie (Dutch), 8

PHOTO CREDITS

Bettmann Archives: 70, 96. George Brace: 79, 84, 86 right, 86 bottom, 97, 141 bottom, 143. Brown Brothers: 27, 47. Burton Historical Collection: 18, 20, 107, 108, 127. Dick Clark: 33. The Detroit News: 76, 145, 176. Jackson County Historical Society: 2, 3, 4, 6, 7, 8, 9, 10, 11. Library of Congress: 26 top, 30, 31 bottom, 32, 34 top, 46, 100, 112. Lucas County Library: 61, 62 top. National Archives: 28. National Baseball Library: ii, vi, viii, 5, 12 bottom, 14, 16, 21, 34 bottom, 43, 44 left, 49, 50, 58, 59, 62 bottom, 63, 64 bottom, 74, 77, 78, 81, 125, 129, 140, 142, 154, 172, 173, 178, 179. New York Mets: 156, 161, 164 right, 167, 168, 169, 171. New York Yankees: 92, 95, 103, 104 top, 105, 111, 116, 117 bottom, 120, 136. Renee Comet Photography: 45. Mark Rucker: 132. Selek Collection: 22, 23, 25, 26 bottom, 113, 114, 146, 147, 156, 157, 166. The Sporting News: 60, 82, 87 bottom, 88, 90 top, 121, 122, 128, 144, 175. UPI/Bettmann Newsphotos: 99 top, 117 top.